DEVELOPING WOMEN AND CHILDREN IN INDIA

Developing Women and Children in India

Edited
by
Ashok Kumar

Commonwealth

Developing Women and Children in India

Edition : 2024

ISBN 81-7169-091-2

Published by :
COMMONWEALTH PUBLISHERS (P) LTD.
4831/24, Govind Lane,
Ansari Road, Darya Ganj,
New Delhi - 110002
Ph. : 23272541, 23242541
e-mail : commonwealthpublishers2016@gmail.com

Distributed by :
ARJUN PUBLISHING HOUSE
4831/24, Govind Lane,
Ansari Road, Darya Ganj,
New Delhi - 110002
Ph. : 23272541, 23242541
e-mail : arjunbooks2001@gmail.com

Laser Typesetting by :
Dimple Computers
Delhi

Printed at :
Milan Enterprises
Delhi

PREFACE

Development of Women and Children has emerged as an important area of scientific work. Several disciplines are involved in understanding the growth and development of this vulnerable group. By its very nature, therefore, this is an inter-disciplinary area of knowledge and work. Social workers and educationists have been for a long time concerned more with women and child development and have contributed a great deal in focusing the attention of the people to the importance of several factors which should be taken care of in helping women and children to develop fully. Considerable public opinion and the pressure of interested groups have led towards greater investment of public funds as well as private funds for the cause of development of women and children. It is, however, necessary to understand the scientific basis of women and child development so that public opinion can be more informed and teachers, social workers and specialists can really contribute in a larger measure towards adequate attention of women and children in our country.

Several research in this field has been done in the more advanced countries of the world, some work has also been done in our country. However, survey and studies which cover several aspects of problems of women and children are many and quantitatively extensive. These studies, whether books or articles, are sometimes repetitive and often very general in their approach and the informations cited therein are still uneven and scanty. A number of studies are projected on various aspects of the problem and are riddled with problems of comparability and allocation. It is, however, very necessary to develop much greater research efforts and mobilise resources for research, both human and otherwise, in order to develop more specific knowledge and understanding of the problems of women and children under Indian conditions.

It was witnessed during eightees that a flood of literature in the field of women and Child Development, particularly following concern and consequent participation of scholars from diverse academic disciplines in analysis of variety of child development problems at different levels. However, very few of these works could serve the desired objective in terms of composite content and perspective. This joint venture is undertaken as an academic exercise to provide an overall view of planning at national and micro-level, includes the valuable contributions from social scientists to present a more comprehensive view on the subject. Thus, the present work is an attempt to provide a comprehensive approach covering aspects of reading materials as well as some critical analysis.

In the present attempt the book covers diverse aspects of the subject and has been organised into two parts, *viz.*, (*i*) women's development; and (*ii*) children development, alongwith a status paper on both in the beginning. The paper aims at comprehending the status of women and children in India. While discussing the status of women, the author observed that the condition of women in India leaves much to be desired and they are still far away from the status of equality with men. While discussing the status of children in terms of nutritional, health and education author hoped that the acceptance of integrated approach to child development a strong foundation will be laid for future adults through ICDS.

The first paper of Part A, highlights that in expecting education to be an effective instrument of social change one has to consider the nature of education which would help in bringing about a desirable change. If we wish to have an enlightened and progressive society, it goes without saying that both men and women should have the right kind of education. Whereas Varshney in his paper concluded that there is need to pay an attention to the problem of education and employment for women—both in rural and urban areas. In India, even after 40 years of planned development, manpower imbalances in certain categories (especially among young women) do persist although these are not desirable from the point of view of either the individual on the society or the nation. To remove imbalances, adjustment of manpower resources available in the country at different levels is very necessary.

After realising the significant role of women in two subsequent papers Dr. Kumar has concluded that the public sector to private sector. Annual growth rate of employment of women in public sector is much higher than the growth rate of total employment in the said sector. Another conclusion that emerges is a corollary of the second. As public sector employment of women is growing at a much faster rate than the same for the private sector relative importance of the two sectors in share of women's employment is undergoing radical change.

Dr. Kumar has made an attempt on the pattern of women's occupational participation in twenty selected states of India for both rural and urban areas. He focussed primarily on household and non-household industry occupations and investigated with two-digit occupational classifications. It has also been determined by the author that whether women workers are relegated to low status ranking occupations and how much scope exists for vertical occupational mobility and identification the major occupations in which women workers are in dominance.

P. K. Saxena in his paper has given an overview of male and female work participation rates in rural Andhra Pradesh. He has examined decadal variation in female work participation rate and established inter-relationship between female work participation rate and influencing variables. Finally, he has concluded that the female work participation rate in rural Andhra Pradesh is reasonably high, but the largest chunk of female workers engaged in low income yielding occupations of the primary sector. While Dr. Kumar in his paper aims to examine women's contribution to the rural economy in general and women's participation in local institutions particular. An attempt has also been made to document the main conditioning factors influencing women's participation in different developmental programmes and local Government.

Part B—Child Development starts with a very interesting paper written by two authors. They have emphasised that the integrated approach to the basic needs of pre-school rural children, has improved the quality of life through activities centred on the mother and child in the inter-related areas of health, nutrition and education. In the second paper of this part Dr. Kumar has concluded that among the different rural child development programmes, ICDS is single comprehensive and selective on clientele and therefore, it is an economic programme. The services complementary to one another are integrated into a package to enhance the overall effect. The earlier programmes for pre-school children took it for granted that if a balwadi was started, related health and nutrition services will be forthcoming from the other agencies like the PHC and ANP, but the ICDS scheme ensures through the budget provisions the necessary direct inputs of health by strengthening the staffing pattern of the PHC, mechanism of proper coordination between health personnel and child development personnel, etc.

Mishra in his paper 'Promoting child development through Rural Development Programmes' has reached to the conclusion that there is a need to include more child development aspects in rural development programmes and the parents, basically mothers should be equipped with required skill to stimulate the development of the child so that both can work simultaneously to create a healthy, intelligent and socially viable child to make our country prosperous. Whereas A. K. Singh and P. S. Singh has stressed upon efficient coordination among departments, better utilisation of existing resources and developing proper linkages among programmes related to child and mother development, will lead to better implementation of child development programme. The child development programme should not be viewed merely as one more government programme, it should be a community programme with Government as one of the aiding organisations. Much of its success will depend on quantity and quality of community participation.

A. K. Jha has written on child monitoring system and is in opinion that in the Indian situation where 80 per cent of births occur at home, it is impossible to collect data on weight at birth. Height by age, although perhaps measurable, cannot be a meaningful indicator across the regions and population groups in the country. Since the genetic and geographic factors have an impact on the height of children irrespective of their nutritional intake. Dr. S. S. Khanka suggests that the various elements of child health development namely, education, nutrition, health, environmental sanitation and fertility reduction are closely inter-related. Therefore, improvements in one area can facilitate improvements in others and reinforce all aspects of development.

About voluntary efforts Dr. Kumar in his paper has written that the role of voluntary agencies needs to be emphasised. The role is not of middleman but of midwife. All the voluntary agencies may not be able to provide assets or direct services to the target group they are serving. But, the voluntary agencies may help the people take advantage of the opportunities available to them there is need for promoting development consciousness among the people. The voluntary agencies alone can undertaken this important but time consuming task. There is one reason because of which the voluntary agencies have entered the development field is that rural development administration is far from satisfactory. The delivery system is imperfect, we should, therefore, study, the imperfections, associated with rural development administration.

The last paper is a case study done by Dr. Kumar. The study was confined to rural ICDS project to make it feasible. It was undertaken with the objective of comparing the effectiveness of delivery of services under two different organisational and administrative system. A total of 10 villages of one block is selected for the purpose by the author. It was observed by the author that at the block level BDO, CDPO and MO are having good coordination between each other but at the grass-root level coordination between the health functionaries and Anganwadi Workers are not so. Another limiting factor is the lack of community participation in the programme.

Finally, I shall be failing in my duty if I do not express my gratitute to the distinguished contributors who have responded to my initiation warmly and spontaneously. A number of colleagues and friends have provided valuable advise and assist in putting this volume together. I must, however, make it clear that the views expressed here are exclusively those of the authors and not of the institutions to which they belong.

It is hoped that the present effort would be found useful for all those who involved in planning, academics, administration voluntary workers and research organisations.

I am indebted to Prof. Moonis Raza, V.C., University of Delhi, Prof. A. Kundu, Dr. S. P. Jain and Dr. A. K. Gopal for their enthusiastic support. I gratefully acknowledge the generous support of Mr. H. P. Joshi and Miss. Harish which was essential in making the initial idea a reality. To my wife, Laxmi, I owe a special debt. She was not only sympathetic in tolerating my self-imposed isolation and oscillating moods, but an active partner in planning and execution of this volume. I would like especially to thank the following for their help and comments in preparing this volume: Mr. S. Mishra and Mr. V. D. Gadker, Mr. R. P. Mamgain, Mr. A. K. Singh, Mrs. P. S. Singh, Mr. Varshney (H. K.), Mr. Y. Grasekar, Mr. R. K. Singh, Mr. Ajay Kumar Singh, Mr. S. K. Yadav, Mr. G. P. Joshi and Mr. R. R. Yadav. Finally, I thank Mr. B. K. Bhattacharjee for typing the manuscript in a very limited time.

I hope this work will bear fruit and of course, the final responsibility for errors of fact and judgement is mine alone.

Ashok Kumar

CONTENTS

Part B

CHILD DEVELOPMENT

CONTRIBUTORS

DR. ASHOK KUMAR
Faculty Member
National Institute of Public Cooperation and Child Development
Lucknow (U.P.)

A. K. JHA
Lecturer in Geography
SNSRKS College
Saharsa (Bihar)

A. K. SINGH, IAS
District Magistrate
Vaishali (Bihar)

MISS HARISH
CSRD/SSS (Research Scholar)
Jawaharlal Nehru University
New Delhi

H. K. VARSHNEY
Faculty Member
IAMR, I. P. Estate
New Delhi

H. P. JOSHI
National Institute of Public Cooperation and Child Development
New Delhi

DR. P. K. SAXENA
Faculty Member
IAMR, I. P. Estate
New Delhi

MRS. P. S. SINGH
Research Scholar
SIS, JNU
New Delhi

DR. SOBHAN SINGH KHANKA
Lecturer
Deptt. of Commerce
Kumaun University
Nainital (U.P.)

SURYAMANI MISRA
Faculty Member
National Institute of Public Cooperation and Child Development
Lucknow (U.P.)

1

Status of Women and Children in India : A Profile

ASHOK KUMAR*

The status of any given section of population in a society is intimately connected with its economic position which depends on rights, roles and opportunities for participation in economic activities.[1] The economic status of women is now accepted as an indicator of a society's stage of development. The recognition of the productive capacities and potential of women in development is very recent, though longover. The extent development paradignes had produced a mind set which saw men as 'producers' and women as 'consumers', assigning men not only the tasks of production but also providing the education and training necessary for the same. Women, on the other hand, were assigned the privileged tasks of familiar nutrition and consumption ignoring their roles as producers.[2] In the world conference on food, and population the status of women was recognised as an important variable in production and reproduction. However, at certain stages of development, capacity for work may provide the highest claim to status. At other stages when society becomes inegalitarian leisure may substitute work as a basic indicator of status.

*Faculty Member at the National Institute of Public Corporation & Child Developmenl, Regional Centre, Lucknow.

The views expressed in this paper are those of the author and not of the institutions to which he belongs.

Status refers to a position in social system sub-systems which is distinguishable from and at the same time related to other positions through to its designated rights and obligation. In the pure sociological sense status does not imply rank or heirarchy but denotes only position *vis-a-vis* rights and obligation. However, the United Nations Women's Development Decade made a definite contribution to the status of women across the world in that governments reviewed their policies regarding women and accepted the integration of women into development as a desirable planning objective.

The greatest advantage of women's participation in National life was that it brought them to the forefront and Indian women after independence received rights that could be won only after a long struggle by women in the west. The right to equality of status and opportunity in education, public employment and participation in political life were guaranteed to all citizens by the Constitution. Article 14,15 and 16 ensure 'equality before law', "prohibits any discrimination and guarantees equality of opportunity for all citizens in matters relating to employment or appointment to any office under the state and forbids discrimination on the grounds of religion, race, caste, sex, descent, place of birth, residence or any one of them".[3]

Partly because of these measures and partly due to the general trend of social change there has been considerable change in the status of women. In the early years after independence the favour of the Gandhian era was still visible. We find urban women becoming famous in almost all the fields of activity. The capacity of women was not underrated by any one the founding fathers and women—mainly from the urban elite—were in the forefront in political, economic, educational and cultural fields, both at home and abroad.

Status of Women

In the past several decades enormous changes have taken place in this developing world. Not least of these have been those related to women's roles and demographic levels. In most developing countries population growth rates (and thus family sizes) have risen due to decreasing mortality rates and more or less constant birth rates (although fertility rates have now begun to fall in many developing countries). There has been large movement of people away from rural areas and towards urban areas ; there has been a tendency for women to marry at later ages; and structure of the family is changing.[4] In addition to the significant effect the movement of women from rural to urban areas and rising education levels have had on women's roles there have also been important changes within rural and urban areas due to non-demographic factors.

Under the ILO Labour and Population Programme, a global research programme was begun to study the 'Role of Women and Demographic Change'.[5] As implied in the project's title the research programme will employ an interdisciplinary approach, and the research will be set in a broad social, economic and cultural frame which takes account of dynamic change over time using three broad types of studies:

(*i*) collection and analysis of socio-anthropological data;

(*ii*) collection and analysis of household survey data; and

(*iii*) analysis of urban labour markets. The first two types of studies are quite complementary, and it is hoped that they will be undertaken in one country in each of the four major regions of the developing World—Sub-Sahara Africa, Latin America, Asia and the Middle East, as well as in the Asian region of the Soviet Union, thereby forming 'representative' indepth country case studies for each of these distinctive regions.[6] The third type of the study will be treated somewhat independently of the other two, although wherever feasible it will also be done on a country where the others are being done.

In the Asian region the concern for incorporating women's studies in the University system has been the feature of the last decade. Further, the development as well as nature and thrust of women's studies in the region are strikingly different from the way women's studies emerged and grew in the west.[7] In sum, in the Asian region during the last decade considerable progress has been made in systematic studies focusing on women's issues.

India is the second largest populated country in the world and so is its female population. In 1981, the female population of India was 331 millions as against 117 millions at the beginning of the country, *i.e.*, 1901. Thus, over the eight decades 1901-81, the female population has increased by 233 millions or by 193 per cent. For improving the lot of females it is imperative to know as to where do they live and where lies their concentration as methods and measures for improvement would have to match with their way of living and situations and conditions in which they are placed. The analysis that follows brings out the position in this regard.

The distribution of population by sex and location as per the last 3 censuses is given in Table 1.

It is evident from Table 1 that as per 1981 census, 77.4 per cent females live in rural areas and 22.6 per cent in urban areas. The status of male population in this respect is not materially different. However, it will be more clear if we will analyse the state-wise data.

The spatial variations of female population can very well observed from Table 1. The maximum rural population among the states of India is seen in Arunachal Pradesh whereas the minimum is in the state of Maharashtra. The percentage of female population to total population is high in the states of Kerala (50.79 per cent) and Nagaland and Tamil Nadu (49.41 per cent) as compared to other states of India. Looking at the rural urban population distribution we find that in the Union Territories of Delhi and Chandigarh, the rural population is negligible, *i.e.*, 7.26 per cent and 6.37 per cent respectively.

The population was growing at rate of below one per cent

TABLE 1

Population of India by Sex and Location

(in lakhs)

Location	Male			Female		
	1961	1971	1981	1961	1971	1981
Total	2262.9 (100.0)	2840.5 (100.0)	3440.5 (100.0)	2129.4 (100.0)	2641.1 (100.0)	3307.8 (100.0)
Rural	1835.0 (81.8)	2253.2 (79.3)	2693.6 (78.3)	1767.9 (83.0)	2137.3 (80.9)	2560.9 (77.4)
Urban	427.9 (18.9)	587.3 (20.7)	746.9 (21.7)	361.5 (17.0)	503.8 (19.1)	746.9 (22.6)

Note: Figures within brackets are percentages.

per annum till 1921 and below 1.50 per cent per annum during 1921-1951. The growth rate increased to 1.96 per cent per annum in 1951-61 to 2.20 per cent in 1961-71 and 2.25 per cent in 1971-81. Among the 14 states (excluding Assam) with more than 10 millions population in 1981, eight states namely, Gujarat, Haryana, Kerala, Madhya Pradesh, Maharashtra, Orissa, Tamil Nadu and West Bengal have shown a decline in growth rate in the 1971-81 decade compared to the 1961-71 decade. In Andhra Pradesh, Bihar, Karnataka, Punjab, Rajasthan and Uttar Pradesh, the growth rate in 1971-81 has been above that of the previous decade. The population of those states where the growth rate has increased, accounts for 52.91 per cent of the total population of India (Table 2). However, it is interesting to note that the sex ratio in India has declined from 972 in 1901 to 933 in 1981. The sex ratio has been adverse to females in the country in all the censuses. It has been declining till 1971 but has shown a slight improvement in 1981. Among the states and union territories, only Kerala has a sex ratio favourable to females. Among the major states, in Haryana, Gujarat, Karnataka, Kerala, Maharashtra, Punjab, Rajasthan, Uttar Pradesh and West Bengal, the sex ratio has increased during 1971-81. Among these states the sex ratio in 1981 is above the all-India sex-ratio in the states of Kerala, Orissa, Tamil Nadu, Andhra Pradesh, Karnataka, Bihar, Gujarat, Madhya Pradesh and Maharashtra (see Table 2).

However, this differential growth has brought about a decline in sex ratio. This ratio for 1986 has been computed on the basis of estimates by the IAMR, New Delhi, as 936 per 1000 males. The female population of India in 1986 has been estimated as 368 millions. The estimated female population for 1991 is 406 millions and that for 2001 is 480 millions. So the problem before the country is development of 480 millions of women by the turn of the century—much more than population of any other country excepting of course, China.

However, in spite of the spread of education among women and their life of the country, the Indian women are still

TABLE 2

Sex Ratio and Growth Rate of States/Union Territories, 1971-1981

Sl. No.	India/State/ Union Territory	Sex Ratio		Growth Rate	
		1971	1981	1961-71	1971-81
(1)	(2)	(3)	(4)	(5)	(6)
	India	930	933	24.80	25.00
1.	Andhra Pradesh	977	975	20.90	23.10
2.	Assam*	896	901	34.95	36.05
3.	Bihar	954	946	21.95	24.06
4	Gujarat	934	942	29.39	27.67
5.	Haryana	867	870	32.23	28.75
6.	Himachal Pradesh	958	973	23.04	23.71
7.	Jammu and Kashmir	878	892	29.65	29.69
8.	Karnataka	957	963	24.22	26.75
9.	Kerala	1,016	1,032	26.29	19.24
10.	Madhya Pradesh	941	941	28.67	25.27
11.	Maharashtra	930	937	24.45	24.54
12.	Manipur	980	971	37.53	32.46
13.	Meghalaya	942	954	31.50	32.04
14.	Nagaland	871	863	39.88	50.05
15.	Orissa	988	981	25.05	20.17
16.	Punjab	865	879	21.70	23.89
17.	Rajasthan	911	919	27.83	32.97
18.	Sikkim	863	835	29.38	50.77
19.	Tamil Nadu	978	977	22.30	17.50
20.	Tripura	943	946	36.28	31.92

(Contd.)

(Contd.)

(1)	(2)	(3)	(4)	(5)	(6)
21.	Uttar Pradesh	879	885	19.78	25.49
22.	West Bengal	891	911	26.87	23.17
23.	Arunachal Pradesh	861	862	38.91	35.15
	Union Territories				
1.	Andaman & Nicobar Islands	644	760	81.17	63.93
2.	Chandigarh	749	769	114.59	75.55
3.	Dadra & Nagar Haveli	1,007	974	27.96	39.78
4.	Delhi	801	808	52.93	53.00
5.	Goa, Daman & Diu	989	981	36.88	26.69
6.	Lakshadweep	978	975	31.95	26.53
7.	Mizoram	946	919	24.93	48.55
8.	Pondicherry	989	985	27.81	28.15

*Population of Assam is projected.

Source: Census of India, 1986, Series 1.

discriminated against and are at a disadvantage. The condition of women in India today leaves much to be desired and they are still for away from the status of equality with men.

Education, however, is the key to progress and unless Indian women are educated, they will not be able to enjoy their rights. The education of Indian women has been sadly neglected in the past. Though the percentage of literacy among women has increased from what it was 40 years ago, the disparity between boys education and girl's education is still very high.

In expecting education to be an effective instrument of social change one has to consider the nature of education which would help in bringing about a desirable change. The question is what are the factors that come in the way of women's education? To think of it, it is the society itself with is orthodox beliefs and customs which is responsible for the state of women's education.

The long term trend in economic participation of women indicates an overall decline both in percentage workers to total female population in their percentage to the total labour force after 1921, and a slight increase from 1971 to 1981. The participation of women in industry, however, shows a general stagnation, and a distinct decline after 1961. In the post-independence period with rapid increase in modern and organised sector of industry, the shave of household industries declined rapidly. Since they constituted the biggest source of women's employment outside agriculture women were the greatest victims of this process of economic transformation the other reason for the exclusion of women from industry was technological change and rationalisation of the process of production which reduced the demand for unskilled labour. Most of the women in the modern industrial sector were employed as unskilled workers.

Status of Children

To have a clear understanding about the importance of

TABLE 3

Growth of Child Population

Year	Population in Age-Group 0-14 (in Million)	Proportion to the Total Population
1951	137	38.4
1961	280	41.0
1971	230	42.0
1981	264	39.0
1991 (Estimated)	274	34.3
2001 (Estimated)	289	30.3

child, one should be aware of the status of the child. The following figures indicate the growth of child population during the last 15 years.[8]

In 1981, out of 261 million children, there were about 121 million in the age group of 0-6 years. Of these, rural children account for 89.7 million tribal children for 7.3 million and urban children for 24.0 million. About 40 per cent of these children were below the subsistence level a staggering total of about 46 million children between 0-6 years were living in conditions below the minimum for survival. Moreover, it is estimated that by 2001 A.D., Indian child population would increase to about 300 million.[9]

However, it is said that in India, a child is born every one and a half second which means 21 million births a year. The national infant mortality rate was 94 in 1988. There were significant differences in these figures between rural and urban areas and from state to state. The Table 4 indicate Birth Rate, Death Rate and Infant Mortality Rate of the states for the year 1987 and 1988.

The above statistics exhibit that there is a large variations in the infant mortality rates from 28 in Kerala to 127 in Uttar Pradesh. However, the national average is 95 and 94 for the year 1987 and 1988 respectively. Deaths among children (0-5 years) in rural areas represent nearly 50 per cent of the total deaths as against about 38 per cent in urban areas. Female mortality is higher than that of males in the first year of life but in the higher age group, female mortality rate decreases. This indicates neglect of the health of female children. On the other hand it can be inferred that high infant mortality rate is due to many health hazards, malnutrition and lack of timely maternal and child health care.

Indian constitution were well aware of the necessity of providing special concessions and priviledges to children and mothers in the constitution. The constitution specially provides that nothing shall prevent the State from making any special provision for women and children. Article 24 of the consti-

TABLE 4

Vital Statistics

Sl. No	State/Union Territories	Birth Rate		Death Rate		I.M.R.	
		1987	1988*	1987	1988	1987	1988*
(1)	(2)	(3)	(4)	(5)	(6)	(7)	(8)
1.	Andhra Pradesh	30.3	26.8	9.9	9.9	79	82
2.	Assam	30.2	32.5	11.6	11.7	102	100
3.	Bihar	36.6	37.3	13.1	12.6	101	97
4.	Gujarat	30.8	29.3	9.8	10.9	97	91
5.	Haryana	34.5	33.5	8.8	9.7	87	89
6.	Karnataka	28.9	28.7	8.7	8.8	75	74

(Contd.)

(Contd.)

(1)	(2)	(3)	(4)	(5)	(6)	(7)	(8)
7.	Kerala	21.7	19.9	6.1	6.3	28	28
8.	Madhya Pradesh	36.4	35.8	13.3	14.2	120	120
9.	Maharashtra	28.3	29.2	8.3	8.8	66	68
10.	Orissa	31.0	31.6	13.1	12.2	126	122
11.	Punjab	28.7	28.5	8.1	8.4	26	62
12.	Rajasthan	35.1	32 8	11.6	13.2	102	103
13.	Tamil Nadu	24.0	22.5	9.9	9.2	76	74
14.	Uttar Pradesh	37.9	36.9	14.5	13.1	127	123
15.	West Bengal	30.7	28.1	8.8	8.3	71	70
16.	Himachal Pradesh	30.8	31.9	8.5	9.5	82	79
17.	Jammu and Kashmir	31.4	32.6	7.7	8.3	71	73
18.	Manipur	25.9	25.2	5.6	6.7	N.A.	N.A.
19.	Meghalaya	34.9	36.2	9.1	9.1	N.A.	N.A.
20.	Nagaland	21.7	23.7	4.9	5.0	N.A.	N.A.
21.	Sikkim	33.3	33.8	10.8	10.1	N.A.	N.A.

22.	Tripura	28.2	26.6	9.2	8.1	N.A.	N.A.
23.	A & N Island	26.9	19.0	6.1	5.1	N.A.	N.A.
24.	Arunachal Pradesh	36.3	39.6	13.2	17.0	N.A.	N.A.
25.	Chandigarh	23.9	22.1	3.8	5.4	N.A.	N.A.
26.	D. & N. Haveli	35.3	38.3@	11.3	9.8@	N.A.	N.A.
27.	Delhi	30.4	28.2	7.5	7.4	N.A.	N.A.
28.	Goa	18.9	17.6	7.5	7.8	N.A.	N.A.
29.	Daman & Diu	27.2	27.9	7.1	8.9	N.A.	N.A.
30.	Lakshadweep	30.5*	25.5	6.3	6.6	N.A.	N.A.
31.	Mizoram	N.A.	N.A.	N.A.	N.A.	N.A.	N.A.
32.	Pondicherry	22.4	22.3	8.0	7.7	N.A.	N.A.
	All India	32.2	31.3	10.9	10.9	95	94

Note: *Provisional

@Rural only

N.A. Not Available.

Source: Ministry of Health and Family Welfare, Government of India.

tution prohibits employment of children in hazardous occupation, Article 45 directs the states to provide, within a period of 10 years from the commencement of the constitution, free and compulsory education for all children until the age of 14 years.[10]

It may thus, be seen that these provisions in the Indian constitution provide the basic safeguards for care, protection and welfare of the children. In order to give concrete share to the constitutional provisions, several legislations concerning women and children were enacted. One of them is the children's Act of 1960 which provides for care, protection, maintenance and rehabilitation of destitue, neglected and delinquent children.[11]

However, to understand the different components of child status, if becomes imperative to have a look on the following components:

(*a*) Health status;

(*b*) Nutritional status; and

(*c*) Educational Status.

(*a*) **Health Status.** In India, about 46.3 per cent of the child population (0-14 years) lives below the poverty line with no access to proper food, shelter or sanitary facilities, the situation is, naturally, far from satisfactory. The young child, barely out of the mother's womb, has not had a chance to adopt to the hostile environment or to build-up his defences against the vagaries of the situation. He is vulnerable, and not unexpectedly he succumbs. Infant mortality rate is 94 (1988) per thousand live births as against a death rate of 10.9 per thousand population. Despite the concerted efforts at reducing the infant mortality rate, infant mortality in the last fifty years has been reduced only by about half of the decline in the general mortality rate.

Safe drinking water is not available to 163 million rural Indian Children (1-14 years). In 113,000 villages, water supply is adequate in quantity but open to pollution hazards while in another 185,000 villages, the supply is both inadequate and unprotected. It is estimated that in rural India, about 33 per cent deaths among 1-4 years old are due digestive disorders while respiratory disorders account for another 22 per cent. Inadequate food further sets into operation the synergistic cycle of infection and malnutrition. Eye ailments and blindness due to vitamin A deficiency are common. About 25,000 children go blind[12] every year because of preventable causes. Tuberculosis is widespread even among young children.

As far as immunisation is concerned, only 20 per cent of women and almost the same percentage of school children in the country have been immunised against tetanus. This is indeed a pitiable situation in view of the fact that the cost of fully immunising a child against the six preventable target diseases—TB, Diptheria, Whooping cough, tetanus, measles and poliomyletis—average a paltry sum of Rs. 24.[13] Despite preventive costs being much lower (and preventive action much more desirable) than curative costs, a very few children in rural area have been immunized.

A detail analysis of this situation indicates that the availability and utilisation of health services in inversely related to the needs of the community, the extent of utilisation of the available services is also inversely proportionate to the need. Even within the available framework, the utilisation is much more by the comparatively better-off rural population. Thus, while village leaders, teachers, and other priviledged sections of the village population avail of PHC services regularly, hardly any of these services percolate to the poorer population.

(*b*) **Nutritional Status.** About 46 million children exposed to hazards of malnutrition. According NNMB reports (1981), about 85 per cent of the children have body weights below the normal standards. Prolonged and chronic malnutrition not only leads to high morbidity and mortality, but influences growth adversely. Protein energy Malnutrition (PEM) is a najor nutritional problem affecting young children. It is estimated that about 25,000 children in India go blind every year. Of these, it is estimated that 12,000 to 14,000 children go blind every year due to Vitamin A deficiency. The incidence of iron deficiency-anaemia—is estimated to be as high as 85 per cent among pre-school children. Many factors other than low intake of iron are responsible for the development of anaemia. Children born to anaemia mothers have very low iron stores and have low birth weights. The incidence is particularly high among children between 6 months and 2 years due to inadequate dietary supplementation.[14] However, anaemia is also responsible for the high rate of maternal mortality found among the women. It is observed that nearly 10 per cent of the maternal deaths are due to anaemia.

(*c*) **Educational Status.** Article 45 of the constitution makes provision for free and compulsory education for all children up to the age of 14 years. The target of hundred per cent coverage of this age group was to be met with a period of ten years. However, even after 41 years, we have not been able to achieve this goal. Of course, the Five Year developmental plans have made tremendous efforts to expand educational facilities especially in the rural areas; yet, the seriousness of the problem still remains. The Fourth Annual Educational Survey conducted by National Council of Educational Research and Training in 1978 has identified 9,64,664 rural habitations all over the country with an estimated population of 50,91,63,428. The States of Bihar, Madhya Pradesh and Uttar Pradesh account for nearly 46 per cent of total rural habitations and 7.1 per cent of the rural habitation are predominantly populated by scheduled castes and 15.9 per cent by scheduled tribes.[15]

The number of primary schools in the country had increased from 1,34,966 at the time of independence 5,70,010 in 1978. Out of these, 5,08,164, *i.e.*, 91.2 per cent are in rural areas.[16] However, the existing educational facilities for the age group 6-10 years have been able to cover only 80.24 per cent of the rural habitation. Thus, approximately 20 per cent of habitations do not have a primary school even within two kilometres of their habitat. The problem is more severe in rural areas where the population slab is low, *i.e.*, 300 and less. It is estimated that 50 per cent of the total rural habitations have a population of less than 300. It is these areas which need increased attention and a beginning should be made by establishing of least non-formal educational Centres. It is interesting to note that about 89 per cent of the habitations predominantly populated by scheduled castes are served by a primary school within or at a distance of 1 km.

In rural areas, 40.5 per cent of primary schools are managed by the government and 54.13 per cent by local bodies. The structure of the schools varies from one-room and one teacher establishment to five teachers establishment. Another very important factor in any educational system is the pupil-teacher ratio. This ratio for the country is 41, and surprisingly, it is almost the same in rural and urban areas.[17] The school buildings are also inadequate to a great extent. A little one 91 per cent primary schools need additional accommodation, around 50 per cent need playground facilities and about 70 per cent need library facilities. The provision for free text-books is available in 37.90 per cent schools in rural areas.

The need of pre-school education as also the day-care facilities for the pre-school child is felt in the case of children of working mothers. However, the organised pre-school education has not been a part of the Indian education system. Gandhi's philosophy of basic education gathered momentum in the thirties. As a part of larger scheme of basic education enunciated by Gandhi, experiments were also made on establishing pre-basic centres which were the counterpart of the pre-school education centres. This led to the establishment of the Kasturba Gandhi National Memorial Trust under whose auspices many rural welfare centres were started which included balwadis as part of their activities. Gram sevikas were trained for running balwadis, craft centres, etc. Teacher's training programme was also started first at Bodhi in Maharashtra and later at kosbad Hills. Between 1960 and 1980, a number of other committees and study groups were set-up to suggest ways and means for expanding provision of pre-school education facilities. Some of the important studies are: Working Group on Production and Supply of Educational Equipment and Toys for Children (1962); Report on Committee on Child Care by the Central Social Welfare Board (1962); Ganga Saran Sinha Committee (1968); and Study Group on Pre-school Child (19 2). All these groups emphasised the importance of pre-school education but the recommendations remained mostly on paper. However, a great impetus to the provision of pre-school education was provided by the declaration of a National Policy on Children in 1974 which recognised children as the supreme asset of the nation. This was followed by the launching of Integrated Child Development Services Scheme (ICDS).

Summing-up

In the foregoing discussions, an attempt has been made to bring together the status of women and children in India. While discussing the status of women, it is observed that the condition of women in India today leaves much to be desired and they are still far away from the status of equality with men. In expecting education to be an effective instrument of social change one has to consider the nature of education which would help in bringing about a desirable change. The question is what are the factors that come in the way of women's education?

The economic participation of women indicates an overall decline both in percentage workers to total female population in their percentage to the total labour force after 1921, and a slight increase from 1971 to 1981. The participation in industry shows a general stagnation, and a distinct decline after 1961. After independence, with rapid increase in modern and organised sector of industry, the share of household industries declined rapidly. Since they constituted the biggest source of women's employment outside agriculture women were the greatest victims of this process of economic transformation.

The second part of the paper has been devoted to the status of children in India. While discussing the status of children in terms of their nutritional deficiency, health conditions and educational status, etc., their access to various facilities have been discussed. The services to for pre-school children leading to the concept of package of services in the scheme of Integrated Child Development Services, which has not only come to stay but has covered a larger population of pre-school children, particularly those belonging to the weaker and vulnerable sections like the scheduled castes, scheduled tribes and OBC. It is hoped that with the acceptance of integrated approach to child development, a strong foundation will be laid for future adults through ICDS which aims at providing services in the field of health, pre-school education, nutrition and health education.

NOTES & REFERENCES

1. Report of the Committee on the status of women in India, "Towards Equality". Govt. of India, Deptt. of Social Welfare, Ministry of Education, p. 148.
2. Women produce 44 per cent of world's agricultural produce, in Africa their is 70 per cent.
3. Kalpana Dasgupta (1976) (Ed.): *Women on the Indian Scance*, Abhinav Publications, New Delhi, pp. 8-9.
4. Richard Anker, Mayra Burinic and Nadia H. Youssef (Ed) (1983): *Women's Roles and Population Trends in the Third World*, Croom Helm, London & Canberra, p. 29.
5. *Ibid.*, p. 29.
6. Easter Boserup (1970): *Women's Roles in Economic Development*, London, George Allen and Unwin, p. 32.
7. There have been two or three major efforts to the situation of women's studies in Asia. Leela Dube in 1980, under the auspices of *UNESCO*, Bangkok carried out a 'Review of Studies on Women in South-east Asia'. An expert meeting was organised, again by the UNESCO, Bangkok in October, 1982 to review the status of women's studies and Social Sciences in Asia and suggest recommendations for Development of Research and Teaching on Women's studies in the region. Bina Agarwal in November 1983, prepared a report of the 'Current Status and needed Priorities of women studies in Asia and Pacific', a project supported by Asian and Pacific Development Centre (APDC), Kuala Lumpur. All these works provides information and analysis of development and features of women's studies in Asia.

8. "UNICEF Assistance for Rural Women and Children Programme", An Approach Paper, Association of Voluntary Agencies for Rural Development, New Delhi, 1980.

9. D. Paul Chowdhury (1984): 'Programmes for Youth and Children in Rural Areas', in ed. book of NIRD, *Rural Transformation—Readings*, A Silver Jubilee Volume, NIRD, Hyderabad, pp. 403-404.

10. *Ibid.*, p. 405.

11. *Ibid.*, p. 405.

12. UNICEF, *Child Atlas of India*, New Delhi, 1981, p. 32.

13. Shanti Ghosh (1980): 'Priorities in Child Health', in *Profile of Child in India*, Ministry of Social Welfare, Government of India, New Delhi, p. 76.

14. Chowdhury (1984), *op. cit.*, p. 410.

15. D. Paul Chowdhury (1961): *Voluntary Social Welfare in India*, Sterling Publishers, New Delhi.

16. 'National Seminar on Education in India', Indian Association for Pre-school Education, 1968.

17. *Promotion of Voluntary Action in Rural Development-Scheme for promotion and Strengthening of Yuvak Mandals & Scheme for promotion and strengthening of Mahila Mandals*, Ministry of Agriculture and Irrigation, Department of Rural Development, Government of India, New Delhi.

PART A

WOMEN'S DEVELOPMENT

2

Educational Structure of Women in India

ASHOK KUMAR*

The role of education in the development of the traditional people has been very well stressed by educationists and sociologists. Education may mean formal or non-formal education. Formal education means learning in the structured school setting. It is necessarily organized and the vast bulk of formal education either receives state support or is organised by the state itself. Non-formal education would be learning in any organized setting which takes place apart from the specific school programme.[1] Which of these two systems is more utilitarian is a matter of opinion. It all depends upon the conditions under which the people receive education. For those who have already crossed the normal age-limits for formal education, non-formal education is the only alternative. 'Non-formal education especially if viewed as a set of alternative to the formal systems of education, offers a way to devise an effective approach to learning and education'.[2]

Education is needed for a cultural revolution is brought out

*Faculty Member at the National Institute of Public Cooperation & Child Development, Regional Centre, Lucknow.

The views expressed in this paper are those of the authors and not of the institutions to which he belongs.

by Ivan Illich.[3] According to Bane and Jencks[4], and Coleman[5] schools provide equal opportunities for children from unequal groups. Wynee[6] has observed that it is through education alone that better socialization takes place. Freire[7] says that education is essential for creating awareness among the people. However, much of rural women's education depends upon the general conditions in the villages. Mridula[8], Ahuja[9] and Bhatty[10] have made certain useful comments on women's education in Indian situation.

The education of girls and of women was regarded as the legitimate responsibility of Indians ; it neither suited nor interested the rulers to take much initiative in this area.[11] However, disparities in male-female literacy rates have clearly been pointed out by Mazumdar and Pandey.[12]

The present section deals with the position of education among women in general. However, the various items included on education are literacy level, girls in elementary and secondary education, drop-out rates in schools, female in higher and professional education.

Literacy Amongst Females

Education is one of the most important factors which determines the status (both social and economic) of a person. For the purpose of getting any job the level of education plays a very significant role in determining ones suitability or otherwise. Literate women force constitutes an important input in the process of socio-economic development of a nation ; but the literacy among women in India still appears like a farfetched cry. However, the literacy rates in regard to males and females are given in Table 1.

It can be observed from Table 1 that literacy amongst women has gone up from 0.69 per cent in 1901 to 24.82 in 1981. The progress, statistically, is no doubt substantial but still in absolute terms, it is far from satisfactory. That is, still three-fourths of women are illiterate. Further, the pace of increase in percentage of literacy amongst females has been less than that of males. During the last 80 years the increase in literacy amongst males had increased by 37 percentage points whereas in case of females it had increased by 24 percentage points.

TABLE 1

Progress of Literacy Rates in India

Census Year	Percentage of Literates to Total Population			
	Males		Females	
	%	Increase in a Decade	%	Increase in a Decade
1901*	9.83	—	0.69	—
1911*	10.56	0.73	1.05	0.36
1921*	12.21	1.65	1.81	0.76
1931*	15.59	3.38	2.93	1.12
1951**	24.95	9.36	7.93	5.00
1961	34.44	9.49	12.95	5.02
1971	39.45	5.01	18.72	5.77
1981†	46.89	7.44	24.82	6.10

*For Undivided India.

**Excludes Jammu and Kashmir.

†Excludes Assam.

Source: Census of India 1981, Key pop. stat.

The literacy rates by sex and by rural and urban areas after independence are presented in Table 2.

It would be seen from Table 2 that the literacy amongst females in rural areas in only 17.9 per cent as against 47.8 per cent in urban areas. This indicates that more efforts in regard to increasing the literacy are required in the rural areas. However, the data regarding literacy rates by states, sex and loca-

TABLE 2

Literacy Rate (Per cent) by Sex and Location—India, 1951-81

Location	Male				Female			
	1951	1961	1971	1981	1951	1961	1971	1981
Total	23.5	34.5	39.5	46.8	7.6	13.0	18.7	24.8
		(46.8)	(14.5)	(18.6)		(17.1)	(43.8)	(32.7)
Rural	19.0	29.1	33.7	40.7	4.9	8.6	13.1	17.9
		(53.1)	(16.0)	(20.8)		(75.5)	(42.1)	(37.3)
Urban	45.1	57.5	61.2	65.8	22.3	34.5	42.0	47.8
		(27.4)	(6.5)	(7.5)		(54.7)	(21.8)	(13.7)

Note: Figures in brackets are percentages.

tion are presented in Table 3 which shows very slow improvements in female literacy in the states of Rajasthan, Madhya Pradesh and Andhra Pradesh. A Comparison of the sex ratios of literates in the age groups will indicate that the gap between the literacy rates of males and females is being steadily bridged. In the rural areas the sex ratio among literates, or the number of females per 1,000 males who are literates steadily increase towards the younger ages.

In view of the above discussions, it can be stated that the women lag far behind so far as the educational achievements of the women force in India are concerned. However, in the preceding sections we will review the progress of education made by women at different levels of education, *i.e.*, elementary, secondary and higher education as well as in professional education and try to identify the tasks ahead.

Girls in Elementary Education

The enrolment of girls at primary and middle levels of education for the years 1951 to 1981 at decennial intervals and as percentage to the total enrolment is presented in Table 4.

It can be seen from the Table 4 that as many as 59 per cent of the female in the age group 6 to 10 were enrolled in primary classes, while this ratio for middle stages of education works out at only 21 per cent in the year 1971, which has gone up to 69.24 per cent and 27.70 per cent in the respective stages upto 1981. It appears that enrolment of women is steadily increasing. However, the limitation of these statistics is also to be borne in mind before drawing any conclusions. The actual enrolments also include students from lower/higher age groups and render higher enrolment ratios in relation to the corresponding age groups population. Further, these enrolment statistics do not necessarily indicate the attendence of the children in the school. The figures are collected from the numbers entered on the enrolment registers of schools. As a consequent of the adoption of no detention policy upto Class II in some states, the names of the students continue on roll irrespective of the consideration whether they attend the school or not.

TABLE 3

Literacy Rates for All Ages by Sex and Rural/Urban, 1971 and 1981—India and States

Sl. No.	India/State	Stratum	1971 Persons	1971 M	1971 F	1981 Persons	1981 M	1981 F
(1)	(2)	(3)	(4)	(5)	(6)	(7)	(8)	(9)
	India	T	29.48	39.52	18.70	36.23	46.89	24.82
		R	23.69	33.76	13.08	29.65	40.79	17 96
		U	52.37	61.24	42.05	57.40	65.83	47.82
1.	Andhra Pradesh	T	24.57	33.18	15.75	29.94	39.26	20.39
		R	19.19	27.31	10.92	23.24	32.25	14 08
		U	47.08	57.30	36.31	51.99	61.89	41.55

2. Bihar	T	19.94	30.64	8.72	26.20	38.11	13.62
	R	17.17	27.64	6.39	22.50	34.38	10.17
	U	44.92	55.43	31.89	52.18	62.47	39.81
3. Gujarat	T	35.79	46.11	24.75	43.70	54.44	32.30
	R	28.33	38.92	17.19	36.20	47.85	24.06
	U	54.90	63.96	44.77	60.31	68.62	51.13
4. Haryana	T	26.89	37.30	14.89	36.14	48.18	22.25
	R	21.71	32.57	9.24	30.33	43.44	15.37
	U	51.00	59.12	41.48	56.86	64.98	47.35
5. Karnataka	T	31.52	41.62	20.97	38.46	48.81	27.71
	R	25.13	35.40	14.54	31.05	42.06	19.77
	U	51.43	60.40	41.61	56.71	64.98	47.78
6. Kerala	T	60.42	66.62	54.31	70.42	75.26	65.73
	R	59.28	65.57	53.10	69.10	74.13	64.25
	U	66.31	71.99	60.62	76.11	80.10	72.20
7. Madhya Pradesh	T	22.14	32.70	10.92	27.87	39.49	15.53
	R	16.81	27.05	6.10	21.22	32.91	8.99
	U	49.55	60.46	36.98	54.02	64.41	42.26
8. Maharashtra	T	39.18	51.04	26.43	47.18	58.79	34.79
	R	30.63	43.22	17.84	38.15	51.25	24.88
	U	58.07	66.88	47.33	63.92	71.80	54.65

(Contd.)

('ontd.)

(1) (2)	(3)	(4)	(5)	(6)	(7)	(8)	(9)
9. Orissa	T	26.18	33.29	13.92	34.23	47.10	21.12
	R	24.09	36.14	12.06	31.49	4.51	18.45
	U	49.00	59.94	3 .05	54 77	65.13	42.72
10. Punjab	T	33.67	40.38	25.90	40 86	47.16	33.69
	R	27.81	34.69	19.88	35.21	41.91	27.63
	U	52.49	58.55	45.41	55.63	60.72	49.72
11. Rajasthan	T	19.07	28.74	8.48	24.38	38.30	11.42
	R	13.85	22.87	4.03	17.99	29.65	5.46
	U	43.46	55.52	29.68	48.35	60 55	34.45
12. Tamil Nadu	T	39 46	51.78	26.86	46.76	58.26	34.99
	R	32.12	45.14	18 98	38.56	51.16	25.80
	U	56.36	66.76	45.42	63.45	72.'0	53.99
13. Uttar Pradesh	T	21.70	31.50	10 55	27.16	38.76	14.04
	R	18 13	28.02	6.99	23.06	35.18	9.49
	U	43.63	52.08	33.33	45.88	54.73	35.43

14. West Bengal	T	33.20	42.81	22.42	40.94	50.67	30.25
	R	25.72	35.80	15.02	33.12	43.58	22.06
	U	55.93	62.01	4.78	62.66	69.08	54.82

Source: Census of India, 1981, Series-1, Part II, Special.

TABLE 4

Enrolment of Girls at Elementary School Stage

Year	Enrolment of Girls (in Million)			Percentage at Girls Enrolment to Total Enrolment		
	Primary	Middle	Elementary	Primary	Middle	Elementary
1951	5.39	0.54	5.93	28.13	17.25	26.60
	(24.6)	(4.5)	(17.49)			
1961	11.40	1.63	13.03	32.58	24.33	31.25
	(14 4)	(12.0)	(13.69)			
1971	21.31	3.89	25.20	37.34	29.20	35.80
	(59.1)	(20.77)	(45.99)			
1981	29.41	6.57	35.98	39.75	33.10	38.34
	(69.2)	(27.70)	(54.33)			

Source: Manpower Journal, IAMR, New Delhi, p. 72.

In view of this, it may be mentioned that the picture which emerges from the enrolment statistics is not satisfactory when analysed in terms of achieving the ultimate goals of literacy. The major problem is of retaining the students upto a standard that a minimum knowledge of literacy and numeracy is attained and they do not further lapse into illiteracy is quite serious. This phenomenon refers to the problem of drop out. The drop-out rate is noted to be more than 60 per cent from Classes I to V.

Girls in Secondary Education

Secondary education is a critical sector for study. It is here that diversification or streaming occurs, and, women close their options earlier than men to enter higher scientific and professional education and consequently on the prestigious levels in modern occupations.

There were 53,000 Secondary Schools in 1982 compared with 4000 in 1947. At the Secondary Stage (14-17 years), only 20 out of every hundred girls are in schools a against 39 boys. Educational opportunity at this level is confined to middle and upper middle class in urban areas to some rural upper and middle class sections. Girls from less than one-third of the total enrolments at the secondary level. Their position is slightly worse in vocational, professional and special education schools at school level. In vocational/professional/special and other schools at the secondary level, the tendency of girls is to go in for female sex typed courses, for example, only 90 girls are present in agricultural schools with a total enrolment of 4,119. In any case, there is only one agricultural school for girls against 60 such institutions for boys. In nursing, there were 3 institutions for boys and 95 for girls with an enrolment of 44 and 3,699 respectively. Girls out-number men in teacher training institutes (preparing primary teachers). In 1977-78, there were 7,182 girls receiving teacher training in 41 institutions whereas there were 6,986 boys enrolled in 72 teacher training institutes for boys. In the industrial training institutes for boys, there were 48,308 girls compared to 80,821 boys but even here the girls were to be found in traditional female crafts and trades and boys were in technical courses leading to middle level participation in mechanized industry. In music and fine arts schools, there were 15,595 girls and 9,871 boys enrolled at that time.

Further, secondary education of girls being an urban phenomenon, the position of rural girls is weaker compared to urban girls. There are as yet, much fewer rural secondary schools for girls and the ones that do exist are rather poorly equipped. On the whole vocationalisation of Secondary Education is a distant dream considering only around 1.5 million students were receiving vocational education at the school level in 1977-78. Some breakthrough in vocational education courses has since been made in Tamil Nadu. Even in this case the reports are that girls tend to take to home science based on vocational courses, *i.e.*, food and nutrition, stitching and handicrafts, the traditional skills associated with women's nuturant family roles. A case study of Delhi Secondary Schools shows a preponderance of girls in arts and lower participation in Commerce, Science and Vocational streams. Even within the SUPW courses, girls are predominantly in female sex-typed courses. Education of woman is, in general, status quoist and does not equip them for anything but primary teaching or low level white collar work.

Drop-out Rates in Schools

The drop-out rates in schools from Class I to Class X during the period 1971-1980 is presented in Annexure I. It would be noticed that although the average drop-out rate for all classes in case of girls has come down, yet it is still higher than that of boys by about 5 per cent. The average drop-out of all classes in 1980 for boys is 12.58 per cent whereas it is 17.30 in case of girls. It would further be noticed that there had been almost no decrease in drop-out rate in case of girls in Classes VI and above. This suggests that girls still continue to be casualties on account of domestic duties which they are required to perform as per tradition in their houses the moment they attain the age of 12 or so. In addition the large number of drop-outs amongst girls could also be on account of the thinking that since girls would not be required to pursue any career further education acquired by them would be infrastuous. To some extent, the large drop-out rate could also be attributed to social restrictions on movements of grown-up girls outside the vicinity of their homes. Since education plays an important role in securing employment, the attitude and outlook of parents towards the education of females requires a change.

Female in Higher Education

Higher education among women (17-23 years) is confined mostly to urban middle and upper classes. Women form 28.5 per cent of the total enrolments at this stage (1982-83). The proportion of woman is higher at post-graduate stage than at the under-graduate stage. The number of degree colleges in Arts, Science and Commerce has increased from 263 to 3,457 in 1982. Female enrolments in higher education have gone up by more than twenty times from 40,000 to 8,93,000 during 1950-51 and 1982-83 while the proportion of women to every hundred men has gone up from 14 and 40 during this period. The number of exclusively, girls' colleges has gone up from 69 in 1947 to 643 in 1982-83. Despite expansion of higher education only 5 per cent girls and 13 per cent boys in the relevant age-group are enrolled in the third level education, the corresponding figures for developed countries being 32 per cent and 28 per cent for boys and girls, respectively.

The faculty-wise enrolment of women in university education shows a large number opting for general arts, science, education courses and medicines. In 1981-82, of every 100 girls enrolled, 56 were in Arts, 21 in Science, 13 in Commerce, 7 in Engeering and 3.6 were in Medicine. Number of women per 100 men in education faculty-wise was 60.5 in arts, 40.4 in science, 19.2 in commerce, 91.9 in education, 4 in engineering and technical education, 32.5 in medicine, 2.5 in agriculture and 7.4 in law, for instance. The curricular openings for women at secondary and higher secondary levels limits there economic participation to a limited numbers of jobs. It may also be noted that the levels of unemployment are far lower among women who enter into professional and technical education.

Inter-state comparison of female enrolments indicates the uneven rate of progress not only between states but between different levels of education in some states. Bihar and Rajasthan have maintained uniformly lowest performance at all levels. Andhra Pradesh, Assam, Maharashtra, Karnataka, Uttar Pradesh, Himachal Pradesh, Manipur, Delhi, and Tripura have made rapid improvement in primary education and Assam, Gujarat, Maharashtra, Punjab, Haryana, Jammu & Kashmir, Nagaland, Tamil Nadu, Delhi, Manipur and Tripura at middle level and Tamil Nadu and Delhi at the secondary level. Kerala leads (as in general and female literacy) in primary school enrolments (classes I-V) having enrolled 115.5 per cent girls (including girls below 6 and above 11 years) at this stage in as early as 1966-67.

In higher education, most states have made a rapid progress, Punjab and Delhi leading at this stage also, and Andhra-Pradesh, Madhya Pradesh, Assam, Karnataka, Rajasthan, U.P., Orissa and Bihar falling at the other end of the continuum.*

The inter-state disparities in male and female enrolments in higher education are to be noted in the NSS data (1980-81) for 77 regions. There are only a few regions where women more than 35 per cent of the total enrolments, namely, Northern (37.4) and Southern (53.7), Kerala; Northern (42.6) and Southern (43.5), Punjab; Coastal Maharashtra (53.8); Delhi (41.3), Chandigarh (37.6); A&N Islands (35.5); Inland Eastern Karnataka (39.4); J&K-mountainous (43.4), Outer Hills (41.0) and Jhelum Valley (35.9); Eastern Haryana (35.6); Guja at-Dry Areas (44.4) and Saurashtra (39.4). Even where the share of women in enrolments is high, they predominate in arts course.

*Female share in higher education enrolments statewise in 1981 was: Kerala 46.9%, Punjab 39.8%, Delhi 39.4%, J&K 24.8%, Haryana 32.0%, Wesst Bengal, Tripura and Sikkim all 31.3%, Maharashtra 31.0%, Meghalaya 30.3%, Gujarat 28.9%, Himachal Pradesh 28.3%, Andhra Pradesh 26.3%, Madhya Pradesh 25.5%, Assam 25.1%, Karnataka 24.8%, Rajasthan 20.4%, Uttar Pradesh 19.0%, Orissa 17.8%, Bihar 13.1%, Total India 27.2%, See U.G.C. Annual Reports.

In 30 regions, mostly in educationally backward states, two-thirds of girls are enrolled in arts only. In eastern Gujarat, Coastal Maharashtra, Western and Central U. P., South-Kerala and Central Plains of Bengal, more than 50 per cent of women students are in arts only.

Female in Professional Education

The distribution of student enrolment sex-wise and faculty-wise for the period 1971-72 and 1984-85 is presented in Table 6. It is observed that the outcome of the efforts made to increase the female enrolment is gratifying. In case of faculties likes commerce, Engineering/Technology, Agriculture, Veterinary and Law, the increase in enrolment of girls in 1984-85 had been several times more than that in 1971-72. In Medical and Science faculties also their enrolment had increased by 85.1 per cent and 104.8 per cent respectively. On the whole, the increase in their enrolment was 117.9 per cent as compared to 57.7 per cent increase in case of males in the corresponding period.

The data relating to literacy levels for the period 1961-1981 are given in Table 5.

It would be seen from the Table 5 that the percentage of females having literacy level of matriculation and above is much less than that amongst Males. Out of total literacy of 24.82 per cent, this percentage is only 3.93 whereas this in case of males is 10.48 per cent out of 46.89 per cent. Again, the proportion of graduates is also much less in case of females as compared to males. These percentages are 0.74 per cent our of 24.82 in case of females and 2.07 per cent out of 46 89 in case of males. This means steps will have to be taken to give higher education to greater number of females alongwith increasing the overall pace of literacy.

The enrolment of girls in 1984-85 in all the faculties put together continued to be far lower (*i. e.*, 28.9 per cent only) than their share in population (48.28 per cent). In faculties like medicine and law the percentage of girls enrolled in 1984-85 was only 27.4 per cent and 7.5 per cent as compared to 72.61

TABLE 5

Educational Composition of Population by Sex

(In 000's)

Educational Level	Males			Females		
	1961	1971	1981	1961	1971	1981
(*i*) Illiterate	148,206 (65.54)	167,121 (60 48)	182,645 (53.11)	185,212 (87.04)	209,115 (81.30)	141,611 (75.18)
(*ii* Literate	77,940 (34.46)	109,214 (39.52)	161,285 (46.89)	27,579 (12.96)	48,084 (18.70)	79,746 (24.82)
(*a*) Literate without education level	48,287 (21.35)	34,068 (12.33)	47,389 (13.78)	18,146 (0.53)	17,576 (6.83)	26,648 (8 29)
(*b*) Primary/or Junior Basic	22,700 (10.40)	58,237 (21.07)	77,831 (22.63)	8,158 (3.83)	25,866 (10.06)	40,482 (12.60)

(*c*) Matric/Secondary/ Inter		13,647 (4.94)	27,854 (8.10)		3,812 (1.49)	9,950 (3.10)
(*d*) Non-Tech. Diploma/ Certificate not equal to Degree		359 (0.13)	146 (0.04)		102 (0.04)	78 (0.02)
(*e*) Tech. Diploma/Certificate not equal to degree		298 (0.11)	912 (0.27)		78 (0.03)	229 (0.07)
(*f*) Graduate and above		2,604 (0.94)	7,134 (2.07)		649 (0.25)	2,360 (0.74)
Grand Total	226,146 (100.00)	276,335 (100.00)	343,930 (100.00)	212,791 (100.00)	257,199 (100.00)	321,357 (100.00)
Matric and above	6,953 (3.07)	16,909 (6.12)	36,045 (10.48)	1,275 (0.60)	4,642 (1.81)	12,616 (3.93)

Note: Figures within brackets are percentages.

TABLE 6

Distribution of Student Enrolment: Sex-wise and Faculty-wise, 1971-72 to 1984-85*

Faculty	Enrolment						%age of Girls to Total Students in Faculty		%age Increase from 1971-72 to 1984-85	
	Total		Boys		Girls					
	1971-72	1984-85	1971-72	1984-85	1971-72	1984-85	1971-72	1984-85	Boys	Girls
Arts	906068 (43.9)	1429728 (40.4)	603005 (37.0)	864191 (34 3)	303063 (64.7)	565537 (55.4)	32.4	39.6	43.3	86.6
Science	505925 (24.5)	697169 (19.7)	404710 (25.3)	489829 (19.5)	101215 (21.6)	207340 (20.3)	20.0	29.7	21 0	104.8
Commerce	289946 (14.0)	747175 (21.0)	279397 (17.5)	607023 (24.0)	10549 (2.2)	136130 (13.3)	3.6	18 3	113.3	1190.6
Education	63658 (3.1)	84934 (2.4)	39655 (2.5)	44181 (1.8)	24003 (5.1)	40753 (4.0)	27.7	48.0	11.4	69.8

Engineering/ Technology	82804 (4.0)	159252 (4.5)	81840 (5.1)	150979 (6.0)	958 (0.2)	8273 (0.8)	1.2	5.2	84.5	763.6
Medical	89921 (4 3)	134479 (3.8)	70002 (4.4)	97607 (3.9)	19919 (4.2)	36872 (3.6)	22.2	27.4	39.4	85.1
Agriculture	25971 (1.3)	46006 (1.3)	25697 (1.6)	44168 (1.7)	274 (0.1)	1838 (0.2)	1.1	4.0	71.9	570.8
Vaterinary Science	6086 (0.3)	10617 (0.3)	6027 (0.4)	10106 (0.4)	59 (Neg.)	511 (0.1)	1.0	4.8	67.7	766.1
Law	84443 (4.1)	212336 (6.0)	79892 (5.0)	196505 (7.8)	4551 (1.0)	15831 (1.5)	5.4	7.5	146.0	247 9
Other	10219 (0.5)	21234 (0.6)	6114 (0.4)	12961 (0.5)	4105 (0.9)	8273 (0.8)	40.2	39.0	112.0	101.5
Total	2065041 (100.00)	3538930 (100.00)	1596345 (100.00)	2517552 (100.00)	468696 (100.00)	1021378 (100.00)	22.7	28.0	57.7	117.9
%age to total	100	100	77.30	71.14	22.70	28.86				

*Estimated.

Note: Figures in parenthesis denote percentage to total.

Source: UGC Annual Reports.

per cent and 92.5 per cent respectively for boys. It is, therefore, suggested that there is still need for putting more efforts in this direction, particularly in professions like medicine and law, where their suitability is as good, if not better, than that of boys and work environment is also congenial. And same is the case with the professsion like education.

Conclusions

Education, however, is the key to progress and unless Indian women are educated, they will not be able to enjoy their rights. The education of Indian women has been sadly neglected in the past. Though the percentage of literacy among women has increased from what it was 40 years ago, the disparity between boy's education and girl's education is still very high. Education is considered the most effective instrument of bringing about social and economic change. That our society particularly rural, has remained static and tradition-bound is due to the fact that a vast majority of women in rural areas are not educated. The question is what are the factors that come in the way of women's education ? To think of it, it is the society itself with its orthodox beliefs and customs which is responsible for the state of women's education.

The data presented in this paper reveal that there are disparities in male-female literacy rates. However, there were 1,055 illiterate women to a 1,000 illiterate men in 1911 the former figure went up to 1,322 women to a 1,000 illiterate men in 1981. This gender gap is due mainly to the growth in absolute numbers. Further, there are substantial regional imbalances and differences ; in Kerala, a state known for its general level of awareness, female literacy is as high as 73 percent, where in Rajasthan, one of the nine states officially recognised as being educationally backward, less than 12 percent of women are literate. Again, though the overall female literacy figure according to the 19·1 Census is 24.8 per cent, in rural areas it is around 18 per cent, while in the towns and cities women's literacy has gone up to 47.8 per cent.

On the whole, girls constitute only one-third of total enrolments at every level of schooling and their drop-out rate is higher than that of boys. Though overall enrolments have been steadily rising with each Census recording, there remain substantial differences in male-female participation rates. At the secondary levels while only 1[illegible] per cent of girls in the relevant age group are in school, a meagre 17 per cent of these are from the villages. There are a number of reasons which keep girls away from school. Important among these are: (*i*) the high opportunity cost of education in relation to the poverty of families; (*ii*) social factors such as early marriage and a widespread belief in female seclusion, increasing the demand for girls schools and women teachers; and (*iii*) discriminatory processes at work within the school system itself.

As regards women's participation in professional education, there is still need for putting more efforts in this direction, particularly in professions like medicine and law, where their suitability is as good, if not better, than that of boys and work environment is also congenial.

In expecting education to be an effective instrument of social change one has to consider the nature of education which would help in bringing about a desirable change. If we wish to have an enlightened and progressive society, it goes without saying that both men and women should have the right kind of education. While entrenched attitude are not easy to root out, a concerted strategy organised by governmental agencies together with others in the area may well work much better than having several conflicting scheme supposedly working for the promotion of girl's education.

REFERENCES

1. A number of scholars have defined the terms, 'Formal education' and 'Non-formal education' and differentiated between the two. For instance:

   (*a*) George H. Axinn, '*Non-formal Education and Rural Development*', East Lansing, Michigan State Univ., 1976.

(b) Beatrice Paolucci *et. al.*, *Women's Families and Non-formal Learning Programmes*', Michigan State Univ., East Lansing, Michigan, 1976.

2. Ted W. Word and William A. Herzog Jr. (1977), '*Effective Learning in Non-formal Education*', Michigan State University, p. 76.

3. Iran Illich (1970), '*The Need for a Cultural Revolution*', Risk, Vol. IV, No. 4, pp. 37-38.

4. Mary, Jo, Bane and C. Jencks (1972), the 'Schools and Equal opportunity', *Saturday Review*, Sept. 16, p. 41.

5. James, S. Coleman (1966), Equality of Educational Opportunities, Washington, Government Printing Press.

6. Edward Wynee (1972), 'Education and Socialization—a Complex Education', *Education Researcher*, December.

7. Paulo Frieve (1970), 'Education for awareness', *Risk*, Vol. IV., No. 4, p. 14.

8. Mridula Seth (1978), 'Educating Women through economic activities', *Social Welfare*, Vol. XXV, No. 8, November, p. 14.

9. Ram Ahuja (1973), 'Female Education in India' *Social Welfare*, Vol. XX, No. 9, December, p. 2.

10. Zarina Bhatty (1975), 'Muslim Women in U.P., 'Social Mobility and Directions of Change', in Alfred D'Souza (ed.), *Women in Contemporary India*, Delhi, Manohar.

11. Neera Desai and Maithreyi Krishnaraj (1987), *Women and Society in India*', Ajanta Publications, Delhi, p. 149.

12. Vina Mazumdar and Balaji Pandey (1985), '*Perspective on Women's Education*, 1971-81', Unpublished paper, p. 1. R.K. Bhandari, '*Education Dev. of Women in India*', New Delhi, History of Ed. and Culture 1982 (Statistics for the graph), p. 13.

3

Initiatives for Educational Development of Women in Five Year Plans and National Policy on Education

ASHOK KUMAR AND H.P. JOSHI*

Education is the most important instrument for human resource development. Education of women, therefore, occupies top priority amongst various measures taken to improve the status of women in India. In recent years, the focus of planning has shifted from equipping women for their traditional roles of house-wives and mothers to recognizing their worth as producers, making a major contribution to family and national income.

Since Independence, the policy makers have argued for universal education and for making education as a tool for bringing about social equality. Efforts have been made during different plan periods to enrol more girls in schools and encourage them to stay in schools, to continue their education as long as posssible, and to provide non-formal education opportunities for women. However, in the present study an

*Working in the National Institute of Public Cooperation and Child Development, Lucknow & New Delhi.

The views expressed here are those of the authors and not of the Institute to which they belong.

attempt has been made to review the initiatives taken for educational development of women during plan era and in the National policy on Education-1986.

Women's Education in the Five Year Plan

Women's education has assumed special significance in the context of the country's planned development. This is because women constitute nearly half nation's population representing a valuable human resource, and play an important role in the development of the community and the national economy. Education enables women to acquire basic skills and abilities, and fosters a value system which is conducive to raising their status in society. Recognizing this fact, great emphasis has been laid on women's education in the five year plans. The First Five Year Plan advocated the need for adopting special measures for solving the problems of women's education. It held that women "must have the same opportunities as men for taking all kinds of work and this presupposes that they get equal facilities so that their entry into the professions and public services is in no way prejudiced". It further added that "at the secondary and even at the university stage it should have a vocational or occupational basis, as far as possible, so that those who complete such stages may be in a position, if necessary, to immediately take up some vocation or other". Accordingly, the educational facilities for girls continued to expand in the subsequent plans. The major schemes undertaken encompassed elementary education, secondary education, university education, post-graduate education and research, technical education, scholarships social/adult education and physical education. The Second Plan continued the emphasis on overall expansion of educational facilities. The Report of the National Committee on Women's Education (1959) made a strong impact on the Third Five Year Plan. It launched important schemes like condensed school courses for adult women, Bal Sevika training and child care programmes. Subsequent plans supported these measures and also continued incentives such as free text-books and scholarships for girls. This trend continued in the Fourth and Fifth Year plans.[1]

Although there was a large scale expansion of facilities for education upto the Fourth Plan vast disparities existed in the relative utilisation of available facilities by boys and girls at various stages of education. Hence, the major thrust in the Fifth Plan was to offer equality of opportunities as part of the overall plan of ensuring social justice and improving the quality of education imparted. To promote enrolment and retention in schools in backward areas and among under-privileged sections of the population, in addition to the incentives like distribution of text-books, mid-day meals, etc., girls were to be given uniforms and attendence scholarships. Inspite of these schemes, it was noticed that insufficient numbers of women teachers resulted in low enrolment of girls. To remove this bottleneck, scholarships were given to local girls to complete their education and training leading to a teaching career. Besides, condensed and correspondence courses were organised for the less educated women. Emphasis was also laid on the need for orientation of the curriculum to meet the special needs of girls.[2]

A landmark in the Sixth Plan was the inclusion of women's education as one of the major Programmes under Women and Development which was an outcome of the publication of the report of the Committee on the Status of Women in India. The programmes for universalisation of elementary education were specially directed towards higher enrolment and retention of girls in schools. It was envisaged to promote balwadi-cum-creches attached to the schools to enable girls responsible for sibling care at home to attend schools. Women teachers, where necessary, were to be appointed in rural areas to encourage girls' education. Science teaching in girls schools and colleges had to be strengthened to achieve greater participation of women in science and technology. Streamlining the admission policies to promote greater enrolment of women in engineering, electronics, agriculture, veterinary, fishery and forestry courses was stressed. For boosting the education of women belonging to backward classes, the number of girls' hostels were to be increased. Instead of adding more separate women's polytechnics, which were developed as multi-purpose institutions for imparting training in arts, crafts, etc., co-educational institutions were encouraged as far as possible. The adult education programme too received a fillip.[3]

The Seventh Plan envisages restructuring of the educational programmes and modification of school curricula to eliminate gender bias. Enrolment of girls in elementary, secondary and higher education courses, formal as well as non-formal, has been accorded high priority. At the elementary stage, education has been made free for girls. Sustained efforts are to be made through various schemes and measures to reach 100 per cent coverage in elementary education. Financial assistance schemes to voluntary agencies to run early childhood education (pre-school centres) as adjuncts of primary/middle schools are to be expanded, particularly to help evolve innovative models suited to specific learner groups or areas. Efforts are to be made to enrol and retain girls in schools, especially in rural areas, and also to enrol children belonging to scheduled castes, scheduled tribes and other weaker sections. Teacher training programmes are to receive continued priority with a view to increase the availability of trained women teachers, and thereby to enhance girl's enrolment and retention in schools. Incentives by way of distribution of uniforms, free text books and attendence scholarships to needy girls are to be continued. Non-formal elementary education is to be set up and programmes for vocationalization of education are to be expanded.[4]

To expedite education among the girls of the scheduled castes and scheduled tribes, additional facilities will continue to be provide under the "Development of Backward Classes" sector. Girls above matriculation stage will get higher scholarships/stipends than boy students. Financial assistance is envisaged for construction of hostel buildings for girls at the district level and for purchase of equipment, furniture utensils, books periodicals in these hostels.

However, under the National Sports policy, participation of women and girls in sports and games is to be encouraged. Stress is to be laid on the identification of sports talent among women, and provision made for sports scholarships, coaching and nourishment support for promising girls with a view to improve the standards of their performance in competition, health, nutrition and family planning. An effort was made to build up awareness about these subjects among women through discussions, talks, and distribution of relevant literature.[5]

Under the Adult Education Programme, apart from increasing adult literacy, the content of education was to be modified to incorporate new value systems regarding the role of women in the family and community. The Seventh Plan also envisages, among other schemes, the preparation of district level plans with local community participation both for activating and implementing the literacy programme, and the creation of special mechanisms to monitor the progress of implementation at the State level. The integrated Rural Development Programme (IRDP). National Rural Employment Programme (NREP). Training of Rural Youth in Self-Employment (TRYSEM), and other such programmes, are also to have a component of functional literacy for women beneficiaries. The programme of Functional Literacy for Adult Women (a component of the ICDS programme) was unfortunately abandoned, though the concept of utilising Anganwadi Workers, who belonged to the villages and were in contact with young mothers, could have been an effective mechanism for imparting non-formal education. The scheme has since been revised to focus on issues of immediate relevance to women but has yet to be introduced.[6]

The various programmes, however, have not yet been able to make any significant impact on literacy levels of the Indian population, particularly on women. According to a World Bank Report, in 2000 A.D. there will be 500 million illiterates in India, constituting 54 per cent of the world's population of illiterates. As per the Seventh Plan, the total number of adult illiterates is about 900 lakhs, of whom 580 lakhs are women.[7] Although it is encouraging to note that the proportion of women in the adult education centres has gone above 50 per cent (52.34 per cent in 1984-85), women still constitute about

57 per cent of the illiterate population. Among these, literacy levels of SC and ST women are still worse. Even those treated as literates, have very low levels of literacy, scant opportunities for continuing education and use of literacy skills. Therefore, they often relapse into illiteracy.

Initiatives for Women in National Policy on Education-1986

The National policy on Education (NPE)-1986 is a landmark in the approach to women's education. It has attempted for the first time to address itself to the basic issues of women's equality. In the section titled "Education for Women's Equality", the policy states:

> "Education will be used as an agent of basic change in the status of women. In order to neutralize the accumulated distortions of the past, there will be a well conceived edge in favour of women. The National Education System will play a positive, interventionist role in the empowerment of women. It will foster the development of new values through redesigned curricula, textbooks, training and orientation of teachers, decision makers and administrators".

It gives over-riding priority to the removal of women's illiteracy and obstacles inhibiting their access to and retention in elementary education. Emphasis has been laid on women's participation in vocational, technical and professional education at different levels as also to promote women's participation in non-traditional occupations and existing and emergent technologies.

The Programme of Action for implementation of NPE (POA) spells out the meaning of women's empowerment:

> "Women become empowered through collective reflection and decision making. The parameters of empowerment are:

—Building a positive self-image and self-confidence.

—Developing ability to think critically.

—Building up group cohesion and fostering decision making and action.

—Ensuring equal participation in the process of bringing about social change.

—Encouraging group action in order to bring about change in the society.

—Providing the wherewithal for economic independence..."

The programme entails the following:

(*a*) A phased time bound programme of elementary education for girls, particularly upto primary stage by 1990 and upto the elementary stage by 1995;

(*b*) A phased time bound programme of adult education for women in the age-group 15-35 by 1995;

(*c*) Increased women's access to vocational, technical professional education and existing and emergent technologies; and

(*d*) Review and re-organization of educational activities to ensure that they make a substantial contribution towards women's equality, and creation of appropriate cells/units therefore.

A number of measures have been suggested to achieve the stated objectives of the National Policy on Education. The Action Plan enunciates that every educational institution should take up by 1995 active programmes for the development of women. All teachers and non-formal education/adult education instructors should be trained as agents of women's development. Special programmes should be developed by research institutions to promote general awareness and positive self-image amongst women through programmes like discussions, street plays, wall-papers, puppet shows, etc. Preference in recruitment of teachers upto school level should be for women.

National Literacy Mission (NLM) which aims at eradication of illiteracy in 15-35 age-group by 1995 concretises what is envisaged in NPE as regards literacy aad adult education. The Mission document emphasises the importance of imbibing the values of national integration, conservation of environment, women's equality, observance of small family norm, etc., and goes on to say that "the focus of NLM would be on rural areas, particularly women and persons belonging to the Scheduled Castes and Scheduled Tribes".

For universalisation of elementary and adult education, the present programme of non-formal centres for girls needs to be extended to all educationally backward pockets of the country. Increased assistance should be given to voluntary organisations to run non-formal education centres for girls. In rural areas, special support services should be provided to relieve the girls from sibling care and other household work like fetching water, fuel, etc. Skill development linked to employment opportunities in the villages is required to be given priority so that there is an incentive on the part of the parents to educate girls. It is necessary to develop adult education programmes for women linked with upgradation of their skills and income generating activities. Skill development for girls should be a continuous process of learning and should be supported by programmes administered by other agencies such as polytechnics. Industrial Training Institutes (ITIs), Women's Centres in Agricultural and Home Science Colleges, etc. Continuing Education Centres should be set up in a phased manner to organize vocational training, provide opportunities for retention of literacy skills, and application of this learning for improving their living conditions. There are 104 ITIs functioning exclusively for women and 97 wings in general ITIs reserved for women. These would need to be revamped during 1988-90 in terms of diversification of trades and courses, keeping in view the job potential, and facilities for vocational counselling, imparting information about credit, banking, entrepreneurial development and women's access to technical education, etc.

Women's studies programmes would also have four dimensions, *viz.*, teaching, research, training and extension. Women's issues would be incorporated in courses under various disciplines. Research would be encouraged on identified areas/ subjects. Seminars/workshops would be organized on the need for women's studies, and for dissemination of information and interaction. Educational institutions would be encouraged to take up programmes like adult education, awareness building, legal literacy, information and training support for socio-economic programmes of women's development, instructional programmes through media, etc., which directly benefit the community and bring about the empowerment of women.

All the foregoing endeavours will be planned, coordinated, monitored and evaluated continuously both at the national and state levels. The Women's Cell in the National Council for Educational Research and Training would be revived and strengthened. National Institute of Educational Planning and Administration and Directorate of Adult Education would have cells to plan and administer women's training programmes. The Women's Cell in the University Grants Commission would be strengthened to monitor the implementation of various programmes at the higher education level. It is proposed that women's cells should be set up in all the states.

Perspective for Women's Education Upto 2000 A.D.

The programmes for women's education will have to be implemented as a priority so that women attain a comparable level of education by 2000 A.D. The strategy to be adopted for raising literacy levels and education among women has to keep in view the vast cultural, geographical and ecological variations as also the problems relative to poverty and ignorance. The cultural and geographical variations call for decentralization of educational planning. Within the national perspective, planning, implementation and monitoring of educational programmes has to be done at district and block levels, keeping in view the socio-economic and geographic parameters of the area. The vocational and occupational components have to be designed in accordance with the availability of resources and job opportunities in the regions. Voluntary organisations and women's groups active in the area should be involved in the task.

In view of the social and cultural handicaps that have operated against women's education and taking account of the multiple roles that women are required to play, the need for adopting a set of objectives specific to women's education is imperative. The objectives to be achieved by 2000 A.D. in regard to women's education are:

(*i*) Elimination of illiteracy, universalisation of elementary education and minimization of the dropout rate in the age group 6-14 years and stagnation to negligible proportions;

(*ii*) Ensuring opportunities to all women for access to appropriate level, nature and quality of education and also the wherewithal for success comparable with men;

(*iii*) Substantial vocationalization and diversification of secondary education so as to provide a wide scope for employment and economic independence of women;

(*iv*) Making education an effective means for women's quality by (*a*) Addressing ourselves to the constraints that prevent women from participating in the educational process; (*b*) Eliminating the existing sexist bias in the system; (*c*) Making necessary intervention in the content and processes of education to inculcate positive and egalitarian attitudes; and (*d*) Ensuring that teachers' perceive this as one of their essential roles;

(*v*) Providing non-formal and part-time courses to women to enable them to acquire knowledge and skills for their social, cultural and economic advancement;

(*vi*) Impetus to enrol in various professional degree courses so as to increase their number in medicine, teaching, engineering and other fields substantially;

(*vii*) Creating a new system of accountability, particularly in respect of the basic educational services, to the local community, *inter alia*, by active involvement of women.

In brief, it is reiterated that the goals and strategies spelt out in the National Policy on Education, POA and the National Literacy Mission will ensure a much larger access for women to education.

High priority has to be accorded to creating awareness, through the various communication media, of the need for women's education and their active participation in economic and political development of the nation.

However, women should be entitled to a package of services at the block level created by the convergence of schemes such as Development of Women and Children in Rural Areas (DWCRA), Integrated Child Development Schemes (ICDS), Adult Education, Health Care, etc., at the grass roots administrative level. Every district should have a coordinator to assist in the integration of these programmes aimed at the development of women. The coordinator will also be responsible for motivating local planning of programmes and assist in their implementation and provide feed back for effective planning and evaluation. Since decentralization of planning monitoring and implementation of development programmes for women is suggested as also devolution of finance at district level, appointment of District coordinators for women's programmes would facilitate this process, and control over finance would empower them. The National Commission on Self Employed Women and Women in the Informal Sector has also recommended the appointment of District coordination officers to be responsible for planning, monitoring, coordination and evaluation of the programmes affecting women. Rationalization of functionaries at the block and village level to ensure coordination of programmes affecting women at the grass roots level also needs to be undertaken.

REFERENCES

1. Govt. of India (1988): National Perspective Plan for Women: 1988-2000 A.D., Ministry of Human Resource Development, Deptt. of Women and Child Development, New Delhi.

2. *Ibid.*, p. 70.
3. *Ibid.*, p. 71.
4. *Ibid.*, p. 71.
5. *Ibid.*, p. 75.
6. A. Kumar (1988): *Indian Women Towards 21st Century*, Criterian Pub., New Delhi.
7. *Ibid.*, p. 11.

ANNEXURE 1

—National Committee on Women
—Inter-ministerial Coordination and Monitoring (Department of Women and Child Development)
—Cells in Mainline Ministries
—State Departments for Women
—District Coordinator for Women's Programmes.

Department of Women and Child Development

(Policy, Planning, Programmes, Training, Information Monitoring at the National Level)

- Programme Implementation
  - CSWB (Welfare and Supportive Programmes)
  - Women's Development Corporations (Economic Programmes)
- Training & Information
  - National Resource Centre for women
- Enforcement of Women's Rights
  - (Commissioner of enforcement to liaise with Special Cells for Women (Police) and with the Department of Public Grievances, etc.)
- Planning Policy
  - Monitoring

Functions:

—Documentation/Policy research
—Advocacy and coordination
—Information dissemination
—Training and sensitization

Source: National Perspective Plan for Women—1988-2000 A.D., Government of India, Min. of HRD, Deptt. of Women and Child Dev., New Delhi.

4

Education and Employment Planning for Young Women

H.K. VARSHNEY*

Introduction

Our Government is committed to improve the status of women in India. The Indian constitution provides for not only equal rights and privileges for all citizens; but specifically mentions the need for making special provision for women. Since the First Five Year Plan, various welfare and development schemes have been introduced to improve the living conditions of women and to increase their access to and control over material and social resources. The last assessment was made in 1975, at the beginning of the Decade for Women. The facts contained in the report prepared by the Committee on the Status of Women (CSWI) were startling as they revealed how little had been done for women in the 28 years since Independence despite the promises and provisions contained in the Constitution. The report outlined how certain development programmes, instead of enhancing women's status, had adversely affected a large section of women and had led to, among other things, a decline in the sex ratio, a lowered life expectancy

*The views expressed in this paper are solely of the author and not of the organisation (IAMR) to which he belongs. The author is grateful to Dr. Tarlock Singh, I.C.S. (Retd.), ex-member Planning Commission, for his valuable comments and suggestions on an earlier version of this paper.

at birth, higher infant and maternal mortality, declining work participation rate among women, greater illiteracy and raising migration.

Past Attempt

These facts necessarily meant that future development plans would have to be devised to ensure that their impact on women was not ignored. The report emphasised the need to integrate women with development, to see them as 'critical input', rather than the recipients of welfare. The key shift in approach was from organising programmes that resulted in women depending on government generosity to those that would equip them with the skills and wherewithals to attain economic independence.

To implement this new thinking, a National Plan of Action was devised in 1976 and a Women's Welfare and Development Bureau was set up under the Ministry of Social Welfare.

The CSWI report, therefore, played an important role in setting up the structures to monitor programmes for women and in turn also influenced the direction of the Sixth Five Year Plan which accepted that women's lack of access to resources was an important constraint in their development. The Seventh Plan has gone a step further by first of all recognising that it is not enough to aim programmes at the family as a unit but at women specifically. Secondly, it attempts to implement the twin concerns of 'equity and empowerment'. For the first time, in the Sixth Five Year Plan, a special chapter was devoted to women which outlined various schemes to promote employment opportunities for women at different levels and to create the needed channels for women to participate effectively in decisions that affect their lives. It was also emphasized that grass root level organisations would be promoted and mahila mandals and other voluntary organisations would be encouraged. However, various empirical studies have shown that women have not benefited adequately from development efforts made in the country.

The development of women, who constitute about 50% of

the human resources of the country has been recognised as a crucial factor in national progress and development. Various conferences and seminars have brought out the point forcefully that women's integration in all sectors of economic and social policy is necessary for national development. Therefore, in recent years there has been a growing awareness in the country of the need to involve women in development programmes in a systemetic way. Social change, advancement in education alongwith the economic need to supplement the family income has brought forward women as a potential labour force in the economy. As such, it becomes imperative for the manpower planners to provide necessary facilities for education and skill development to young women and also ensure ample employment opportunities for them on equal footing with men.

Education is the key that opens the door to life. Education is widely accepted as a necessary tool for attainment of development goals. Education leads to political consciousness-awareness of rights and duties among the people of a nation. In the areas of family planning, the higher the level of women education the fewer children she is likely to have and the later she will start having them. This link between female education and lowered fertility is crucial, some uncontrolled fertility aggravates many women own specific health problems and also affects the health of the whole family. Therefore, it becomes the responsibility of the educational system to provide adequate facilities to women, equip them with knowledge, skills and attitudes so that they may be able to get into avenues relevant to their respective fields. In short, the quality of education is a crucial element in shaping the 'women resources' for economic development.

Despite the large expansion in educational facilities from primary to university levels, women's education still lags. It may be worth mentioning here that all the drafts plans and policies for uplifting the women-folk has not resulted in much progress. It is desirable that the current 'Draft National' perspective plan on development policies for women for the next 12 years, *i.e.*, 2000 A.D. deals with certain basic issues raised in that paper. It may be noted that about 75 per cent of India women are still illiterate. Between 1951 and 1981, the number of illiterate women had increased by 50 per cent (from 162 million in 1951 to 242 million in 1981) and that for every 100 illiterates among men, the number of illiterate women had risen from 105 in 1951 to 122 in 1981. A considerable proportion of workers, especially women workers, in public and private enterprises and in government and quasi-government organisations still continue to be illiterate.

An analysis had been made in this paper regarding young women in the age-group of 15-34 years—their educational and employment pattern based on the 1981 Census and the Directorate General of Employment and Training data, in order to highlight the problems areas which needed attention of the planners. Section I deals with the composition and general characteristics of young women. Section II deals with employment situation and section III gives the conclusion.

Human Resource Development covers the development and productive utilisation of male as well as female manpower. After more than three decades of manpower planning and development, one is compelled to admit that not much attention has been given to the development and proper utilisation of women human resources.

SECTION I

COMPOSITION AND CHARACTERISTICS

The latest population figures are available from the 5 per cent sample data of the census of India-1981. Table 1 shows that out of India's total population of 665 million in 1981, youth (in the age group of 15-34 years) accounted for 214.5 million (about 32 per cent of the total population). The female population in 1981 was 321 million: 247 million females living in rural areas and 74 million females living in urban areas. The young women population in the age group of 15-34 years was 104 millions or 32.47 per cent of the total female population. Distributing the youth population in the

TABLE 1

Young Women Population in India—Census—1981

(In thousand)

Age Group (Years)	Total Population	Women Population		
		Total	Rural	Urban
(1)	(2)	(3)	(4)	(5)
All Ages	665,288	321,257	247,554	73,804
15-19	64,037	30,160	22,342	7,808
20-24	57,308	28,345	20,872	7,473
25-29	550,747	24,998	18,512	6,486
30-34	42,442	20,843	15,378	4,965
Youth Total	214,535	104,336	77,604	25,732

Note: Due to rounding during estimation, totals may not tally exactly in some cases.

Source: Census of India, 1981, series-I (India), Part II, Special Report and Tables based on 5% sample data.

age groups of: 15-19, 20-24, 25-29 and 30-34 years, it was observed that the proportion of young women was maximum in the age group of 15-19 years and decreased steadily in the following groups both in the case of rural and urban areas. In the rural areas, young women population was 77.6 million (31.35 per cent of the total rural female population) whereas urban young women population was 26.7 million (36.22 per cent of the total urban female population).

Table 2 shows, that according to 1981 Census, the All India literacy rate was 36.23 per cent; 26.65 per cent for rural areas and 57.4 per cent for urban areas. Literacy rate in case

TABLE 2

Young Women Literacy Rates by Age and Strata in India—Census—1981

(Per cent)

Age Group (Years)	Persons			Women		
	T	R	U	T	R	U
(1)	(2)	(3)	(4)	(5)	(6)	(7)
All Ages	36.23	29.65	67.80	24.82	17.96	47.82
15-19	55.37	47.74	76.86	43.28	33.66	70 40
20-24	52.02	43.11	74.71	37.18	27.16	65 16
25-34	45.10	36.25	69.50	28.96	19.64	56.98

of females at all India, rural and urban areas were 24.82 per-cent, 17.96 per cent and 47.82 per ent respectively. The wide difference between the literacy rates of total population and female population is alarming. There is still a wide gap between the educational status of males and females. More-over, the literacy rates of females in urban areas was two to three times the literacy rates in rural areas which indicates that education is still out of reach to a very large proportion of women. The higher literacy rates in the age group of 15-19 years as compared to the higher age groups suggests that with the passage of time the literacy is also going up. Some of significant findings of 1981 census are:

(*i*) Indian girls dropped out of school much faster in 1981 than 1971.

(*ii*) Girls are being pulled out of school and put to work.

(*iii*) In 1981 the percentage of girls completed primary school dropped 33 per cent from 35 per cent in

1971, but in rural areas the dropped out much sharper to 43 from 37 percent.

This has adversely affected our women manpower resources and hence greater emphasis must now be given to this issue.

The 5 per cent sample data of Census, 1981 provide valuable information on the educational and occupational characteristics of the population of literate young women. The 1981 census, has distinguished two categories of workers: Main workers and Marginal workers. The definitions of Main workers and Marginal workers is given as follows:

"Main workers are those who have worked for the major part of the year preceding the date of enumeration and whose main activity was in either cultivation or as agricultural labourer or in household industry or in other work. Marginal workers are those who have not worked for the major part of the preceding year concerned but nevertheless have done some work during any time in the reference period. In other words, such workers while not being capable of being classified as main workers, nevertheless perform some work".

In the 1981 census, total work force was 244.61 million, of which 222.52 million were main workers and 22.09 million marginal workers. Thus, of the total Indian population, 36.77 per cent are in the working force and 33.45 per cent are main workers and only 3.32 per cent are marginal workers of the total main workers, 44.97 million are females which is about 14 per cent of the total female population and 20.21 percent of the total main workers. Total female marginal workers in the Indian economy account for 18.55 millions which are 5.77 per cent of the total female population and about 84 percent of the total marginal workers.

Table 3 shows that in the rural areas, more than 80 per cent of the workforce consists of main workers but in the case of females, the share of marginal workers is as large as 31 per cent. About half of the main workers belong to young age, both in the aggregate as well as for females. The relative

TABLE 3

Main Workers and Marginal Workers Among Young Women in Rural India by Age-Group—Census—1981

(In thousand)

Age Group	Total Work Force		Women Work Force	
	Main Workers	Marginal Workers	Main Workers	Marginal Workers
(1)	(2)	(3)	(4)	(5)
All Ages	176,434	30,874	39,603	17,785
15-19	19,595	2,936	5,088	2,286
20-24	21,847	3,953	5,069	2,423
25-29	21,918	2,612	.4,840	2,280
30-34	19,381	2,208	4,394	2,081
Youth Total	82,741	10,709	19,391	9,010

shares of women main workers in the age-groups of 15-19, 20-24, 25-29 and 30-34 years are 26.24 per cent, 26.14 per cent, 24.96 per cent and 22.66 per cent respectively. Out of female marginal workers, 55.66 per cent belong to the young age group (15-34 years). Table 4 shows that in urban areas, more than 97 per cent of the workforce comprises main workers and the proportion in case of females being 87.5 per cent. Over one half of main workers, both in the aggregate and for females, belong to the young age group. It is important to note that females, account for only 11.65 per cent of the total main workers. In the case of marginal workers, more than 85 per cent are females. The maximum (29 per cent) and minimum (20 per cent) employment of female marginal workers were observed in the age of 25-29 years and 30-34 years.

Occupational and educational analysis in this paper is

TABLE 4

Main Workers and Marginal Workers Among Young Women in Urban India by Age-group—Census—1981

(In thousand)

Age Group	Total Work Force		Women Work Force	
	Main Workers	Marginal Workers	Main Workers	Marginal Workers
(1)	(2)	(3)	(4)	(5)
All Ages	46,083	1,214	5,370	767
15-19	3,309	201	483	121
20-24	6,188	200	691	98
25-29	7,163	182	790	124
30-34	6,396	121	730	86
Youth Total	23,064	704	2,694	429

confined to 'main workers' only. It is evident from Table 5 that 43.4 per cent of female main workers in urban areas are literate, while only 11.8 per cent are literate in rural areas. The proportion of literates among the principles industrial groups for both rural and urban areas are shown in this Table. It is clear from the table that both in rural and urban households, literate female main workers are being absorbed in Transport, Trade and allied activities. Given opportunities for gaining education and skills, non-household industry could also merge in the future as a significant venue for providing employment to female workers in rural and urban areas. Therefore, it becomes necessary for manpower planners to develop the skills of women for tertiary activities for proper manpower utilisation.

The special reports of the Registrar General on the basis of

TABLE 5

Female Main Workers in India Classified by Industrial Category and Literacy—Census—1981

Industrial Category	Female Main Workers			
	Rural		Urban	
	Number (000)	Literacy (%)	Number (000)	Literacy (%)
(1)	(2)	(3)	(4)	(5)
I. Cultivators	14,682	11.7	250	20.8
II. Agricultural Labourers	19,878	7.6	890	11.1
III. Livestock, Forestry, Fishing, Hunting and Plantations, Orchard and Allied Activities	233	15.0	100	27.0

(Contd.)

(Contd.)

(1)	(2)	(3)	(4)	(5)
IV. Mining and Quarrying	134	3.7	29	13.8
V. (*a*) Manufacturing, Processing, Servicing and Repair, Household industry	1,501	20.9	563	32.7
(*b*) Manufacturing, Processing, Servicing and Repair, Non-household Industry	830	30.7	768	44.7
VI. Construction	201	7.5	157	13.4
VII. Trade and Commerce	438	21.2	479	42.4
VIII. Transport, Storage and Communication	47	44.7	123	62.6
IX. Other Services	1,159	53.7	2,012	65.9
Total	39,603	11.8	5,370	43.4

Note: Due to rounding during estimation, totals may not tally exactly in some cases.

the 5 per cent sample provided significant information on the educational level of young women and reveals an inherent weakness in the education system in our country. Table 6 and 7 give date regarding literacy among young women for both rural and urban areas.

Table 6 gives the literacy rates in the various age groups of young women for rural areas. Of the total 19.4 million young women main workers, only 3.16 million (16.28 per cent) are literate. Among them 2 .7 per cent are without any formal education, 42.8 per cent are educated upto primary level and 15.2 per cent are educated upto middle level. On the other hand, technical/non-technical diploma or certificate holders are only 1.5 per cent; and 2.4 per cent are graduate and above.

The decline in the proportion of young women persuing education beyond primary level is mainly due to economic compulsions, lack of educational facilities and social constraints like early marriage. Further, rural young women who are going in for higher education largely prefer general education as compared to technical education. The reason for this can be attributed as much to availability of enough employment opportunities in rural areas for non-technical services as to lack of technical training facilities in rural areas.

Table 7 gives literacy rates and educational levels in the various age groups of young women for urban areas. Of the total 2.7 million young women main workers, 1.5 million (54.1 per cent) are literate. Among them 9.9 per cent are without any formal education, 16.8 per cent are educated upto primary level; 10.4 per cent middle and 23.4 per cent have obtained matriculate/secondary certificate. Though only 3.3 per cent females are technical/non-technical diploma holders, 27.7 percent are graduate and above. Hence it can be safely deduced that after higher secondary, females are attracted towards conventional education, *viz.*, B. A. , M. A., etc. and not towards vocational education.

Table 9 gives the distribution of young women main workers in India by age-group and industrial category. Of the total 45

TABLE 6

Young Women Main Workers in Rural India by Age-Group and Literacy—Census—1981

(In thousand)

Educational Level	Age Group (Years)						Col. (7) as Percentage
	All Ages	15-19	20-24	25-29	30-34	Youth Total	Literate Youth Total
Literate (without educational level)	1,561	303	242	202	158	905	28.7
Primary	1,905	453	393	302	203	1,351	42.8
Middle	616	151	154	109	65	479	15.2
Matriculation/Secondary	329	36	79	77	58	250	7.9
Hr. Secondary/Intermediate/ Pre-University	56	4	15	17	10	46	1.5

Non-Technical Dip./Cert. not equal to degree	18	—	2	4	4	10	0.3
Technical Dip./Cert. not equal to degree	76	—	7	13	19	39	1.2
Graduate and above	103	—	17	33	25	75	2.4
Total Literates	4,664	949	910	755	543	3,157	100.0

Note: Due to rounding during estimation, totals may not tally exactly in some cases.

TABLE 7

Young Women Main Workers in Urban India by Age-Group and Literacy—Census—1981

(In thousand)

Eucational Level	Age Group (Years)						Col. (7) as Percentage to Literate Youth
	All Ages	15-19	20-24	25-29	30-34	Total Youth	Total
Literate (without educational level)	286	41	37	36	30	144	9.9
Primary	410	75	67	55	48	245	16.8
Middle	249	37	46	37	32	152	10.4
Matriculation/Secondary	538	27	95	113	105	340	23.4

Hr. Secondary/Intermediate/ Pre-University	171	7	39	44	32	122	8.4
Non-Technical Dip./Cert. not equal to degree	18	—	2	3	4	9	0.5
Technical Dip./Cert. not equal to degree	73	1	9	14	16	40	2.7
Graduate and above	588	4	109	169	122	401	27.8
Total Literates	2333	192	404	471	389	1456	100.00

TABLE 8

Distribution of Youths Attending School/College by Age, Sex and Strata

(Per cent)

Age Group (Years)	Total			Rural			Urban		
	Persons	Males	Females	Persons	Males	Females	Persons	Males	Females
15-19	26.4	36.0	15.5	20.5	30.9	8.9	42.9	50.2	34.5
20-24	7.2	11.3	3.0	4.7	8.2	1.3	13.4	18.5	7.5
25-34	1.1	1.7	0.5	0.8	1.3	0.3	3.0	2.7	1.1

TABLE 9

Young Women: Main Workers in India by Age-Group and Industrial Category

(In thousand)

Industrial Category	Age-Group (Years)					
	All Ages	15-19	20-24	25-29	30-34	Youth Total
(1)	(2)	(3)	(4)	(5)	(6)	(7)
I	14,932	1,787	1,856	1,777	1,632	7,052
II	20,768	2,772	2,668	2,518	3,293	10,251
III	832	100	107	105	84	396
IV	163	20	22	25	24	91

(Contd.)

(Contd.)

(1)	(2)	(3)	(4)	(5)	(6)	(7)
Sub-Total : Primary Sector	36,695 (81.6)	4,679 (84.0)	4,653 (78.6)	4,425 (78.6)	4,033 (78.7)	17,790 (80.5)
V(*a*)	2,064	321	289	258	222	1,090
V(*b*)	1,598	267	255	216	187	925
VI	358	56	55	51	43	205
Sub-Total: Secondary Sector	4,020 (8.9)	644 (11.5)	599 (10.4)	525 (9.3)	452 (8.8)	2,220 (10.1)
VII	917	46	92	100	109	366
VIII	170	12	30	34	26	102
IX	3,170	190	387	525	505	1,607

Sub-Total:	4,257	248	508	679	640	2,075
Tertiary Sector	(9.5)	(4.5)	(8.8)	(12.1)	(12.5)	(9.4)
Total: All Industries	44,973	5,571	5,760	5,630	5,124	22,085
	(100.0)	(100.0)	(100.0)	(100.0)	(100.0)	(100.0)

*I: Cultivators.
II: Agricultural Labourers.
III: Livestock, Forestry, fishing, etc.
IV: Mining and quarrying.
V: Manufacturing, Processing, Servicing and Repairs:
(a) Household.
(b) Non-household.
VI: Construction.
VII: Trade and Commerce.
VIII: Transport, storage and communication.
IX: Other services.

Note: (*i*) Due to rounding during estimation totals may not tally exactly in some cases.
(*ii*) Figures in brackets represent percentage to grant total.

million female main workers, 31.6 per cent are engaged in the primary sector; 8.9 per cent in the secondary sector; and 9.5 per cent in tertiary sector. Among female main workers, 22.1 million (*i.e.*, 49 per cent) belong to the young age category between age groups of 15-34 years. Among the young age category 80.5 per cent women main workers are engaged in the primary 10.1 per cent in the secondary and 9.4 per cent in the tertiary sectors. The maximum concentration for both primary (84 per cent) and secondary (11.5 per cent) sector was observed in the age groups of 15-19 years whereas in the tertiary sector, the maximum concentration was observed in the age group of 30-34 years.

The work participation rates for young women main workers by various age groups and strata have been given in table 10. The overall work participation rate for females was 14.0 per cent whereas for rural and urban areas the participation

TABLE 10

Work Participation Rates for Young Women Main Workers by Age and Strata: Census—1981

(Per cent)

Age Group (Years)	Work Participation Rates		
	Total	Rural	Urban
(1)	(2)	(3)	(4)
All Ages	14.0	16.0	7.3
15-19	18.5	22.8	6.2
20-24	20.3	24.3	9.3
25-29	22.5	26.1	12.2
30-34	24.6	27.7	14.7
Youth Total	21.2	25.0	10.0

rates were 16.0 per cent and 7.3 per cent respectively. The work participation rates for young women in the aggregate and for rural and urban areas were 21.2 per cent, 25.0 per cent and 10.1 per cent respectively. This indicates that young women account for a higher proportion of female employment especially in rural areas. Among young women, work participation rate increases with age, both in rural and urban areas. In rural areas, in increased from 22.8 per cent in 15-19 years to 27.7 per cent in 30-34 years whereas in urban areas it increased from 6.2 per cent in 15-19 years to 14.7 per cent in 30-34 years.

This is inspite of the efforts made by the government in recent years for the vocationalisation of education, especially for the females. These tables bring out a significant fact that inspite of spread of primary and secondary education and adult education programmes, development of potential female human resources still lags behind seriously. This must now be a matter of utmost concern for educational planners specially in the wake of the new educational policy.

The concept, whether a person was attending an educational institution, *i.e.*, school/college was first introduced in the 1981 census. The distribution of youths attending school/college by sex and strata has been presented in table 8. Among the given age groups the largest proportion of students is in 15-19 years age-group, which stands at 26.4 per cent; however the proportion of young men and young women in this age-groups. This male-female differential is higher in rural areas as compared to urban areas in all the age-groups. The proportion of young women fell sharply from 15.5 per cent in the 15-19 years age-group to 3.0 per cent in 20-24 years age group and further to 0.5 per cent in the 25-34 years age-group. The same trend was observed in rural and urban areas. The possible reasons for the low studentship of women in higher age groups may be due to:

(*i*) Lack of educational facilities;

(*ii*) Early marriage and other social constraints;

(*iii*) Financial constraints.

SECTION II

EMPLOYMENT SITUATION

The information on the employment condition, future prospects for youths and their distribution according to various characteristics is available with the Directorate General of Employment and Training in the Ministry of Labour. Some relevant data which have a bearing on the policy formulation are presented in brief in Tables 11-14.

Table 11 shows the number of work-seekers registered with employment exchanges for the years 1975 to 1985 classified by sex, along with the percentage variation over the previous year. The number of work-seekers increased from 93.3 lakhs in 197- 262.7 lakhs in 1985, *i.e.*, registering an increase of 166.1 per cent during the last decade. The growth of women work-seekers was significantly higher than that of their counter-part; their number increased from 11.2 lakhs in 1975 to 44.5 lakhs in 1985, *i.e.*, an increase of 295.4 per cent. This fact may be attributed to the accelerated growth in women's education and the changing value of the society where the working women is becoming a status symbol. Certain relaxations and facilities provided by the government may also be responsible in attracting educated women in the labour market.

Distribution of Work-seekers by Age-groups

The work-seekers are mainly concentrated in four age group *viz.*, 15-19 years, 20-24 years, 25-29 years and 30-34 years and these four groups together account for about 95 per cent of the total registrants. Table 12 presents the distribution of young work seekers by sex and age-groups as on the end of December, 1984. This table shows that out of 195.4 lakh men and 40.0 lakh women work-seekers, the relative shares in the age-groups 15-19 years, 20-24 years, 25-29 years and 30-34 years for men were 19.8 per cent, 38.5 per cent, 26.4 per cent and 10 per cent respectively and the respective shares in the case of women were 21.4 per cent, 37.9 per cent, 24.5 per cent and 10 per cent. However, the maximum concentration of

TABLE 11

Number of Work-Seekers Registered with Employment Exchanges by Sex During the Years 1975-1985

Year (Ending 31st December)	Number of Work-Seekers ('000)			Percentage Change Over Previous Year		
	Total	Men	Women	Total	Men	Women
(1)	(2)	(3)	(4)	(5)	(6)	(7)
1975	9326.3	8201.4	1124.9	10.6	9.9	15.6
1976	9784.3	8553.6	1230.7	4.9	4.3	9.4
1977	10924.0	9513.7	1410.3	11.6	11.2	14.6
1978	12677.8	11006.2	1671.6	16.1	15.7	18.5
1979	14333.9	12429.6	1904.3	13.1	12.9	13.9
1980	16200.3	13855.1	2345.2	13.0	11.5	23.2

(Contd.)

(Contd.)

(1)	(2)	(3)	(4)	(5)	(6)	(7)
1981	17838.1	15105.2	2732.9	10.1	9.0	16.5
1982	19753.0	16614.6	3138.4	10.7	10.0	14.8
1983	21953.3	18371.7	3581.6	11.1	10.6	14.1
1984	23546.8	19544.7	4002.1	7.3	6.4	11.7
1985	26269.9	21322.4	4447.5	11.6	11.7	11.1

Source: Directorate General of Employment and Training (unpublished data from EMI-unit).

TABLE 12

Distribution of Work-Seekers by Sex and Age-Group

Age-Group (Years)	No. of Work-Seekers as on 31st December, 1984 ('000)			Percentage to Total		
	Total	Men	Women	Total	Men	Women
(1)	(2)	(3)	(4)	(5)	(6)	(7)
15-19	4722.0 (100.0)	3866.8 (81.9)	855.2 (18.1)	20.1	19.8	21.4
20-24	9039.8 (100.0)	7522.0 (83.2)	1517.8 (16.3)	38.4	38.5	37.9
25-29	6134.1 (100.0)	5154.3 (84.0)	979.8 (16.0)	26.0	26.4	24.6

(Contd.)

(Contd.)

(1)	(2)	(3)	(4)	(5)	(6)	(7)
30-34	2357.6 (100.0)	1958.3 (83.1)	399.3 (16.9)	10.0	10.0	10.0
Total (All Ages)	23546.8 (100.0)	19544.7 (83.0)	4002.1 (17.0)	100.0	100.0	100.0

Note: Figures in the brackets are percentages to the total of the respective age-groups.

Source: Directorate General of Employment and Training (unpublished data from EMI-unit).

work-seekers (about 38 per cent) for both the sexes was in the age-group of 20-24 years followed by work-seekers in the age-group 25-29 years (25-26 per cent). This table further depicts that while the relative share of women work-seekers (all ages) to total work-seekers (all ages) was 17 per cent, their relative share to the total registrants in various age-groups varies between 16 per cent to 18 per cent. Thus the women work-seekers are distributed over various age-group in the same pattern as the male work-seekers.

Educated Work-Seekers

The work-seekers in the employment exchanges are registered without any regard to their educational qualifications. Thus illiterates, less educated as well as educated persons are on the live register of the employment exchanges. Since educated general, interested in white collar jobs, the problem of unemployment in the case of educated persons needs greater attention.

The distribution of work-seekers by educational level, sex and age-group has been provided in Tables 13 and 14. It may be observed from these tables that out of 195.4 lakh men and 40.0 lakh women work-seekers, the proportion of educated work-seekers for males and females was only 51 per cent and 63 per cent respectively. Thus about half of the registrants were either illiterate or had qualifications below matric level. Again, of the total 125.4 lakh educated (matric and above) registrants, 100.1 lakh were men and 25.3 lakh were women. It may be noted that among the educated work-seekers, both in the case of men and women, about 60 per cent were matriculates/higher secondary and about 40 per cent were graduate and above.

While analysing the data in respect of educated work-seekers (matric & above) by sex, it may be observed that the proportion or educated young women is higher as compared to men in all the educational levels. It is a pity that the Indian economy is not able to absorb the educated women and they have to wait for long period to get gainful employment. If this trend

TABLE 13

Distribution of Women Work-Seekers by Educational Level and Age-Group (At the End of Dec. 1984)

('n thousands)

Educational Level	Age Group (Years)									
	15-19		20-24		25-29		30-34		Total	
Below Matric	1710.9	271.7	3512.8	520.2	2604.1	394.0	1085.4	175.9	9535.9	1477.0
Matric	1430.8	400.5	2286.9	572.3	1355.5	303.6	489.7	123.9	5825.4	1475.8
Under-Graduate (including Intermediate/Hr. Sec.)	560.2	129.7	1031.1	223.1	630.1	121.7	207.1	40.6	2526.2	549.3
Graduate	159.5	51.8	639.3	178.8	503.6	136.0	156.7	48.2	1503.7	435.6

Post-Graduate	5.4	1.5	61.9	28.4	61.0	24.5	19.4	10.7	155.5	64.4
Total	3866.8	855.2	7522.0	1517.8	5154.3	979.8	1958.3	399.3	19544.7	4002.1

Source : Directorate General of Employment & Training (unpublished data from EMI-unit).

TABLE 14

Percentage Distribution of Work-Seekers by Educational Level and Age-Groups
(At the End of Dec. 1984)

Educational Level	Age-Group (Years)									
	15-19		20-24		25-29		30-34		Total (all ages)	
Below matric	44.3	31.8	46.7	34.3	50.5	40.2	55.5	44.0	48.8	36.9
	(17.0)	(18.4)	(36.8)	(35.2)	(27.3)	(26.7)	(11.4)	(11.9)	(100.0)	(100.0)
Matric	37.0	46.8	30.4	37.7	26.3	31.0	25.0	31.0	29.8	36.9
	(24.6)	(27.1)	(39.3)	(38.8)	(23.3)	(20.6)	(8.4)	(8.4)	(100.0)	(100.0)
Undergraduate (including Intermediate/	14.5	15.2	13 6	14.7	12.2	12.4	10.6	10.2	12.9	13.7
Hr. Secondary	(22.2)	(23.6)	(40.4)	(40.6)	(24.9)	(22 2)	(8.2)	(7.4)	(100.0)	(100.0)
Graduate	(4.1	6.0	8.5	11.8	9.8	13.9	8.0	12.1	7.7	10.9
	(10.6)	(11.9)	(42.5)	(41.1)	(35.5)	(31.2)	(10.4)	(11.1)	(100.0)	(100.0)

Post-graduate	0.1 (3.5)	0.2 (2.3)	0.8 (39.8)	1.5 (36.3)	1.2 (39.2)	2.5 (38.0)	1.0 (12.5)	2.7 (16.6)	0.8 (100.0)	1.6 (100.0)
Total	100.0 (19.8)	100.0 (21.4)	100.0 (38.5)	100.0 (37.9)	100.0 (26.4)	100.0 (24.5)	100.0 (10.0)	100.0 (100.0)	100.0 (100.0)	100.0 (100.0)

Source : Directorate General of Employment & Training (unpublished data from EMI-unit).

continues it will hamper the urge for education, and the educational standards of women in the country will not improve. The women will continue to lag behind. It is, therefore, very necessary that special attention is given to see that all the educated women get employment within reasonable time. There should also be part time employment opportunities for child-bearing and rearing women.

SECTION III

CONCLUSIONS

It is apparent from the present analysis that inspite of the development that has taken place, the economy still lacks the capacity to absorb annual additions to the labour force. Young women largely find employment in unorganised sector. The emphasis on educational development of young women as envisaged in various plans, on the one hand, and the inability of the economy to create adequate employment opportunities for them, on the other hand, is likely to further widen the mismatch between education and employment.

The salient points that emerged from the analysis are :

— the young women are about 32.5 per cent of the total female population. Their distribution in rural and urban areas is three-fourth and one-fourth. (Table 1)

— literacy rate among the young women in urban area is 2 to 3 times higher than that in the rural area. (Table 2)

— among the total young women workers in rural areas, about 68 per cent are main workers, whereas in urban areas, the proportion is as high as 86 per cent. (Table 3 & 4)

— literacy among young women "main workers" is 16.28 per cent in rural areas as compared to 54.1 per cent in urban areas. (Table 6 & 7)

— work participation rates for young women on the criterion of "main workers" in rural and urban areas are 25 per cent and 10 per cent respectively. (Table 10)

— the number of young women work-seekers on the live-register recorded an increase of 295.4 per cent during 1975-85 whereas in the case of men, the increase was only of the order of 166.1 per cent.

— the proportion of educated young workmen work-seekers is in general higher a compared to the men at all educational levels.

Thus, it can be safely conclude, that there is need to pay an attention to the problem of education and employment for women—both in rural and urban areas. Literacy rates and educational levels among young women are far from satisfactory. The fulfilment of the constitutional directive to satisfactory. The fulfilment of the constitutional directive to provide free and compulsory education up to the age of 14 years continues to remain a distant dream as far as women are concerned. No wonder the high illiteracy ratio (75%) among workmen still worries the planners. At present women are largely employed in the unorganised sector which lures them at comparatively low wage and poor facilities. The employment pattern as envisaged in our economy is a reflection of the type of training facilities available for women in India.

In India, even after 40 years of planned development, manpower imbalances in certain categories (specially among young women) do persist although there are not desirable from the point of view of either the individual or the society or the nation. In order to remove these imbalances, adjustment of manpower resources available in the country at different levels is very necessary. Manpower planning *viz-a-viz* educational planning can to a great extent help in reducing these imbalances.

5

Occupational Structure of Women in India

ASHOK KUMAR*

After independence, however, most of our leaders have also realised that people's participation and the economic role of women cannot be isolated from the total framework of development. Despite concerted efforts at improving the status of women, Indian women are observed to be lagging behind in many spheres. It has been emphatically articulated in many debates among forums connected with the development of women that the Indian society has not succeeded in framing the required norms for institutions to enable women to fulfil the multiple roles (as a mother, housewife and a unit of human capital) that they are expected to play.[1] Policy debates in India during the International Women's Decade, have even ironically characterised women as a weaker section. There has even been a fervent plea to treat women with sympathy and compassion, and to provide for job reservations in the field of self-employment generation and employment in organised industries and services.[2]

*Faculty Member at the National Institute of Public Cooperation & Child Development, Regional Centre, Lucknow.

The views expressed in this paper are those of the author and not of the institutions to which he belongs.

It is in the light of the above broad issues, the present section proposed to analyse available evidence on trends in economic participation with a view to identifying critical issues for further consideration. However, the main sources of data on women in the labour fource can be grouped as:

(a) Decennial census of population and economic establishments and National Sample Surveys designed to collect data on the economic and related characteristics of the population;

(b) Returns under various Acts relating to regulation of economic establishments regarding the workers, working conditions, wages and related characteristics therein, and similar voluntary returns from establishments; and

(c) Employment Exchange recording job-seekers, vacancies and job-placements.

Sources at (a) have a comprehensive coverage of the total population, all economic activities, all types of establishments, irrespective of employment, size, location and nature. Sources (b) usually are establishment surveys and have a limited coverage, to either certain industries or certain employment or capital size of establishments.[3] However, sources at (c) provide information more frequently that the sources at (a) but largely in respect of the organised sectors of the economy. The last source at (c) has a limited scope; covering job-seekers and job-placements, and further covers only a small section of the economically active population on a voluntary basis. Data on vacancies are comprehensive in respect of only the organised sector.

Women Work-Force as Per NSS Data

The National Sample Survey Organisation has been collecting the data on labour force, employment and unemployment through their successive rounds since 1952. But more reliable source of information on economic participation of women among the survey of NSSO are the comprehensive enquiries starting from 1972-73, namely the 27th Round (1972-73), the

32nd Round (1977-78) and the 38th Round (1983). In all these three quinquennial surveys, the main objective was to measure the nature and extent of employment and unemployment in quantitative terms disaggregated by meaningful correlates, such as sex, age, education, residence, status, etc.[4] To achieve this objective the attempt in all the three surveys was to classify the population of age 5 years and above as belonging to different activity categories adopting three different approaches:

(*a*) Usual status approach with a reference period of 365 day preceding the date of survey;

(*b*) Current weekly status approach with a reference period of days preceding the date of survey; and

(*c*) Current daily status approach reference period being each day of the 7 days preceding the date of survey.

The data regarding percentage of workers for various categories of population separately for 'usual status'; 'current status' and 'current day status' are presented in Table 1. It is evident from Table 1 that though there was not much variation in respect of the male labour force but there are significant differences in case of the female labour force. It is evident that the 'usual status approach' yielded higher estimate of labour force than the 'current status approach'.

The findings of the last 3 rounds relating to labour force, employment and unemployment are presented in the Table 2.

From Table 2 it would be seen that women employment has been steadily going up in rural India. As a percentage of their population in the age-group of 5 and above, it was 37.53 per cent in 1972-73, 38.48 per cent in 1977-78 and 38.74 per cent in 1983. In case of males between 1972-73 and 1983 there was a drop in their employment from 63.84 per cent to 63.23 per cent. In urban India also the women employment went up from 15.53 per

TABLE 1

Percentage Distribution of All Workers According to Usual Status, Current Status and Current Day Status Approaches During the 27th, 32nd and 38th Rounds of NSS

	27th Round				32nd Round				38th Round			
	Rural		Urban		Rural		Uaban		Rural		Urban	
	Male	Female	Male	Female	Male	Female	Male	Female	Male	Female	Male	Female
Usual Status	63.84	37.53	57.09	15.53	64.06	38.48	57.48	17.80	63.23	38.74	57.71	17.31
Current Weekly Status	61.42	30.52	56.34	13.98	59.94	25.92	56.05	14.75	58.98	25.02	56.02	13.81
Current Day Status	57.9[illegible]	25.22	54.72	12.19	56.12	21.63	54.13	13.00	55.43	21.76	53.77	12.49

TABLE 2

Percentage of Labour Force Employment and Unemployment in India (Rural and Urban)

NSS Rounds/Year	Ref. Period	Criterion	Female Male	Percentage of Population					
				Rural			Urban		
				Labour Force	Employment	Unemployment	Labour Force	Employment	Unemployment
27th Round	Long	Usual	F	37.71	37.53	0.18	16.53	15.33	1.00
(1972-73)	Period	Status	M	64.59	63.84	0.75	59.96	57.00	2.87
32nd Round	One	Usual	F	39.27	38.48	0.79	20.32	17.80	2.52
(1977-78)	Year	Status	M	64.89	64.06	0.89	60 76	57.48	3.28

38th Round*	One	Usual	F	39.06	38.74	0.32	18.36	17.31	1.05
(1983)	Year	Status	M	64.20	63.23	0.97	60.82	57.71	3.11

*Based on unscrutinised data collected during the first-two sub-rounds of 38th Round of NSSO.

Note: (*i*) Percentages are to total population of age 5 years and above, and (*ii*) Labour force percentages have been computed by adding employment and unemployment percentages.

Source: Sarvekshana, Journal of the NSSO, April, 1986.

cent to 17.31 per cent, the corresponding figures for male being 57.09 per cent and 57.71 per cent.

Women Work Force as Per Census Data

Population Consenses have been the main source of information *inter alia*, on the economically active population on a comparative basis. Table 3 gives the percentage of the economically active population for the decennial population censuses of India. The fluctuations observed over the period 1901-1981 particularly noticeable in the case of females are partly due to the differing concepts and definitions relating to the economically active population adopted in the various censuses as is evident from the Table 3 and partly due to changing trends. It has, however, been difficult to involve trends due to these two reasons. This has resulted in the census data not being strictly comparable from one census to the other comparative position of male and female work force and their participation rate, according to the last 3 censuses, is given in Table 3.

However, the data presented in Table 3 are not strictly comparable since concepts and definitions adopted kept on changing from census to census. In 1961 census any person engaged in gainful work for even an hour per day in the greater part of the working season was counted as a worker, whereas in 1971 the person was asked as to what was his main activity and he was classified as worker or non-worker accordingly. Thus, the concept of main worker brought down substantially the participation rate of females. In 1981, the concept of 'main worker' and 'marginal worker, were adopted. As per 1981 main workers are those who have worked for the major part of the reference period and the marginal workers are those who have worked not for the major period but nevertheless have done some work during the reference period. Hence, while 1981 main workers are comparable with the workers of 1971, the work are comparable with the workers of 1971, the work force participation rate of 1981 (main and marginal together) is not comparable to 1961.

TABLE 3

Work Force and their Participation Rates in Rural and Urban Areas, by Sex as Per 1961, 1971 and 1981 Census

Year	Category of Workers	Total			Rural			Urban		
		P	M	F	P	M	F	P	M	F
1961*	Total Workers	188676 (—)	129171 (57.11)	59505 (27.96)	162246 (—)	106751 (58.22)	55495 (31.42)	26430 (—)	22410 (52.40)	4010 (11.09)
1971**	Total Workers	176396 (—)	145379 (52.75)	31017 (14.15)	144781 (—)	117078 (52.78)	27703 (15.84)	31615 (—)	28301 (48.86)	3314 (7.15)
1981	Marginal Workers	22089 (—)	3537 (1.03)	18552 (5.77)	20874 (—)	3090 (1.19)	17784 (7.18)	1214 (—)	477 (0.53)	767 (1.04)
	Total Workers	222516 (—)	177543 (52.62)	44973 (13.99)	176434 (—)	136831 (52.2)	39603 (16.00)	46083 (—)	40713 (48.54)	5570 (7.28)

*Includes Assam.
**Excludes Assam.

Other Surveys

Apart from the NSSO and population censuses, there have been some all India surveys covering certain sections of the population. An All-India Agricultural Labour Enquiry (ALE) was conducted first in 1950-51, followed by a second enquiry in 1956-57. The scope of such an enquiry was later enlarged to cover rural labour households (RLH) during 1963-65, followed by a second RLH during 1974-75. These surveys have been more comprehensive in scope than either the censuses or NSS surveys on employment/unemployment in as much as substantive details like earnings of individuals and number of days in wage-paid employment in a year were also enquired into by them. These details provide an insight into the working conditions of female workers.

Economic Census. The first Economic Census of non-agricultural establishments conducted by the CSO in 1977 collected some information on workers by size of establishment and the second Economic Census 19 0, has a similar provision. However, these censuses do not contain sex-wise break-up of average employment.

Employment Market Information (EMI)

The EMI was established around 1966, the scope of which envelopes almost the entire organised non-agricultural sector of the national economy. While the data on total employment is released quarterly, detailed information on educational level and occupation is collected once in two years for public and private sectors separately.

Employment Exchanges

Over the last 25 years or so the number of employment exchanges rose to 535 and these constitute an important source of information on the number of job seekers. It should however, be noted that the number of job seekers is not necessarily the number of unemployed persons as registration is not compulsory and also multiple registration, and registration of employed seeking better employment are also permitted. Further, registrants have been largely urban based, as there are no rural employment exchanges.

Limitation of the Data Base

The data base available in respect of employment and unemployment is thus restrictive and is subject to limitation. Despite long series of data available on labour force and employment from the population censuses and NSS rounds, the results are largely non-comparable and elaborate research is needed to draw valid inference on inter-temporal variation in the economic participation of women. Comparability among sources is also a problem because of varying concepts and reference periods.

REFERENCES

1 *Towards Equality*, Report of the Committee on Status of Women in India, Deptt. of Social Welfare, Min. of Ed. & Social Welfare, Govt. of India, Dec. 1974, p. 101.

2. *Critical Issues on the Status of Women*, ICSSR, New Delhi, 1977, pp. 10-11.

3. Usha Nayar, *Cultural Roots of Oppression: Patterns of Women's Education in India*, in Sushila Kaushik (Ed.) Women's Oppression: Patterns and Practices, New Delhi, Shakti Books, 1985.

4. *Towards Equality*, *Ibid*, p. 110.

6

Trends in Economic Participation of Women

ASHOK KUMAR*

The long term trend in economic participation of women indicates an overall decline in percentage of workers to total female population in their percentage to the total labour force after 1921. And a slight increase from 1971 to 1981.

Table 1 reveals that work participation rates have been falling since last half a century, both for males and females. But the fall is sharper for females.

Agriculture continued to receive the burden of the surplus labour force all through period of 81 years. Variation in participation rates, in agriculture during different decades mainly show a slight decline before 1847 and a steady rise after 1947.

The participation of women in industry, however, shows a general stagnation, and a distinct decline after 1961. In the post independence period with rapid increase in modern and

*Faculty Member at the National Institute of Public Cooperation & Child Development, Regional Centre, Lucknow.

The views expressed in this paper are those of the authors and not of the institutions to which he belongs.

TABLE 1

Percentage of Economically Active Population

Census	Male	Female
1901	61.11	31.70
1911	61.90	33.73
1921	60.52	32.67
1931	58.27	27.63
1941	DNA	DNA
1951	54.05	23.30
1961	57.10	37.96
1971	52.75	14.15
1981	52.65	19.76

organised sector of industry, the share of household industries declined rapidly. Since they constituted the biggest traditional source of women's employment outside agriculture women, were the greatest victims of this process of economic transformation. The other reason for the exclusion of women from industry was technological change and rationalisation of the process of production which reduced the demand for unskilled labour. Since the majority of women in the modern industrial sector were employed as unskilled workers, they were the main victims of this change.

However, to examine the trends of women's employment, different sectors can broadly be divided into two categories, *i.e.*, unorganised and organised sector.

Women in Unorganised Sector

According to the report of the Committee on the status of women in India about 94 per cent of the women workers are engaged in the unorganised sector of the economy, 81.4

per cent in agriculture and the rest in non-agricultural occupations.

Agriculture has received somewhat more attention from Government agencies and experts engaged in socio-economic research. Consequently, relatively more information is available on the role and conditions of women worker in this field. The non-agricultural industries and services in the unorganised sector, however, have been neglected by most of the investigators, with the result that there is practically no reliable data on this field.

Taking the industrial categories of census which are primarily rural in character, *viz.*, cultivators and agricultural labour, while more male work as cultivator and more female work as agriculture labourers. In fact, half of the female workers (50.86 per cent) in 1971 and almost in same proportion (46.18 per cent) in 1981 worked as agriculture labourers. The predominance of men as cultivator is obviously because of the inheritance laws which are loaded in favour of males. As is well known agricultural labourer's job is lowest paid and so called requiring very little skill. Thus, female workers of rural areas are crowding the lowest paid jobs.

The other industrial category where women outnumber men in household industry. This is another factor which not regulated by any law or code to be enforced by the state and hence, situation permitting, leaves scope for exploitation irrespective of employment status of the workers, whether self-employed or wage employed. If self employed, lack of access to market (both for factors and commodities) renders opportunity to unscrupulous middlemen and others to exploit the women. The employed on wage, in absence of any rule or authority to enforce the right of workers, scope of exploitation is enormous.

It can be seen from Table 2 that women engaged in agricultural activities has declined marginally (1.3 per cent) as compared to men (4.1 per cent) during 1971 to 1981. Whereas increase in female cultivators from 29.84 per cent to

TABLE 2

Percentage Distribution of Main Workers by Industrial Categories

Industrial Category	1971		1981	
	Male	Female	Male	Female
1. Cultivator	45.90	29.84	43.70	33.20
2. Agril. Labourers	21.54	50.86	19.56	46.18
3. Livestock, Forestry, Fishery, Hunding, etc.	2.24	1.31	2.34	1.85
4 Mining, Quarrying	0.54	0.40	0.62	0.36
5. (*a*) Household Industry	3.42	4.24	3.18	4.59
(*b*) Industry other than household	6.70	2.77	8.92	3.55
6. Construction	1.36	0.65	1.81	0.80
7. Trade and Commerce	6.37	1.[illegible]8	7.33	2.04
8. Transport	2.86	0.47	3.32	0.38
9. Other Services	9.07	7.08	9.22	7.05
All Categories	100.00	100.00	100.00	100.00

33.20 per cent and decline in male cultivators from 45.9 to 93 7 per cent in the respective period. An explanation of this could be found from the nature of distribution of asset holdings (mainly land) of these workers.

Women in Organised Sector

While discussing Census data which has a comprehensive coverage it was pointed out that only a small proportion (6 per cent) of women are employed in organised sector, which are regulated through state intervention. But since employment in organised sector have a large element of formality, it becomes visible to public eye. Further, establishment in this sector are usually concentrated in urban and sub-urban areas as a result of which there is great communication among workers engaged in this sector, giving opportunity for unionisation and trade union activity. The trade unions being vocal and politically volatile certain rights of workers have given legal sanction and employers are obliged under law to acceed to them. Because of these regulations by the state and their periodic reporting being obligatory fairly large amount of data is available on organised sector. In spite of its share in total employment being not at all substantial. The data on organised sector is available separately from public and private sector (see Table 3).

From Table 4 three conclusicns emerge. Firstly, while the public sector offer more employment as compared to the private sector, the latter employs more number of women than the former. Secondly, over the pericd of twelve years, women's employment in public sector has been rising faster than the private sector. Thus, as shown in the Table 4 employment of women in the public sector has been rising at an annual rate of 5 to 7 per cent as compared to only 2 per cent in the private sector. Moreover, annual growth rate of employment of women in public sector is much higher than the growth rate of total employment in the said sector. This is an indication of the public policy after 1975, in which International Women Year was declared by the United Nations and some emphasis was laid down on women's status on the one hand and on the other is the education intensity. The third conclusion that emerges is a corollary of the second. As public sector employment of women is growing at a much faster rate than the same for the private sector relative importance of the two sectors in share of women's employment is undergoing radical change. Thus, while in 1971 about 45 per cent of organised employment of women was accounted for by the public sector it rose to 54 per cent ten years later. In other words there was a reversal of the position between the two sectors, so far as share in women's employment is concerned.

TABLE 3

Distribution of Male and Female Workforce in Unorganised and Organised Sector—1971 and 1981*

Industrial Categories	Unorganised Sector				Organised Sector				%age Share of Female in			
	Male		Female		Male		Female		Male		Female	
	1971	1981	1971	1981	1971	1981	1971	1981	1971	1981	1971	1981
(1)	(2)	(3)	(4)	(5)	(6)	(7)	(8)	(9)	(10)	(11)	(12)	(13)
Agriculture, Hunting, Forestry Fishing & Allied Activities	103498 (77.5)	118977 (72.2)	25487 (87.7)	36547 (85.5)	677 (4.4)	864 (4.3)	396 (20.6)	456 (16.3)	19.8	23.5	36.9	34.5
Mining & Quarrying	266 (0.2)	272 (0.2)	71 (0.2)	78 (0.2)	533 (3.4)	861 (4.3)	53 (2.8)	87 (3.1)	21.1	22.3	9.0	9.2
Manufacturing**	10067 (7.5)	15947 (9.8)	1765 (6.0)	3097 (7.2)	(4804) (30.9)	6153 (30.6)	431 (22.4)	612 (21.9)	14.9	16.3	8.2	9.0

(Contd.)

(*Contd.*)

(1)	(2)	(3)	(4)	(5)	(6)	(7)	(8)	(9)	(10)	(11)	(12)	(13)
Construction	1056 (0.8)	2198 (1.3)	145 (0.5)	304 (0.7)	959 (6.2)	1102 (5.5)	59 (3.1)	59 (2.1)	12.1	12.1	5.8	5.1
Transport, Storage & Communications	1987 (1.5)	3331 (2.1)	99 (0.3)	90 (0.2)	2270 (14.6)	2688 (13.4)	47 (2.4)	82 (3.0)	4.7	2.0	2.0	3.0
Trade, Commerce & Services	16740 (12.5)	21800 (13.4)	21848 (6.3)	2643 (6.2)	6237 (40.5)	8418 (41.9)	938 (48.7)	11977 (53.6)				
Total	133616	162575	29415	42759	15530	20036	1924	2793	18.0	20.8	11.8	13.9

*Includes estimated work force of Assam which has been computed by applying the work participation rates for the year 1971 to the projected population of Assam.

**Includes Electricity, gas and water.

Note: Figures in parentheses denote percentage of the total.

Source: (*i*) Employment Reviews, DGE&T, Min. of Labour, New Delhi.
(*ii*) Censuses of India, RGO, India, New Delhi.

TABLE 4

Employment of Women in Public and Private Sectors

(Employment in lakhs)

Year Ending March	Public Sector			Private Sector			Total Public & Private Sector		
	Total	Women	Per Cent	Total	Women	Per Cent	Total	Women	Per Cent
(1)	(2)	(3)	(4)	(5)	(6)	(7)	(8)	(9)	(10)
1971	107.11	8.61	8.0	67.43	10.63	15.8	174.54	19.24	11.0
1972	112.09	9.11	8.1	67.69	11.05	16.3	179.78	20.16	11.2
1973	119.75	10.05	8.4	68.49	11.30	16.5	188.24	21.35	11.3
1974	124.86	10.72	8.6	67.94	11.11	16.4	192.80	21.88	11.3
1975	138.63	11.19	8.8	68.04	11.02	16.2	196.67	22.31	11.3

(Contd.)

(Contd.)

(1)	(2)	(3)	(4)	(5)	(6)	(7)	(8)	(9)	(10)
1976	133.63	12.20	9.1	68.44	11.77	17.2	202.07	23.97	11.9
1977	138.76	12.96	9.3	68.67	11.98	17.4	207.43	24.94	12.0
1978	144.41	14 12	9.8	70.43	12.44	17.7	214.84	26.56	12.4
1979	146.70	13.69	9.3	70.08	12.46	17.3	218.78	26.15	11.9
1980	150.78	14.47	9.6	70.27	12.55	17.4	223.05	27.02	12.1
1981	154.84	14.99	9.7	73.95	12.94	17.5	228.79	27.93	12.2
1982*	159.48	15.80	9.9	76.11	13.20	17.3	235.59	29.00	12.3
Growth rate	3.7	5.7	2.0	1.0	2.0	0.8			

*Figures for 1982 is provisional.

Source: Min. of Labour, Statistics relating of employment and unemployment of women (Mimeograph).

7

Women's Share in Household and Non-Household Industry

ASHOK KUMAR*

I. INTRODUCTION

The status of any given section of population in a society is intimately connected with its economic position which depends on rights, roles and opportunities for participation in economic activities.[1] Economic development is the progress towards an increasingly intricate pattern of labour specialization. The position of women differs in many basic features in the community groups. The extant development paradigms had produced a mind set which saw men as 'producers' and women as 'consumers', assigning men not only the tasks of production but also providing the education and training necessary for the same. Women, on the other hand, were assigned the privileged tasks of familiar nutrition and consumption ignoring their roles as producers. In the World Conference on food and population the women's status was recognised as important variable in production and reproduction.

Wh le discussing the partcipation of women in production process, one has to keep in mind the gender role ideology in

*Dr. Ashok Kumar is a Faculty Member of the Institute of Applied Mannpower Research, New Delhi.

the mode of production. One line of thinking is to analyse the development of housewife role as a historical product of changes in the economic function of the household and the physical and conceptual separation of domestic work from other kinds of work (Gulati, 1957, Oakley, 1976, Kanther, 1977, Srinivas, 1978). From the second point of view women constitute labour reserve: being defined first and foremost as domestic workers and may be drawn into the industrial work force or excluded from it according to the needs of capitalist production (Sinha, 1972, Papnek 1973, Bland *et. al.* 1979, Sharma, 1980). Some micro level studies (Gadgil, 1965, Mitra, 1979, Sharma, 1980, Alikhan and Ayesha 1982, Jain, 1983) reveals womens's participation has been declining since 1921. Reasons for the decline of women's participation in the workforce differ in urban and rural areas which are mainly rooted from a strong view that wife's leisure might be taken as a sign of status rather than indigence.[2] The other factors that exhibit women's employment are heavy domestic work load, lack of assumed work, irregular and underpayment of wages, absence of transport facilities, lack of child care centres and other supportive structures.[3] It is, however, well documented as well as empirically shown that women are no longer a protected dependent sex in modern India but an active member of this developing nation.

After realising the significant role of women, an attempt has been made in the present exercise on the patterns of women's occupational participation in twenty selected states for which 1981 census is available. The focus is primarily on household and non-household industry occupations and investigated with two-digit occupational classifications. It has also been determined whether women workers are relegated to low status-ranking occupations and how much scope exists for vertical physical and occupational mobility and identified the major occupations in which women workers are in dominance.

II. METHODS OF ANALYSIS

For the purpose of this exercise, the major groups of Industry in the Indian Standard Industrial Classification (ISIC)[4] answering to household[5] and non-household industry[6], rural and urban are statewise identified.[7] The idea is to examine specifically the extent of females participation relative to males in the household manufacturing sector, which is usually regarded as the stronghold of female workers. The index of assessing female participation relative to male is to work out the sex ratio (F/M$\times$1000) of participants in each major groups and study the behaviour of this ratio in household and non-household activity by major groups, rural and urban and different regions.

For the purpose of analysis of variance, a two-way ANOVA test (with one observation per cell) was applied. The mathematical details are as follows:

Let, n_{ij} be the value from the *i-th* group and *j-th* region.

The linear mathematical model, *i.e.*,

$$n_{ij}=\mu+\alpha_i+\beta_j+E_{ij} \qquad (1)$$

Where,

μ is the general mean effect,

α_i is the effect due to *i-th* group,

β_j is the effect due to *j-th* region, and

E_{ij} is the error effect due to chance,

and

$$\sum_{i=1}^{k} \alpha_i=0=\sum_{j=1}^{h} \beta_i \qquad (1.2)$$

Null Hypothesis

The null hypothesis is that the groups as well as regions are homogenous. In other words, the null hypothesis for groups and regions are respectively,

$$Hg : \alpha_1=\alpha_2= \quad \ldots= \quad =0$$

$$Hz : \beta_1=\beta_2= \quad \ldots= \quad =0 \qquad (1.3)$$

i.e., there is insignificant difference between groups as well as between regions.

Now, $S_t^2 = S_g^2 + S_z^2 = S_e^2$ .... (1.4)

where ; S_t^2—is the total sum of squares.

S_g^2—is the S.S. due to Groups.

S_z^2—is the S.S. due to regions.

S_e^2—is the S.S. due to Error.

For numerical computation of the various sum of squares the following formulas are used.

Total sum of squares = R.S.S. (Row Sum of Squares)

(T.S.S.)—C.F. (Correction factor)

$$= \sum_i \sum_j n_{ij}^2 - \frac{G^2}{N}$$

$$\left[C.F. = \frac{G^2}{N} \right] \qquad (1.5)$$

Where, G is the grand total of all the cell observation and $N = k \times h$ or (rows × columns)

Groups Sum of Squares

$$(C.S.S.) = \frac{1}{h} \sum_{i=1}^{k} T_i^2 - C.F. \qquad (1.6)$$

Regions Sum of Squares

$$(R\ S.S.) = \frac{1}{k} \sum_{i=j}^{h} T_j^2 - C.F. \qquad (1.7)$$

Error Sum of Squares is then calculated by subtracting the total of Group Sum of Squares and Regions Sum of Squares from the Total Sum of Squares.

ANOVA Table for Two-way Classified Data

Source of Variation	Sum of Squares (S.S)	*d.f.*	M.S.S.	Variance Ratio
(1)	(2)	(3)	(4)	(5)
Groups	S_g^2=C.S.S.	$(k-1)$	$S_g^2/(k-1)$	$F_g=\frac{S_g^2}{S_E^2} \sim F_{(k-1),\ (k-1),\ (h-1)}$
Regions	S_z^2=Z.S.S.	$(h-1)$	$S_z^2/(h-1)$	$F_z=\frac{S_z^2}{S_E^2} \sim F_{(h-1),\ (k-1),\ (h-1)}$
Error	S^2_E	$(k-1)\times(h-1)$	$S_E^2/(k-1)$	$(h-1)$
Total	T.S.S.	(N—1) or $(hk-1)$		

The degrees of freedom (*d. f.*) for Groups, Regions and Error should add up to total *d. f.*

If the observed value of F_g obtained is greater than the tabulated value of F for $(k-1)$, $(k-1)$ $(h-1)$ *d. f.* at specified level of significance (usually 5% or 1%) then H_g is refuted as that level otherwise it may be retained.

Similarly for F_z.

If the Error mean Sum of Squares is less than the M. S. S. of any factor of classification then F is calculated by keeping M. S. S. (Error) in the numerator.

In the ANOVA Table, the valuable of the variance ratio F which are significant at the given level of significance, has been marked with one asterisk (*). Double asterisk (**) represents highly significant value.

Since variance is independent of change of origin, the shifting of origin to some arbitrary point, if necessary, also reduces arithmetic to a great extent.

III. ANALYSIS OF DATA

It is decided to limit the present exercise to the six political regions of India to fiind out whether significant regional differences exist. Besides, analysis on the basis of all the states and union territories would be a very large undertaking. The analysis has been thus confined to variations in the sex ratio of participation in rural and urban areas of each of the six political regions of India distributed by Major Groups of the industrial Classification of household and non-household industry.

Ranking of Regions. The first three Major Groups (MG, in order of total number of workers employed in different regions are given Table 1. It is evident from the table that out of 6 Regions, in 4 Regions Major Group 27 (*i.e.*, Manufacture of wood and wood products, furnitures and fixtures) occupies first order followed by Major Group 26 (*i.e.*, Manufacture of Textile Products, other than Footwear).

Non-household industry classification runs through all the 9 Divisions of the Industrial Classification. Among the different Divisions the Divisions 2 and 3 (Manufacturing and Repair) occupies the first position followed by, Division 9 (Con munity, social and personal services) and Division 6 (wholesale and Retail Trade Hotels). The highest ranking is occupied by Division 2 and 3 for all the regions, followed by Division 9 and 6, although not always in that order in every region.

Ranking of Sex-Ratio of Workers

The sex ratio of workers (*i.e.*, 1000×Female/Male) other than in cultivation was computed for all industrial major groups. In the ideal circumstances of men and women partici-

TABLE 1

(A) First-Three Major Groups Employed in Household Industry in Different Regions

Region	First Order Groups	Second Order Groups	Third Order Groups
India	MG-23 (Manufacture of Cotton Textiles)	MG-27 (Manufacture of wood and wood products, furnitures and fixtures)	MG-39 (Repair)
Northern	MG-26 (Manufacture of Textile Products other than Footwear)	MG-27 (Manufacture of wood and wood products, furnitures and fixtures)	MG-39 (Repair)
Central	MG-26 (Manufacture of Textile Products (other than Footwear)	MG-39 (Repair)	MG-27 (Manufacture of wood and wood products, furniture and fixtures)
Eastern	MG-27 (Manufacture of wood and wood products, furnitures and fixtures)	MG-23 (Manufacture of Cotton Textiles)	MG-32 (Manuf.cture of Non-Metallic Mineral Products)

(*Contd.*)

(Contd.)

Region	First Order Groups	Second Order Groups	Third Order Groups
North-Eastern	MG-27 (Manufacture of wood and wood products, furnitures and fixtures)	MG-39 (Repair)	MG-26 (Manufacture of Textile Products other th n Footwear)
Southern	MG-27 (Manufacture of wood and wcod products, furnitures and fixtures)	MG-39 (Repair)	Mg-26 (Manufacture of Textile Products other than Footwear)
(B) First-Three Major Groups in Non-Household Industry in Different Regions			
India	MG-65 (Retail Trade in Food and Articles, Bever ges, Tobacco and Intoxicants)	MG-70 (Land Transport)	MG-90 (Public Admn. and Defence Services)
Northern	MG-70 (Land Transport)	MG-65 (Retail Trade in Food and Food Articles, Beverages, Tobacco and Intoxicants)	MG-02 (Live stock Production)
Central	MG-65 (Retail Trade in Food and Food Articles, Beverages, Tobacco and Intoxicants)	MG-70 (Land Transport)	MG-99 (Services not elsewhere classified)

Eastern	MG-65 (Retail Trade in Food and Food Articles, Beverages, Tobacco and Intoxicants)	MG-90 (Public Admn. and Defence Services)	MG-70 (Land Transport)
North-Eastern	MG-90 (Public Admn. and Defence Services)	MG-65 (Retail Trade in Food and Food Articles, Beverages, Tobacco and Intoxicants)	MG-70 (Land Transport)
Western	MG-70 (Land Transport)	MG-90 (Public Admn. and Defence Services)	MG-65 (Retail Trade in Food and Food Articles, Beverages, Tobacco and Intoxicants)
Southern	MG-65 (Retail Trade in Food and Food Articles, Beverages, Tobacco and Intoxicants)	MG-70 (Land Transport)	MG-90 (Public Admn. and Defence Services)

pating equally in every industry or activity, this ratio would be 1000. However, the sex ratio for rural/urban and household and non household industry has been calculated for all the Major Groups are rearranged according to sex ratio category. The consolidated Table 2 gives frequency of each of the sex ratio categories. The percentage frequency columns convert the absolute frequencies in the frequency column into percentages, categories I to VI together being taken as 100. The cumulative percentage frequency (to identify the greater-than-type groups) column adds up the percentage frequencies from bottom upwards to the figure 100 in each case.

For household industry in India as a whole, 80 per cent (85% for rural and 80% for urban) of the Major Groups fall in the low frequency category IV (250- 99). While in non-household industry this percentage is as high as more than 90 per cent. In other words, the proportion of women employed is less than half of men in more than two-third of the Major Groups. This does not bring out the gravity of the situation quite fully. In fact, in one-fifth (20 per cent in rural and 25 per cent in urban) the proportion of women employed is in the very low grading, being as little as between twentieth and a quarter of men employed.

The corresponding picture in non-household industry is much more distributing, in fact alarming. The maximum participation frequency (34 rural and 36 urban) occurs in the low category V (5o to 249) and 42 per cent of rural and 44 per cent of urban the Major Groups fall in category VI (Lowest). This means that only in one per cent of the Major Groups in rural non-household industry does the participation of women exceed half that of men. The great bulk of rural non-household industry Major Groups have a participation rate of women which varies between a twentieth and a quarter (50-250) of that of men.

As reflected by the sex ratio figures for household and non-household industry, the position of female workers in both rural and urban areas is quite alarming, verging on the precarious. Generally speaking, more than 85 per cent of the

TABLE 2

Percentage Frequency of Participation Sex Ratio in India and Six Regions by Rural Urban Household and Non-Household Industry, 1981

(Sex Ratio Categorisation: I: Over 1000, II: 750-999, III: 500-749, IV: 250-499, V: 50-249, VI: Below 50)

Category	Rural			Urban		
	Frequency	Percentage Frequency	Cumulative Percentage Frequency	Frequency	Percentage Frequency	Cumulative Percentage Frequency
(1)	(2)	(3)	(4)	(5)	(6)	(7)
			HOUSEHOLD INDUSTRY			
			India			
I	1	5	100	3	15	100

(*Contd.*)

(Contd.)

(1)	(2)	(3)	(4)	(5)	(6)	(7)
II	1	5	95	0	0	85
III	1	5	90	1	5	85
IV	8	40	85	3	15	80
V	5	25	45	8	40	65
VI	4	20	20	5	25	25
Total	20	100		20	100	
NON-HOUSEHOLD INDUSTRY						
India						
I	0	0	100	0	0	100
II	1	1	100	0	0	100
III	0	90	99	2	3	100
IV	7	10	99	2	3	97

V	34	47	89	36	50	94
VI	31	42	42	31	44	44
Total	73	100		73	100	

Major Groups in household and non-household industry, rural and urban, have sex ratio falling in category IV and below. In other words, not more than 15 per cent of the Major Groups have sex ratios which can be called High, Moderate or Low Moderate, with female participation rates of 500 and above.

IV. ANALYSIS OF RESULTS

An examination of the results in Table 3 of analysis of variance dealing with rural household industry workers shows that there is no significant variation in the number of females per 1000 males between regions. But the variation in sex ratio between Major Groups is significant at 1 per cent level. In point of fact, statistically speaking, the mean sex ratios for six regions are not quite different from each other. On the other hand, all Major Groups do not have equal mean sex ratio. This inequality of mean sex ratio for all Major Groups having been established, the next obvious question will be to identify the Major Groups that has the highest mean sex ratio.

However, Table 4 shows the results of analysis of variance for urban household industry work. The results are significant

TABLE 3

Analysis of Variance for Rural Household Industry Workers, 1981

Source	Degree of Freedom (D.F.)	Sum of Squares (S.S.)	Mean Sum of Squares (M.S.S.)	F-value
Major Group	18	38974794	2165266	28.213**
Region	5	37160228	7432045	96.83**
Error	90	6907223	76747	—
Total	113	83042245	—	—

Note: Double Asterisk indicates insignificant at 1% level.

at 1 per cent level, meaning thereby is significant variations exist in both Groups as well as regions. Hence, we have not calculated the critical differences for this particular Table, whereas for other three tables ranking and critical differences have been worked out. The task thereafter will be to rank all other Major Groups by the decreasing mean sex ratio. This is what is done in the first three column of Table 7, with the first column containing the description of the Major Groups of of the highest six and the lowest six mean sex ratios.

TABLE 4

Analysis of Variance for Urban Household Industry Workers, 1981

Major Group	18	466397038	25910947	1.074*
Region	5	159224271	31844854	1.32*
Error	90	2171957121	24132857	—
Total	113	2797578430	—	—

Note: Single Asterick indicates significant at 1% level.

After ranking the Major Groups, one would like to know whether one Major Group was statistically different from another, that is, to go in for pairwise comparisons in terms of mean sex ratio. The comparison of one Major Group with another next in rank is done by comparing the mutual mean difference given in the fourth column of Table 7 with the computed critical differences given at the bottom of the table.

The differences in the ranking of regions in rural household industry is presented in the first left hand column in Table 7. This shows the significant differences between regions: the North-Eastern commands the highest mean sex ratio followed by Southern, Eastern, Northern, Central and Western respectively. The mean sex ratio for North-Eastern region is significantly different from that of Southern.

Tables 5 and 6 show that the variance among regions as well as among major Groups is not significant at 1 per cent level. The ranking of regions presented in the Table 7 puts the Southern (in rural non-household industry) North-Eastern (in urban non-household industry) at the top. The ranking of Regions in terms of mean sex ratio, with the qualifying observation that the mean sex ratio for each of them is very low..

TABLE 5

Analysis of Variance for Rural Non-Household Industry Workers, 1981

Source	Degree of Freedom (D.F.)	Sum of Squares (S.S.)S_E *	Mean Sum of Squares (M.S S.)S_E *	F-Value
Major Group	63	5747390	89802	4.79**
Region	5	565605	113121	6.04**
Error	320	7305441	18731	—
Total	389	13618436	—	—

Note: Double Asterisk indicates insignificant at 1% level.

Since regions show significant differences, instead of calculating students 't' for different pairs of regions. We calculated the least significant difference at the given level of significance. This least difference is known as the critical difference (C. D.) and calculated by the formula given below:

$$\sqrt{\frac{2\,S_e^2}{r}} \times t\ 0.05 \text{ for error } d.f. \qquad (1.8)$$

Where,

S_e^2 = Mean Sum of Square (M.S.S.)

r = Regions, *i.e.*, 6

TABLE 6

Analysis of Variance for Urban Non-Household Industry Workers, 1981

Source	Degree of Freedom (D.F.)	Sum of Squares (S.S.)	Mean Sum of Squares (M.S.S.)	F-Value
Major Group	63	7561988	120031	2.65**
Region	5	1212066	242413	5.34**
Error	315	14290799	45367	—
Total	383	23064853	—	—

Note: Double Asterisk indicates insignificant at 1% level.

We arrange the region's mean in their descending order of magnitude. However, the results are presented in the Tables. We therefore, conclude that the difference between means of North-Eastern region and Southern region are significantly different from each other, since the differences between their mean, *viz.*, 1437 exceeds critical difference, *i.e.*, 313.49. All the remaining differences are not significant.

V. FINDINGS

The discussion in this paper is proof of the limited number of industries in which women participate to any significant degree. Activities engaging higher rates of female participation in house-hold industry are industries relating to different textiles, tobacco products or forestry and logging which are characterised by high labour intensity and tediousness, less mobility, less skill, coupled—with less remuneration. On the other hand, some of the Major Groups in non-household industry are commandnig higher rates of female participation. This marked difference in work participation for women in many

TABLE 7

Rural Household Industry

Region	Mean	Mutual Mean Difference
North-Eastern	1778	1437
Southern	341	84
Eastern	257	23
Northern	234	4
Central	230	39
Western	191	—

Critical Difference
(5% Level)=313.49

Rural Non-Household Industry

Region	Mean	Mutual Mean Difference
Southern	178	6
North-Eastern	172	24
Western	148	22
Central	126	19
Eastern	107	39
Northern	68	—

Critical Difference
(5% Level)=154.87

(Contd.,

Urban Non-Household Industry

Region	Mean	Mutual Mean Difference
North-Eastern	231	77
Southern	154	31
Western	123	45
Northern	78	1
Eastern	77	2
Central	75	—

Critical Difference
(5% Level)=241.02.

Major Groups in household industry and several in non-household industry, where higher female participation is invariably characterised by heavy manual labour, druggery, insanitary conditions of work, and low remuneration, may very possibly have undesirable impacts on society through first, high morality rate of women (the continuous decline in sex ratio in the population since 1901 is disturbing, to say the least) and, second, through the motivation of increasing the family size to lessen the burden of economic struggle.

REFERENCES

1. Report of the Committee on the Status of Women in India, "*Towards Equality*", Govt. of India, Deptt. of Social Welfare Min. of Education, p. 148.
2. Ashok Kumar (1989), "*Indian Women Towards 21st Century*, Criterion Publications, New Delhi, p. 8.
3. *Ibid.*, p. 8.
4. The Study is based on the 1981 industrial classification. The Indian Standard Classification (ISC) classifies the industrial distribution of workers into 9 Divisions and 99 Major Groups.

5. Household industry in strictly limited to manufacturing on the household level and excluded manufacturing outside house.

6. Non-household industry, spous manufacturing, construction, trade and commerce, transport, communication and services.

7. Household industry in the Census of India, 1981 is confined to Division 2 and 3 only and the major and minor groups comprising them.

8

Employment Characteristics of Women: A Case Study of Rural Andhra Pradesh

P.K. SAXENA*

I. Introduction

The female work participation rate (main workers) in rural Andhra Pradesh is reasonably high. The 1981 Census defines main workers as these, "who had work for the major part of the year preceding the date of enumeration, *i.e.*, those who were engaged in any economically productive activity for 183 days or six months or more during the year". According to 1981 Census, in rural Andhra Pradesh, the female work participation rate (henceforth it will be referred as FWPR) was 31.95 per cent against the All India rural FWPR of 16.00 per cent and among 21 states (excluding Assam) it was placed at the fifth place. Interestingly, all the four states (Nagaland, Manipur, Sikkim and Meghalaya) with higher rural FWPR than Andhra Pradesh were hilly states.

According to 1981 Census, in Andhra Pradesh, 77.0 per cent of the female population lived in rural areas and only 23.0 per

*Faculty Member, Institute of Applied Manpower Research, New Delhi. Views expressed in this paper are exclusively those of the author and nor of the Institute to which he belongs.

cent was in urban areas. However, out of 71.43 lakh female workers, 65.06 lakh or 91.1 per cent were from rural areas, and only 6.37 lakh or 8.9 per cent belonged to urban areas. It is due to the reason that urban women in comparison to their rural counterparts had a very low work participation rate, *i.e.*, 10.49 per cent. In such a predominantly agrarian economy like Andhra Pradesh, a proper understanding of the employment characteristics of rural women seeks specific attention.

II. Objective

The paper proposes to:

(*i*) Give an overview of male and female work participation rate in rural Andhra Pradesh.

(*ii*) Examine decadal variation in FWPR.

(*iii*) Highlight sectoral distribution of female work force.

(*iv*) Establish inter-relationship between FWPR and some influencing variables.

This paper is based on 1971 and 1981 Census and takes into account only main workers. The concept of main worker was introduced in 1981 Census, and main workers of 1981 Census are comparable with workers of 1971 Census.

III. Female Work Participation

The intercensal period 1971-81 has witnessed a sharp rise in female work force in rural Andhra Pradesh. During this period, the growth rate of rural female work force has been very higher than that of rural female population. The rural female population increased from 174.0 lakh in 1971 to 203.6 lakh in 1981, thereby showing an annual growth rate of 1.70 per cent. On the other hand, rural female work force increased from 47.62 lakhs to 65.06 lakhs, thereby releasing a highly significant annual growth rate of 3.66 per cent. In comparison to it, rural male work force could increase at the annual growth rate of 1.56 per cent only.

The data in Table 1 gives an overview of male and female work participation rate in rural Andhra Pradesh for the year

TABLE 1

Male and Female Work Participation Rate in Rural Andhra Pradesh—1981

Districts	Male Work Participation Rate	Female Work Participation Rate
(1)	(2)	(3)
Nizamabad	59.34	43.84
Karimnagar	60.50	40.52
Kurnool	57.98	38.23
Mahbubnagar	59.62	37.75
Rangareddy	57.38	35.22
Guntur	60.29	35.13
Prakasam	58.83	34.39
Medak	59.32	34.11
Adilabad	58.83	33.80
Anantpur	58.28	33.23
Warangal	59.08	32.31
Nalgonda	60.19	32.11
Vizianagaram	60.96	31 29
Srikakulam	59.12	31.17
Khammam	58 46	30.71
Nellore	60.01	30.36
Krishna	60.04	28.40
Chittor	60.34	28.40

(Contd.)

(*Contd.*)

(1)	(2)	(3)
Visakhapatnam	61.11	27.76
Cuddapah	58.41	27.50
West-Godavari	60.33	26.68
East Godavari	60.31	19.78
Andhra Pradesh	59.56	31.95
Coefficient of Variation	1.68	15.66

Source: Census of India 1981, Series-2, Andhra Pradesh, Part III-A and B(*i*), General Economic Tables Director of Census Operations, Andhra Pradesh.

1981. It is evident from the table that FWPR exhibits significant inter-district variations, and it ranges from a very low rate of 19.78 per cent for East Godavari to a substantially high rate of 43.84 per cent for Nizamabad. Out of 22 districts, 16 are having FWPR above 30.00 per cent but below 45.00 per cent, while in five it is between 20.00 per cent and 30.00 per cent, and in only one district it is below 20.00 per cent. The measure of inequality, *i.e.*, coefficient of variation is 15.66 which confirms further inter-district inequalities in FWPR.

In comparision to FWPR, male work participation rate is very high and it shows marginal inter district variations. In rural Andhra Pradesh, out of 100 men, 59.56 take up economic work as their main activity against 31.95 for women. The male work participation rate ranges very narrowly from 57.38 per cent for Kurnool to 61.11 per cent for Visakhapatnam, the coefficient to variation being 1.68 only.

The data in Table 2 shows that during the period 1971-81, the FWPR in rural Andhra Pradesh increased from 27.37 per cent to 31.95 per cent, thereby showing a decadal increase

TABLE 2

Decadal Variation in Female Work Participation Rate, and Percentage Share of Female in Total Employment in Rural Andhra Pradesh : 1971-81

District	Female Work Participation Rate				Percentage Share of Female in Total Employment			
	1971	1981	Decadal Increase	Percentage Decadal Increase	1971	1981	Decadal Variation (+) or (—)	Percentage Decadal Variation
(1)	(2)	(3)	(4)	(5)	(6)	(7)	(8)	(9)
Nizamabad	34.60	43.84	9.24	26.71	36.45	43.21	+6.76	+18.55
Karimnagar	33.30	40.52	7.22	21.68	34.81	40.18	+5.37	+15.43
Kurnool	31.75	38.23	6.48	20.41	35.11	38.94	+3.83	+10.19

(Contd.)

(Contd.)

(1)	(2)	(3)	(4)	(5)	(6)	(7)	(8)	(9)
Mahbubnagar	35.80	37.75	1.95	5.45	36.85	38.56	+1.71	+ 4.64
Rangareddy	34.06	35.22	1.16	3.41	35.36	37.32	+1.96	+ 5.54
Guntur	26.33	53.13	8.80	33.42	30 38	36.19	+5.81	+19.12
Prakasam	24.78	34.39	9.61	38.78	29.76	36 69	+6.93	+23.29
Medak	31.88	34.11	2.23	6.99	33.79	36.25	+2 46	+ 7.28
Adilabad	28.15	33.80	5.65	20.07	31.77	36.27	+4.50	+14.16
Anantpur	29.34	33.23	3.89	13.26	32.11	35.10	+2 99	+ 9.31
Warangal	27.63	32.31	4.68	16.94	30.20	34.59	+4.39	+14.54
Nalgonda	28.63	32.11	3.48	12.15	30.10	34.28	+3.48	+11.30
Vizianagaram	27.59	31.29	3.70	13.41	30.92	34 11	+3.19	+10.32
Srikakulum	23.33	31.17	2.84	10.02	32.99	35.11	+2.12	+ 6.43
Khammam	25.60	30.71	5.11	19.96	22.24	33.52	+4.28	+14.64
Nellore	25.69	30.36	4.67	18.18	29.86	33.21	+3.35	+11.22
Krishna	23.53	28.40	4.87	20.70	28.00	31.56	+3.56	+12.71

Chittor	23.58	28.12	4.54	19.23	27.10	31.14	+4.04	+14.91
Visakhapatnam	24.73	27.76	3.03	12.25	28.47	31.14	+2.67	+ 9.38
Cuddapah	22.71	27.50	4.79	21.09	26.82	31.17	+4.35	+16.22
West Godavari	24.14	26.68	2.54	10.52	28.33	30.49	+2.16	+ 7.62
East Godavari	19.60	19.78	0.18	0.92	24.83	24.59	−0.24	− 0.97
Andhra Pradesh	27.37	31.95	4.58	16.73	30.88	34.55	+3.67	+11.88

Source: Census of India 1981, Series India Paper-2 of 1986, Comparative Primary Census Abstract 1971 to 1981, Registrar General of India, New Delhi.

of 4.58 per cent and a percentage increase of 16.73. Though all the districts registered an increase in FWPR, yet the highest increase was realised by Prakasam (38.78 per cent), and lowest by East Godavari, *i.e.*, 0.92 per cent. In 1971, Mahbubnagar had highest FWPR but during this decade, Nizamabad, Karimnagar and Kurnool registered a very high increase in their FWPR, with the result, Mahbubnagar wae relegated to the fourth place. On the other hand, East Godavari continued to be placed at the bottom among 22 districts.

The data in Table 2 shows further the proportion of female in total employment and its decadal variation. This pattern confirms to the similar pattern as showed by FWPR. The relative share of female in total employment for rural Andhra Pradesh increased from 30.88 per cent in 1971 to 34.55 per cent in 1981, thereby achieving a decadal increase of 11.88 per cent. Here also Nizamabad had highest share of its female work force in total employment, and East Godavari had the lowest. During the decade 1971-81, out of 22 districts in 21, the relative proportion of female work force increased, whereas in East Godavari it declined marginally.

The data in the Table 3 documents sectoral distribution of female work force for the year 1981. In rural Andhra Pradesh and its all districts, the bulk of the female work force is engaged in the primary sector, and secondary and tertiary sectors have absorbed a small proportion of it. In Andhra Pradesh, 88.6 per cent of the female work force is in the primary sector, and secondary and tertiary sectors account for 6.4 per cent and 5.0 per cent of the female work force respectively. Regarding district-wise pattern, only Nizamabad shows a somewhat different distribution of female work force. Here 73.6 per cent of the female work force is in the primary sector, and 24.0 per cent in engaged in the secondary sector. However tertiary sector has absorbed only 2.4 per cent of the female work force.

The high incidence of employment of rural female workers

TABLE 3

Sector-wise Distribution of Female Work Force in Rural Andhra Pradesh—1981

(Figures in percentage)

Districts	Primary Sector	Secondary Sector	Tertiary Sector
(1)	(2)	(3)	(4)
Nizamabad	73.6	24.0	2.4
Karimnagar	82.7	12.6	4.7
Kurnool	92.5	3.2	4.3
Mahbubnagar	90.9	5.5	3.6
Rangareddy	88.1	6.3	5.6
Guntur	91.2	3.8	5.0
Prakasam	90.1	4.9	5.0
Medak	89.5	7.2	3.3
Adilabad	87.3	9.6	3.1
Anantpur	93.5	2.8	3.7
Warangal	89.7	5.3	5.0
Nalgonda	88 2	6.1	5.7
Vizianagaram	91.3	3.5	5.2
Srikakulam	88.7	5.6	5.7
Khammam	91.4	3.6	5.0
Nellore	89.6	4.4	6.0
Krishna	88.9	4.0	7.1
Chittor	92.5	3 6	3.9
Visakhapatnam	87.1	5.8	7.1
Cuddapah	88.5	5.7	5.8
West Godavari	88.4	4.5	7.1
East Godavari	85.7	6.4	7.9
Andhra Pradesh	88.6	6 4	5.0

Source: Same as for Table 1.

in the primary sector is due to the reason that rural economy of Andhra Pradesh continues to be a traditional agrarian economy. Its secondary and tertiary sectors have not been able to relieve the pressure of work force on primary sector, with the result the bulk of the work force continues to be engaged in the low income yielding occupations of the primary sector. Moreover secondary and tertiary sectors require educated, better equipped and skilled workers. Therefore employment opportunities for rural women in these sectors are restricted because majority of them is illiterate and they do not possess requisite skill/training.

IV. Analysis of Inter-District Variations in Female Work Participation Rate

As explained earlier the FWPR in rural Andhra Pradesh exhibits glaring inter-district variations. In order to explain these variations, six explanatory variables have been incorporated in the analysis. These variables are shown in Table 4. Out of these six variables, excluding male work participation rate, all five are agricultural variables. These variables have been incorporated in the analysis because in a predominantly rural economy where the bulk of female workers are in the agricultural sector, the variations in agricultural conditions are likely to give a comprehensive explanations of inter-district variations in FWPR. For establishing the inter-relationship between FWPR and these explanatory variables, Spearman's coefficients of rank correlation have been computed and tested by the significance test.

Male Work Participation Rate

The data in Table 5 shows district-wise FWPR and male work participation rate in rural Andhra Pradesh. It is evident from the table that Visakhapatnam has highest male work participation rate followed by Vizianagaram, whereas for FWPR these come at 19th and 13th Place respectively. On the other hand Rangareddy with lowest male work participa-

TABLE 4

List and Type of Variables Used in Rank Correlation Analysis

Sl. No.	Description of Variables	Type of Variable
1.	Female Work Participation Rate.	Dependent Variable
2.	Male Work Participation Rate.	Explanatory Variable
3.	Structure of Employment. It is percentage of workers engaged as Cultivators and Agricultural Labourers to total workers.	,,
4.	Cropping Intensity. It is the percentage of Gross Cropped Area to Net Sown Area.	,,
5.	Cropping Pattern. It has been defined as percentage of area under Rice to Total Gross Cropped Area.	,,
6.	Structure of Operational Land Holdings. It is the percentage of Land Holdings below 1.0 Acre to total Land Holdings.	,,
7.	Tractor Land Ratio. It is availability of one tractor for area operated.	,,

tion rate comes at fifth place for FWPR. The coefficient of rank correlation between the two variables comes as under:

$r_s = -0.3563$ (which is statistically significant at 10 per cent level of significance).

This significant inverse relationship between the two variables implies that in rural Andhra Pradesh, female work participation is sensitive to change in male work participation rate. A higher work participation among males is likely to result in low female work participation rate and *vice versa.*

Structure of Employment

In a traditional agrarian economy like Andhra Pradesh where agricultural sector is dominant, women have an easy

TABLE 5

Female and Male Work Participation Rates in Rural Andhra Pradesh—1981

Districts	Female Work Participation Rate	Male Work Participation Rate	Ranks Assigned in Descending Order of Magnitude	
			Female Work Participation Rate	Male Work Participation Rate
Nizamabad	43.84	59.34	1	12
Karimnagar	40.52	60.50	2	3
Kurnool	38.23	57.98	3	21
Mahbubnagar	37.75	59.62	4	11
Rangareddy	35.22	57.38	5	22
Guntur	35.13	60.29	6	7
Prakasam	34.39	58.26	7	20
Medak	34.11	59.32	8	13
Adilabad	33.80	58.83	9	16
Anantpur	33.23	58.28	10	19
Warangal	32.31	59.08	11	15
Nalgonda	32.11	60.19	12	8
Vizianagaram	31.29	60.96	13	2
Srikakulam	31.17	59.12	14	14
Khammam	30.71	58.46	15	17
Nellore	30.36	60.01	16	10
Krishna	28.40	60.04	17	9
Chittor	28.12	60.34	18	4
Visakhapatnam	27.76	61.11	19	1
Cuddapah	27.50	58.41	20	18
West Godavari	16.68	60.33	21	5
East Godavari	19.78	60.31	22	6

Source: Same as for Table 1.

assess for low income yielding occupations of this sector. Since majority of them is illiterate and they do not possess any skill, their employment opportunities in the secondary and tertiary sectors are very limited. Therefore a positive relationship between FWPR and structure of employment is expected.

It is evident from Table 6 that in rural Andhra Pradesh, the bulk of the work force is engaged as cultivators and agricultural labourers. Anantpur has highest proportion of its work force in the agricultural sector followed by Kurnool, whereas for FWPR these come at 10th and 3rd place respectively. On the other hand, Rangareddy with lowest proportion of its work force in the agricultural sector comes at 5th place for FWPR. The coefficient of rank correlation between the two variables comes as under:

$r_s = +0.1225$ (which is statistically not significant even at 10% level of significance)

Though the coefficient of correlation has assumed a positive sign, yet it is insignificant. Since its value is not significant, a positive or negative sign is as good as zero. Therefore, it can safely he concluded that in rural Andhra Pradesh, FWPR tends to act independently of structure of employment.

Cropping Intensity

It is one of the important indicators of agricultural development. A higher cropping intensity, *i.e.*, more than 100 implies improved cropping pattern due to multiple cropping and is generally considered a proxy for agricultural advancement. The higher cropping intensity discourages female work participation in two main ways, firstly, since it leads to higher income women may withdraw from the work force, and secondly, the higher cropping intensity paves the way for use of modern inputs like improved seeds, fertilizers, more use of agricultural implements, with the resultant the introduction of new agricultural technology may substitute female workers by male workers. In any case, the higher cropping intensity is likely to result in low female work participation rate. Therefore, an

TABLE 6

Female Work Participation Rate and Structure of Employment in Rural Andhra Pradesh—1981

Districts	Female Work Participation Rate	Structure of Employment	Ranks Assigned in Descending Order of Magnitude	
			Female Work Participation Rate	Structure of Employment
Nizamabad	43.84	73.94	1	21
Karimnagar	40.52	75.77	2	19
Kurnool	38.23	83.93	3	2
Mahbubnagar	37.75	83.35	4	4
Rangareddy	35.22	73.37	5	22
Guntur	35.13	83.15	6	5
Prakasam	34.39	81.08	7	10
Medak	34.11	81.79	8	7
Adilabad	33.80	81.51	9	8
Anantpur	33.23	85.55	10	1
Warangal	32.31	80.40	11	13
Nalgonda	32.11	79.83	12	16
Vizianagaram	31.29	81.47	13	9
Srikakulam	31.17	79.64	14	17
Khammam	30.71	82.75	15	6
Nellore	30.36	80.63	16	12
Krishna	28.40	80.76	17	11
Chittor	28.12	83.83	18	3
Visakhapatnam	27.76	77.74	19	18
Cuddapah	27.50	80.02	20	15
West Godavari	26.68	80.25	21	14
East Godavari	19.78	75.23	22	20

Source : Same as for Table 1.

inverse relationship between FWPR and cropping intensity is expected in the analysis.

The data in Table 7 shows that East Godavari has highest cropping intensity followed by Krishna, whereas for FWPR these come at 22nd and 17 place respectively. On the other hand, Adilabad with lowest cropping intensity come at 9th

TABLE 7

Female Work Participation Rate and Cropping Intensity in Rural Andhra Pradesh

Districts	Female Work Participation Rates*	Cropping Intensity**	Rank Assigned in Descending Order of Magnitude	
			Female Work Participation Rate	Cropping Intensity
(1)	(2)	(3)	(4)	(5)
Nizamabad	43.84	121.9	1	7
Karimnagar	40.52	119.4	2	8
Kurnool	38.23	107.4	3	16
Mahbubnagar	37.75	105.8	4	19
Rangareddy	35.22	106.6	5	17
Guntur	35.13	129.6	6	4
Prakasam	34.39	106.0	7	18
Medak	34.11	108.2	8	15
Adilabad	33.80	102.3	9	22
Anantpur	33.23	104.4	10	20
Warangal	32.31	124.5	11	6
Nalgonda	32.11	115.8	12	10
Vizianagaram	31.29	115.0	13	11

(*Contd*)

(Contd.)

(1)	(2)	(3)	(4)	(5)
Khammam	30.71	109.9	15	13
Srikakulam	31.17	118.9	14	9
Nellore	30.36	109.3	16	14
Krishna	28.40	141.9	17	2
Chittor	28.12	112.3	18	12
Visakhapatnam	27.76	126.3	19	5
Cuddapah	27.50	103.6	20	21
West Godavari	26.68	140.0	21	3
East Godavari	19.78	142 9	22	1

*Relates to 1981. **Relates to 1981-82.

Sources: Column 2: Same as for Table 1.

Column 3: Statistical Abstract, Andhra Pradesh (1982) Bureau of Economic and Statistics, Government of Andhra Pradesh, Hyderabad.

place for FWPR. The coefficient of rank correlation between the two variables comes as under:

$r_s = -0.3224$ (which is statistically not significant even at 10% level of significance)

Though the correlation coefficient has assumed negative sign, yet it is insignificant. Therefore, it is difficult to say that cropping intensity is having any impact on female work participation.

Cropping Pattern

In the present analysis, it has been defined as percentage of area under rice to gross cropped area. It largely reflects the existing agricultural conditions in the area. In Andhra Pradesh, the area under rice occupies the highest proportion in gross cropped area. In 1981-82, the area under rice was 29.3 per cent of the gross cropped area. However, in area under food crops, the relative proportion of rice was 37.9 per cent, which shows that rice constitutes the major food crop of Andhra Pradesh. A higher percentage of area under rice depends upon assured irrigation facilities and leads to higher income, which is likely to result in low female work participation rate. Therefore, an inverse relationship between FWPR and cropping pattern is expected in the present analysis.

The data in Table 8 shows district-wise cropping pattern in Andhra Pradesh. It is evident from the table that regarding cropping pattern West Godavari and East Godavari come at 1st and 2nd place respectively, whereas for FWPR these are placed at 21st and 22nd place respectively. On the other hand, Anantpur with lowest cropping pattern comes at 10th place for FWPR. The coefficient of rank correlation between the two variables comes as under:

$r_s = -0.4049$ (which is statistically significant at 10% level of significance).

It implies that in rural Andhra Pradesh, the female work participation is negatively associated with percentage of area under rice to gross cropped area. A relatively high proportion of area under rice is likely to result in low female work participation and *vice versa*.

Structure of Operational Land Holdings

It is one of the most important indicators of existing agricultural conditions in the region. The distribution of operational land holdings is having a direct bearing on employment pattern. A relatively high proportion of small land holdings (below 1.0 acre) which is the result of segmentations and fragmentation of land holdings, is likely to result in low female work participation. Since a relatively small cultivable piece of land does not offer full time work even for male members of the household, then there is hardly any work available for females. Therefore, an inverse relationship between FWPR

TABLE 8

Female Work Participation Rate and Cropping Pattern in Rural Andhra Pradesh

Districts	Female Work Participation Rate	Cropping Pattern	Ranks Assigned in Descending Order of Magnitude	
			Female Work Participation Rate	Cropping Pattern
Nizamabad	43.84	39.8	1	7
Karimnagar	40.52	31.3	2	9
Kurnool	38.23	9.4	3	21
Mahbubnagar	37.75	15.6	4	17
Rangareddy	35.22	14.4	5	19
Guntur	35.13	41.1	6	6
Prakasam	34.39	17.5	7	16
Medak	34.11	23.6	8	14
Adilabad	33.80	11.3	9	20
Anantpur	33.23	8.0	10	22
Warangal	32.31	25.5	11	13
Nalgonda	32.11	28.4	12	10
Vizianagaram	31.29	37.1	13	8
Srikakulam	32.17	53.7	14	4
Khammam	30.71	26.0	15	12
Nellore	30.36	56.1	16	3
Krishna	28.40	50.6	17	5
Chittor	28.12	23.1	18	15
Visakhapatnam	27.76	26.7	19	11
Cuddapah	27.50	14.9	20	18
West Godavari	26.68	72.8	21	1
East Godavari	19.78	62.4	22	2

Sources: Same as for Table 7.

and structure of operational land holdings is expected in the analysis.

The data in Table 9 shows that Srikakulam has highest proportion of small land holdings followed by East Godavari, whereas for FWPR these come at 12th and 50th place respectively. On the other hand, Anantpur with lowest proportion of small land holdings comes at 9th place for FWPR. The coefficient of rank correlation between the two variables comes as under:

$r_s = -0.5426$ (which is statistically significant at 5% level of significance)

Such a high value of negative correlation implies that female work participation is highly sensitive to change in structure of operational land holdings. It concludes that a relatively high proportion of small land holdings in total land holdings restricts female work participation and *vice versa*.

Tractor Land Ratio

It is an important indicator of agricultural mechanisation. A higher level of agricultural mechanisation is likely to displace the labour, and in comparison to male labour, women are first to be retrenched. Therefore, a high tractor land ratio means availability of more employment opportunities and a relatively low ratio is likely to result in low employment potential of the agricultural sector.

The data in Table 10 shows that West Godavari and East Godavari the last two districts with lowest tractor land ratio are also placed at last for FWPR, but their ranking has changed slightly. On the other hand, Visakhapatnam with highest tractor land ratio, comes at 17th place for FWPR. The coefficient of rank correlation between FWPR and tractor land ratio comes as under :

$r_s = -0.4466$ (which is statistically significant at 5% of significance)

TABLE 9

Female Work Participation Rate and Structure of Operational Land Holdings in Rural Andhra Pradesh

Districts	Female Work Participation Rate*	Structure of Operational Land Holdings**	Ranks Assigned in Descending Order of Magnitude	
			Female Work Participation Rate	Structure of Operational Land Holdings
Nizamabad	43.84	52.6	1	9
Karimnagar	40.52	54.2	2	8
Kurnool	38.23	25.0	3	19
Mahbubnagar	37.75	27.0	4	18
Guntur	35.13	55.6	5	6
Prakasam	34.39	40.3	6	14
Medak	34.11	47.8	7	11
Adilabad	33.80	30.1	8	17
Anantpur	33.23	24.9	9	20
Warangal	32.31	46.0	10	12
Nalgonda	32·11	36.5	11	15
Srikakulam	31.17	64.2	12	1
Khammam	30.71	36.3	13	16
Nellore	30.36	55.4	14	7
Krishna	28.40	58.2	15	3
Chittar	28.12	49.7	16	10
Visakhapatnam	27.76	55.9	17	5
Cuddapah	27.50	42.3	18	13
West Godavari	26.68	56.1	19	4
East Godavari	17.78	60.8	20	2

*Relates to 1981.

**Relates to 1976-77.

Source: Same as for Table 7.

TABLE 10

Female Work Participation Rate and Tractor Land Ratio in Rural Andhra Pradesh

Districts	Female Work Participation Rate*	Tractor Land Ratio**	Rank Assigned in Descending Order of Magnitude: Female Work Participation Rate	Rank Assigned in Descending Order of Magnitude: Tractor Land Ratio
(1)	(2)	(3)	(4)	(5)
Nizamabad	43.84	1749	1	10
Karimnagar	40.52	3183	2	7
Kurnool	48.23	3522	3	6
Mahbubnagar	37.75	6864	4	3
Guntur	35.13	490	5	16
Prakasam	34.39	1027	6	13
Medak	34.11	2782	7	8
Adilabad	33.80	6882	8	2
Anantpur	33.23	4834	9	4
Warangal	32.31	2372	10	9
Nalgonda	32.11	996	11	14
Srikakulam	31.17	4829	12	5
Khammam	30.71	1322	13	12
Nellore	30.36	434	14	18
Krishna	28.40	467	15	17
Chittor	28.12	679	16	15
Visakhapatnam	27.76	7319	17	1
Cuddapah	27.50	1513	18	11
West Godavari	26.68	265	19	20
East Godavari	19.78	356	20	19

*Relates to 1981.
**Relates to 1976-77.
Source: Same as for Table 7.

The negative value of correlation coefficient shows that the level of tiacterisation is having a significant negative impact on female work participation. It can safely be concluded that a higher degree of mechanisation in the agriculture results in low female work participation rate and *vice versa.*

V. Conclusions

Main findings of the analysis are summarised as below:

—The female work participation rate in rural Andhra Pradesh is reasonably high, but it exhibits significant inter-district variations.

—In comparison to FWPR, the male work participation rate is very high and shows marginal inter-district inequalities.

—The decadal period 1971-81 has witnessed a fair increase in FWPR in rural Andhra Pradesh and its districts.

—The relative proportion of rural female workers in total rural employment is low, *i.e.*, about 31.00 per cent only. However during the intercensal period 1971 81, it increased fairly to 34.55 per cent.

—The bulk of the female work force is engaged in the primary sector, whereas secondary and tertiary sector could have absorbed a small proportion of it.

—Out of six explanatory variables incorporated in rank correlation analysis for explaining inter-district variations in FWPR, two variables, *viz.*, structure of employment and cropping intensity did not exhibit any significant relationship with FWPR.

—Male work participation rate has been found to be inversely correlated with FWPR. It implies that higher the male work participation rate lower will be the FWPR *vice versa.*

—A higher percentage of area under rice is having a negative impact on female work participation. On the other hand, a low proportion of area under rice is likely to result in higher female work participation.

—The female work participation rate is highly sensitive to structure of operational land holdings. The districts with a higher proportion of small land holdings are having low female work participation rate and *vice versa.*

—A higher level of mechanisation in the agricultural sector has been found to be negatively associated with female work participation rate.

Thus, the preceding analysis has demonstrated that the female work participation rate in rural Andhra Pradesh is reasonably high, but the largest chunk of female workers is engaged in low income yielding occupations of the primary sector. The differences in the agricultural conditions are having a significant impact on female work participation rate in rural Andhra Pradesh.

9

Women's Participation in Local Institution

ASHOK KUMAR*

I. Introduction

In India, rural women constitute about 80 per cent of the total female population and 48.3 per cent of the total population. They contribute largely to country's economy which is mainly agriculture based. Although distributive justice has been categorically underlined in all the development plans, the needs of women have not been adequately addressed.[1] However, a majority of women in rural areas attend to domestic work and those who are engaged in free collection of goods (vegetables, roots, fish, firewood, cattle feed, etc.) and providing services (sewing, weaving, maintenance of kitchen-gardens, orchards, poultry, etc.). The number of rural women in the age group 15-49 years engaged in domestic work is estimated at 43.8 million, and those engaged in free collection of goods and services is 26.6 million.[2] Although rural women constitute a large section of population of the country, their lives are still characterized by hardwork druggery and without any basic amenities. They trapped in the vicious circle of low income, ill-health, low nutrition, low productivity and low

*Faculty Member, IAMR, New Delhi.
The views expressed in this paper are exclusively of those of author and not of the Institute to which he belongs.

wages. As a result women were considered as target groups in the Community Development programme (1952).

As far as political participation, of women are concerned, they won the right to vote as early as 1921 and have held high political offices, yet their participation in the elections has been disappointingly low. For instance, in 1984 election there were only 161 women among the 5493 candidates and Lok Sabha had only 42 members of the fair sex in a House of 545.[3] However, their turnout at this polling booths have increased from 38.8 per cent in 1957 polls to 58 per cent in 1984 elections. The need of the hour, therefore, is to choose more women candidates and encourage them to actively take part in politics too.

During the Second, Third, Fourth and Fifth Five Year Plans programmes for and participation of women did not receive any fresh impetus and continued on the earlier lines. But Rural Development programmes for women have only in recent decades recognised the crucial role of organisation and mobilisation as strategies for women's improvement and development. The programme envisaged under community development had a strong component for women's development, social education, etc. But the emphasis was more on women's role in household activities rather than community participation.

Recognising the importance of democratic institution at grass root level, the Panchayat at village level (village council) was established in 196 .[4] The Panchayati Raj institutions were in fact, considered to be the most effective instruments for realising the goals of economic betterment and social justice for the least privileged. Participation of women, who constitute nearly half of the population, in Panchayati Raj institution has been considered essential for enabling them to participate effectively and independently in democratic and political processes and to influence decision making. It has been recognised as a step towards equal society and a means of realising the developmental goals for women.

In the light of this introductory statement, the aim of this paper is to examine women's contribution to the rural economy in general and women's participation in Panchayati Raj particular. An attempt has also been made to document the main conditioning factors influencing women's participation in different developmental programmes and Panchayati Raj The paper is spilit into five sections, including the present one. The second gives a brief sketch on women's contribution to the rural economy. The third takes the vivid account of women's programmes and their participation therein The fourth part considers women's participation in Panchayati Raj followed by a description and suggesting alternative strategies. The final part offers a closing statement on the problems and highlighting some issues.

The Gram Panchayat

The three levels of local administration-gram panchayat at the anchal level, the panchayat samiti at the block level and the Zilla Parishad at the district level—play an increasingly important role.[5] Their activities relate to the planning of developmental and infrastructural works, the appointment of staff and extension workers, the execution of centrally-sponsored poverty alleviation programmes and the implementation of State initiated reform programmes, such as land reforms, etc. The various functions and duties of the Gram Panchayats are defined under section 15 which includes almost all aspects of rural development. The Ashok Mehta Committee was appointed when the Janata Government came into power in 1977. This Committee submitted its report in August, 1978. This report observed that 'the activities of Panchayati Raj institutions were meagre, their resource-base weak, and the overall attention given to them niggardly.[6] However, the only functions mentioned with regard to women are maternity and child welfare and promotion of family welfare and establishing and maintenance of village primary schools for boys and girls. But in actual practice the gram panchayats are not performing these functions.

According to Panchayat Raj Act, 1947, Section 15, every adult female is a member of Gram Panchayat and has a right to vote and be a candidate for the office of Pradhan and member of the Gram Panchayat. Section 12 (7) of the said Act provides that in case no women member is elected in the Gram Panchayat, then the elected members will coopt a member from amongst the women members of Gram Sabha. Thus, one women member either by election or cooption, has to be in the Gram Panchayat.

However, over the years, women's participation in Panchayati Raj institutions has been marginal because of several socio-economic constraints. Except for Andhra Pradesh, Gujarat, Maharashtra, Karnataka and Punjab, where some women members have been elected to village level Panchayati Raj institutions in respectable numbers in other States, their representation is either non-existent or negligible. Though in some states the balance is sought to be struck through nomination and cooption of women members, it has not brought any perceptible impact on women's participation in Panchayati Raj Bodies. Cooption is done only in letter and not in the spirit of getting women involved in Panchayat activities.

However, the National Conference on Panchayati Raj and Women (May 9, 1989) has recommend that invitations to womens members be made compulsory at Panchayat mee'ings for decision making [7] Government has recently drawn up a National Perspective Plan (1988-2000 A.D.) for effective participation and empowerment of women at the grassroots level in democratic institutions. The plan has recommended that 50 per cent of all grass-roots level functionaries should be women. To facilitate this minimum educational qualifications for them should be relaxed. Some of the other recommendations of the Plan are reservation of seats for women upto 30 per cent of Gram Panchayat to Zila Parishad levels and in local municipal bodies, reservation upto 30 per cent at the level of executive heads of all bodies from Village Panchayat to district level, and the need to declare a certain percentage of constituencies in the lower tier of Panchayati Raj as exclusively women's constituencies [8] But even if everything goes through on schedule, it would be another couple of years before the panchayati raj system gets really going. Secondly, even when it gets going it would be hardly more effective than it has been in some of the states over the years.

II. Women's Participation in Rural Economy

Despite concerted efforts at improving the status of women, Indian women are observed to be lagging behind in many spheres.[9] It has been emphatically articulated in many debates among forums connected with the development of women that the Indian society has not succeeded in framing the required norms for institutions to enable women to fulfil the multiple roles (as a mother, housewife and a unit of human capital) that they are expected to play.[10] However, after realising the significant role of women, it is desirable that a greater emphasis should be given for her all round development.

In the male dominating society, the condition of women crucially depends on the extent of economic independence of females.[11] With this awareness, the present section proposes to analyse available evidence on trends in economic participation with a view to identifying critical issues for further consideration. While the data on female participation rates in urban India is more reliable, one cannot ignore the issues of women's work and employment in rural India. Hence, in the present section we shall confirm our discussion to some of the issues related to women's contribution to rural economy.

The long term trend in economic participation of women indicates an overall decline in percentage of workers to total female population in their percentage to the total labour force after 1921, and a slight increase from 1971 to 1981 (Table 1).

The Table 1 reveals that work participation rates have been falling since last half a century, both for males and females. But the fall is sharper for females. Agriculture continued to receive the burden of the surplus labour force all through period of 81 years. Variation in participation rates in agriculture during different decades mainly show a slight decline before 1947 and a steady rise after that. However, estimates

TABLE 1

Percentage of Economically Active Population[13]

Census	Male	Female
1901	61.11	31.70
1911	61.90	33.73
1921	60.52	32.67
1931	58.27	27.63
1941	DNA	DNA
1951	54.05	23.30
1961	57.10	37.96
1971	52.75	14.15
1981	52.65	19.76

of female participation rates (hereinafter referred to as FPRs) in rural India are derived from two basic sources, namely the decennial population censuses and the national sample surveys. All of these relate only to those workers whose 'main activity' was 'work'.

It is evident from Table 2 that a dramatic decline in the FPR, from 31 per cent to 13 per cent between 1961 and 1971 for India as whole; a similar decline was witnessed in each of of the States, too. This is not a real decline but an apparent one, attributable to changes in the definition of a worker between the 1961 and 1971 censuses.

Now, let us have a look of the 1981 Census estimates and see how these compare with the earlier ones. Main workers were defined in the same way as in the 1971 Census, namely, if they had worked for a major part of the year preceding the date of enumeration.[13] The FPR, exclusive of marginal workers, increased from 13.4 to 16.5 over the decade 1971 to 1981.[14]

These estimates of FPR for all age-groups taken together. Because the age-wise break-up of workers and of population for 1981 is not available. In order to analyse changes in the FPR over time, it is necessary to include marginal workers, as the 'main workers' category tends to exclude a lot of female workers who perceive 'non-work' at their main activity. If we include marginal workers, the increase in the FPR between 1971 and 1981 is much greater from 15.9 per cent in 1971 to 23.9 per cent in 1981, then in the FPR of 'main worker' over the same time period.[15] Once again, this does not signify a 'real' increase in FPRs. The dramatic decline in FPR from 1961 to 1971 and the subsequent increase between 1971 and 1981 are not real, as there has been no dramatic change in the extent and or nature of female employment.

Let us turn to the alternative source, *i.e.*, NSSO. Between 1972-73 and 1977-78 there was some decline in FPRs for India as whole, though this does not hold for individual states. Between 1977-78 and 1983 there was not much change, with the exception of Jammu and Kashmir. From the above discussion, it is clear that inter-temporal comparability poses a high problem. The number of actual women workers is likely to be quite high in rural India, the available statistics do not capture all of them. This, in turn, is due to the fact that neither society nor the women themselves perceive their role in society as anything out marginal in the economic sphere. Another point that required consideration is that female participation rates are highly correlated to poverty and landlessness in rural India. Given that man is the primary bread winner, women go out to work when their household incomes do not suffice for their basic needs; more often then not, the poorest households are also the landless. It was observed that, in areas where incomes had gone up consequent on the Green Revolution, women tended to withdraw from the labour market due to the improved income effect. Of course, it is also likely that women do not learn new skills and techniques because they are deemed to be primarily engaged in housework.[16]

TABLE 2

Female Participation Rates in Rural Areas—Main and Marginal Workers All India and States

India/States	%age of Rural Female Workers to Total Female Population in Rural Areas			Main and Marginal Workers (Female)				Female Participation Rates Based on NSS Data					
								Usual Status			Current Weekly Status		
	1961	1971	1981	1971	1977-78	1981	1983	1972-73	1977-78	1983	1972-73	1977-78	1983
(1)	(2)	(3)	(4)	(5)	(6)	(7)	(8)	(9)	(10)	(11)	(12)	(13)	(14)
All-India	31.4	13.4	16.5	15.8	38.5	23.5	38.7	37.5	28.8	28.4	30.5	25.9	25.0
Andhra Pradesh	46.9	27.4	32.9	31.9	54.7	44.9	53.4	62.5	45.4	46.1	37.0	39.0	37.9

(Contd.)

(Contd.)

(1)	(2)	(3)	(4)	(5)	(6)	(7)	(8)	(9)	(10)	(11)	(12)	(13)	(14)
Assam	32.4	5.6	N.A.	5.6	13.5	N.A.	13.7	9.0	7.5	7.9	6.9	6.6	8.2
Bihar	28.5	9.3	9.3	10.3	24.5	14.5	27.3	23.0	19.1	17.4	18.5	15.2	15.7
Gujarat	34.1	12.1	14.5	15.2	45.2	26.3	43.3	44.5	33.4	34.8	39.8	32.6	32.8
Jammu & Kashmir	29.5	4.2	N.A.	6.8	44.3	N.A.	29.0	27.0	13.6	4.4	21.5	15.7	4.1
Karnataka	36.8	15.8	22.6	19.0	43.5	30.8	46.3	50.4	37.6	37.3	38.7	32.6	33.3
Kerala	20.9	14.1	13.5	15.3	46.3	18.2	34.3	39.3	21.1	19.9	23.5	22.3	18.4
Madhya Pradesh	48.6	20.7	26.1	25.1	49.8	35.5	51.6	52.8	43.4	43.2	41.3	33.5	34.9
Maharashtra	46.7	24.4	31.9	28.9	54.6	40.8	51.8	53.6	42.0	47.1	43.5	38.5	35.4
Orissa	27.4	6.8	11.3	15.2	31.4	20.9	23.6	35.9	25.8	26.50	24.5	17.1	21.5
Punjab	16.5	1.4	3.7	2.0	31.6	12.0	31.2	32.3	10.9	9.8	31.7	19.9	13.4
Rajasthan	40.8	9.3	10.7	16.0	65.7	25.0	53.9	63.1	38.3	40.4	55.6	39.7	40.4
Tamil Nadu	37.1	17.6	28.1	20.4	50.9	34.5	51.0	51.2	39.4	41.8	41.6	38.3	34.7

Uttar Pradesh	19.9	7.3	6.5	7.7	24.9	10.6	30.0	28.1	18.8	17.0	24.6	19.2	18.0
West Bengal	10.6	4.6	6.3	4.6	20.3	9.4	22.6	15.5	10.9	10.6	11.7	10.2	10.9

Source: (*i*) For Columns 2-5 and 7, *Census of India*, 1961, 1971 and 1981.

(*ii*) For Columns 6 and 8, *Sarvekshana*, April, 1986.

(*iii*) For Columns 9-14, National Sample Surveys on *Employment and Unemployment in Rural Areas*, Various Issues.

However, in the preceeding paragraphs we have a bird's-eye view on the women's contribution to rural economy in India. The vital role of women in the Indian labour force and their contribution to the national economy has been established beyond doubt. In the subsequent section we will examine women's participation in the developmental programmes.

III. Women's Programme

India has a surplus labour economy with a high incidence of unemployment and underemployment for both man and women workers, particularly in the countryside.[17] The Government of India has been aware of this and has launched a series of specific programme for women in India. Currently, the Government of India has over twenty seven schemes for women, some women specific and others both for the male and female population.[18] These programmes are being implemented by different Government Departments and Ministries such as Rural Development, Labour, Education, Health, Science and Technology, Welfare, Women and Child Development, etc. The total outlay on the women-specific schemes in the Seventh Plan is 2.4 per cent of the total while a gender break-up of beneficiaries or targets is not available for general schemes (RLEGP, NREP, etc.). The Government has launched special programmes providing supplementary nutrition, health services, health education and other facilities for women.

In almost all the programmes the major thrust was on the following principal categories:

—Strengthening and improvement of women's work and employment in different sectors of economy;

—Economic rehabilitation of women from weaker sections of society in the form of training and employment;

—To bring women into mainstream through offering them better employment opportunities;

—Providing short stay homes for women and girls with counselling, medical care, psychiatric guidance and treatment and development of skills;

—Preventive and rehabilitative services to women and children; and

—To provide general awareness and legal support services.

While the general objectives of development have remained common in all Five-Year Plans, emphasis on specific objectives shifted over the years, keeping in view the national priorities and changing situation. As first Five Year Plan emphasized on 'increased food production, expansion of agricultural inputs' irrigation and power generation got the highest priority. Subsequently, community development programme and National Extension Service were introduced (1952) to enthuse people's participation in development programmes. It was conceived as a multi-dimensional programme, aiming at a process of socio economic transformation of village life and mobilization of both human and material resources. Initially it had not included any programme for women. In one course, women's component under the programme was, however, sought to be provided by the appointment of Social Education Organiser (SEO) to promote women's community participation. The programme which emerged by 1954 was based on the Home Science Extension Approach with the objective of Strengthening women's home making roles.

The programme initiated by the Central Social Welfare Board's Welfare Extension Projects (1954) (Table 3) also emphasized on home based activities. The general thrust of these programme was to promote women's groups or organizations at local level through which the programmes for women welfare could be organised.[19] The potential of the Mahila Mandals was sought to be utilized for some selected development and social welfare programmes, such as Applied Nutrition Programme (ANP), the Integrated Child Development Services (ICDS), and Composite Programme for Women and Pre-School Children.

Two major components of 'Composite Programmes for Women and Children, *i.e.*, Incentive Awards to Mahila Mandals and Training of Associate Women Workers were introduced during Fourth Five Year Plan. Under the former, mandals showing good performance over a year were awarded cash for undertaking economic projects or activities. The latter was designed to provide orientation to selected women having leadership qualities in organizing village women and assist them in implementing various welfare programme. During Fifth Five Year Plan a number of programmes have been initiated and more stress was given to promote voluntary action. The objective of these was to utilise the potential of organisations in the implementation of various programmes meant for women and children.

Three major programmes, *viz.*, Integrated Child Development Services (ICDS), Social Inputs in Area Development and Development of Women and Children in Rural Areas (DWCRA) were lanched specially for women and children during Fifth and Sixth Five Year Plan period. These programmes were jointly sponsored by UNICEF and State Government. The main objectives of these programmes were to provide basic facilities like; proper nutrition, health education/services and employment and income generating activities, etc. Another programme called 'wheat Based Nutrition Programme' was initiated in Seventh Five Year Plan (1986) by the Department of Women and Child Development to provide supplementary nutrition with a view to cover large number of beneficiaries in tribal, urban slums and backward rural areas.

The Seventh Five Year Plan envisaged providing employment to all the unemployed in the rural areas.[20] As a result, 'the Jawahar Rozgar Yojana (JRY) unfolded by the Prime Minister, in parliament recently reflect the Government's anxiety to give a push to the effort at generating rural employment.[21] This is an employment programme announced in the Budget.[22] It is proposed that a little less than one-third or 30 per cent of employment generated to be reserved for women in this Yojana. However, it too early to comment on the success of the JRY, since the programme is yet to reach at the grass root' level.

In most of the development programmes, women as a group have been neglected. Among the various groups of beneficiaries who are below the poverty line, rural women are most difficult to be reached with assistance. As a result, women are benefiting nominally. According to 1981 figures, out of 20,041 beneficiaries in Rajasthan, only 1,466 were women; in Tamil Nadu, out of 54,858 beneficiaries 1,873 were women; and in Gujarat out of 8,089 beneficiaries, 531 were women; in Uttar Pradesh out of 26,561 beneficiaries, 1,087 were women (UNICEF, 1982). However, it is clear from these data that a small proportion of women are benefited through developmental programmes.

The proper utilisation of the existing resources, mobilizing the potential resources for use, release of physical and psychic energies of people, improvement and application of skills are most crucial for bringing about change in any society. The process of mobilization is not envisaged properly in most of the programmes. Alongwith this problem, are the other problems such as lack of political will among the ruling elite, lack of committed personnel to work for the emancipation of women, lack of awareness, illiteracy, tradition values and structural constraints, etc.

However, an attempt has been made below to indicate the difference in the trends of the programmes in the past and in the current decades.[23]

'Before' (Earlier Programmes)	'Now' (Thinking trend)
— Social Welfare Oriented.	— Development oriented.
— All women are treated as homogenous having some responsibilities, needs and problems.	— Accept the women as different in different socio-economic set-up.
— Mainly home makers.	— Both home-makers and providers for the family.
— Women's programme isolated from the main stream.	— Integration in the major programme for development.

— Oriented to the delivery of services. — Participatory in nature.

Notwithstanding, much ground needs to be covered yet to achieve the goal by way of creating an atmosphere of better understanding of the developmental needs for women in the context of national development strategy and a strong infrastructure and other supports to achieve the goal.

In view of the above problems it can be stated that the Panchayati Raj institutions can act as a link between the service agencies at the higher levels and women's group. Such link will be useful in making the different services available speedily and according to local requirements. Panchayats as the bodies at the grass root level can create an atmosphere and awareness in respect of women's programmes and their implementation. It will not only result in better appreciation of women's needs but also facilitate their wider participation in the process of development.

IV. Women's Participation in Panchayati Raj

Participation is generally understood as a process and not as some kind of static and product of development. The concept of time in terms of a process of participation is, of course, related to the task to be undertaken, which itself is a function of the development perspective employed.[24] However, participation of women in the Panchayats has been considered essential for enabling them to participate effectively in democratic processes.

The introduction of 'Democratic Decentralisation' resulted in the establishment of Panchayat. But in most of the Panchayat Raj legislations enacted by different State Governments, women were to be coopted under special category.[25] This did not result into the development of village leadership among women and their participation in the decision-making process. In this connection the Committee on the status of women in the Panchayati Raj institutions has not been effective either in articulating women's needs, or in mobilizing women for adequate participation. Taking not of this fact the Committee on Panchayati Raj Institutions recommended: (*a*) increasing representation of women in these institutions; (*b*) establishing a special committee of women Panchayat members and powers and funds to ensure that the decisions are made by women themselves on priorities and choices in welfare and development programmes specifically for women and children; (*c*) provision of institutional finance and budget support for rural industrialisation projects for women; and (*d*) strengthening the constructive decision-making and managerial roles; (*e*) Mahila Mandals to ensure full access to development resources and services.[26]

The World Conference on Agrarian Reforms and Rural Development (WCARRD) had also recommended that governments should "promote collective action and organisation by rural women to facilitate their participation in the full range of public services and to enhance their opportunities to participate in economic, political and social activities on an equal footing with men".

It is thus, evident that local bodies at village level are required to play a meaningful role in promoting women's participation in development. Hence, it is increasingly felt that after four decades experience what the performance of this institution. For this purpose, state-wise data on number of Panchayati Raj bodies (1979-80) are presented in Table 3.

It is evident from Table 3 that Uttar Pradesh being the largest state in terms of population has the maximum number of Gram Panchayats (72,826), Panchayat Samitis (876) and Zilla Parishads (56), followed by Maharashtra and Madhya Pradesh. Contrary to this, there are some States and Union Territories, *viz.*, Meghalaya, Nagaland and Lakshadweep, Mizoram, which do not have any Gram Panchayat at all.

As per 1980s counts, on an average number of population and village in India come to 2,098 and 2.8 respectively. These two averages were maximum in Kerala because of the densely

TABLE 3

State-Wise Number of Panchayati Raj Bodies (1979-80)

Sl. No.	State/Union Territory	Gram Panchayat (Nos.)	Panchayat Samitis (Nos.)	Zilla Parishad (Nos.)
(1)	(2)	(3)	(4)	(5)
1.	Andhra Pradesh*	16,137	324	21
2.	Assam	7'4	—	20
3.	Bihar	11,378	578	8
4.	Gujarat	12,924	182	19
5.	Haryana	5,260	87	—
6.	Himachal Pradesh	2,355	69	1
7.	Jammu and Kashmir	1,482	—	—
8.	Karnataka	8,184	175	19
9.	Kerala	1,001	—	—
10.	Madhya Pradesh	16,233	459	—
11.	Maharashtra*	24,016	296	25
12.	Manipur	107	6	—
13.	Meghalaya	—	—	—
14.	Nagaland	—	—	—
15.	Orissa	3,832	314	—
16.	Punjab	10,610	118	12
17.	Rajasthan	7,292	236	26
18.	Sikkim	215	—	—
19.	Tamil Nadu	12,582	376	24
20.	Tripura	689	—	—
21.	Uttar Pradesh	72,826	876	56
22.	West Bengal	3,242	324	15

(Contd.)

(Contd.)

(1)	(2)	(3)	(4)	(5)
23.	Arunachal Pradesh	701	48	5
24.	A&N Islands	38	—	—
25.	Chandigarh*	21	1	1
26.	D&N Haveli	10	1	—
27.	Delhi	204	—	—
28.	Lakshadweep	—	—	—
29.	Goa, Daman & Diu	195	—	—
30.	Mizoram	—	—	—
31.	Pondicherry	—	11	—
	Total (All-India)	2,12,248	4,481	251

*Information relates to 1978-79.
Source: Rural Development Statistics, NIRD, Hyderabad, 1982.

TABLE 4

State-wise Coverage of Panchayati Raj Institutions (1980)

Sl. No.	Sate/Union Territory	Average Popula-tion/Gram Panchayat	Average No. of Village/ Gram	Average No. of Gram Panchayat/ Panchayat Panchayat Samiti	Average No. of Panchayat Samiti/Zilla Parishad
(1)	(2)	(3)	(4)	(5)	(6)
1.	Andhra Pradesh	2,281	1.8	49.8	15.4
2.	Assam	18,077	29.1	—	—

(Contd.)

(Contd.)

(1)	(2)	(3)	(4)	(5)	(6)
3.	Bihar	4,458	6.9	19.8	18 6
4.	Gujarat	1,512	1.4	71.0	9.6
5.	Haryana	1,517	1.3	60.5	—
6.	Himachal Pradesh	1,367	7.2	34.1	5.8
7.	Jammu & Kashmir	2,604	4.7	—	—
8.	Karnataka	2,710	3.6	46.8	9.2
9.	Kerala	18,781	1.2	—	—
10.	Madhya Pradesh	2,132	4.7	35.4	—
11.	Maharashtra	1,445	1.6	81.1	11.8
12.	Manipur	5,607	4.8	17.8	—
13.	Orissa	5,245	13.5	12.2	—
14.	Punjab	1,254	1.2	89.9	9.1
15.	Rajasthan	2,910	4.9	30 9	9.1
16.	Sikkim	847	1.9	—	—
17.	Tamil Nadu	2,551	1.3	33.5	15.7
18.	Tripura	2,444	1.3	—	—
19.	Uttar Pradesh	1,043	1.6	83.1	15.6
20.	West Bengal	10,138	11.7	10.0	21.6
21.	A&N Islands	1,763	4.5	—	—
22.	Arunachal Pradesh	583	4.0	14.6	9.6
23.	Chandigarh	2,238	1.0	21.0	1.0
24.	D&N Haveli	7,400	7.2	10.0	—
25.	Delhi	2,941	1.3	—	—
26.	G.D. & Diu	3,287	2.3	—	—
27.	Pondicherry	—	—	—	—
	All India	2,098	2.8	47.4	17.8

Note: There is no Panchayati Raj Set-up in Meghalaya, Nagaland, Lakshadweep and Mizoram.

Source: Same as for Table 3.

populated State. And average number of Gram Panchayats per Panchayat Samiti and Panchayat Samitis per Zilla Parishad in India were 47.4 and 17.8 respectively (Table 4).

The data regarding women's participation in Panchayati Raj bodies (1979-80) for all India, are presented in Table 5. However, the extent of Women's participation in Panchayati Raj bodies is derived from Table 4 and Table 5, and presented in Table 6.

TABLE 5

Women's Participation in Panchayati Raj Bodies 1979-80—All India

Sl. No.	Item	Number
1.	Women Members of Gram Panchayats:	
	(*a*) Elected	41,207
	(*b*) Coopted	1,00,385
	(*c*) Total	1,41,592
2.	Women Members of Panchayat Samitis:	
	(*a*) Elected	595
	(*b*) Coopted	1,136
	(*c*) Total	1,731
3.	No. of Women Sarpanches	506

Source: Same as for Table 3 and 4.

The Table 6 reveals that the participation of women in Panchayati Raj institutions were very marginal. Out of 2,12,248 Gram Panchayats only 506 (0.23 per cent) women sarpanches were elected. The number of elected women member were very few (29.10 per cent) as compared to those of coopted (70.90) in both the cases Gram Panchayats as well as Panchayat Samitis. Further, if we have a look at the elected women members of Gram Panchayat to total number of

TABLE 6

Extent of Women's Participation in Panchayati Raj Bodies

Sl. No.	Item	Percentage
1.	Percentage of elected women member of Gram Panchayats	19.41 (29.10)*
2.	Percentage to coopted women members of Gram Panchayat to total number of Gram Panchayats	47.29 (70.90)*
3.	Percentage of elected women members of Panchayat Samitis to total Number of Panchayat Samitis	13.27
4.	Percentage of coopted women members of Panchayat Samitis to total No. of Panchayat Samitis	25.35
5.	Percentage of women Sarpanches to total number of Gram Panchayats	0.23

Note: Percentage of total, elected plus coopted.

Panchayats, it was only about one-fifth (19.41 per cent). Again in the Panchayat Samitis, a little more than one-forth (25.35 per cent), women members were coopted and only 13.27 per cent were elected.

However, the above statistics exhibit that women's participation in the Panchayati Raj is not upto the mark. It is felt that more reservation will not solve the problem unless women members are given commensurate powers to function effectively. Panchayats should be given real autonomy and not subjected to excessive governmental controls. And then only women members of Panchayats will welcome the concepts of Nyaya Panchayats.

Leadership, Role of Women

Women are considered an extremely pivotal point in the

process of change in rural areas. The establishment of the Institution of village council (Panchayat) at village level in 1961 also provided opportunities to women to participate in the decision making process. Women's participation in these bodies was encouraged by coopting them as a special category.[27] Women's participation in village-based institutions proved to be the most effective instrument in bringing about a change in their way of life in terms of economic well being and adoption of new technology.[28] Although these measures have not yielded the results to the desired extent, it can not be denied that rural women have been exposed to the process of modernization and avenues for interaction with the forces of social change.

While organising women's groups, an attempt was made on a country-wide basis to utilise these institutions to promote people's participation and as catalyst to social change. As these organisational were formed on democratic principles, the rural women tended to get community welfare affairs and participate in the development process by assuming leadership roles. Although the emerging village leadership, as has been found by a number of scholars,[29] is confined to the upper castes/classes in village communities, the poor women also get the opportunity, and assume leadership roles, through to a limited extent, and get exposed to the process of modernization and social change.

Participation of women in the village based formal and non-formal organisations has thus, made significant changes in their social status as well as their position within the family. Further, mere participation of women in these organisation is a clear indication of a change in the traditional norms which restricted free movements of a female member in society for social and political activities ; women were expected to participate in such economic and social activities which were confined to the domestic spheres. Any deviation from this norm naturally resulted in on improvement in her position in the society. Participation of women in different organisations thus have two important cannotations : (*i*) it gives them a status in the society, and (*ii*) it permits contribution of women not only in rural development process but also for their own development. It also gives them an opportunity to (*a*) work in groups on projects of common interest; (*b*) associate with the on-going development programmes; (*c*) participate in the decision-making process; (*d*) articulate women's needs; (*e*) assume leadership in the national development process.[30]

The emerging women leadership in rural areas is to a large extent characterised by middle age, high literacy rate and income. However, in the light of the socio-economic features of the village leadership, it will be found that the characteristics features of women leadership in rural India are at variance in terms of age, education and occupation. As a result, the rural women have, in the first instance, been able to identify themselves as an important segment in the society. It has also helped in attracting the attention of the official functionaries to design and implement programmes for the benefit of women. This is evident from the fact that a number of specific programmes specifically meant for women beneficiaries in the field of education, health, employment, family welfare, vocational training have been designed and implemented in recent years.

As a result, rural women have also started showing considerable interest in organizing joint economic ventures such as thrift societies, dairy cooperatives, poultry and cattle farming, agricultural and allied activities weaving and so on. The nature of these groups vary from place to place depending upon their pattern of work and availability of technical and financial assistance from outside. The change from home based action which has prevailed all along to collective action has made a significant change in the lifestyle of people.

However, the introduction of women's organizations and the consequent emergence of women leadership at the grass roots level has brought about social changes in the rural women's life, in particular and village communities in general. These organisations have the necessary potential for bringing about more changes rapidly and if given proper opportunity and assistance these can provide further strides in the development of rural women.

Women's Economic Motivation

Development programmes for women should be addressed to the problem that concern rural women.[31] Economic motivation is central to rural women's behaviour. Women need money not only to contribute to the family as whole but also to save for emergencies for times when they and their families are in distress. Thus, when a women is urgently concerned with her family's economic and social security, she may not be interested in acquiring modern knowledge in nutrition or health practices or in literacy classes which, though related to her primary needs, are of secondary importance to her. However, once a certain amount of economic security has been achieved, rural women will be interested in other social changes desired for comprehensive development of the community and society. If national policy favours keeping rural women in economically productive work, then training and employment of rural women would be required for their effective participation.

The National Perspective Plan (1988-2000 A.D.) suggested the need for proper training for all women members of Panchayats and other bodies to enable them to exercise their authority adequately. A massive conscientization programme for women in general needs to be taken up and modules designed for this purpose should adequately deal with social economic constraints which restrict their participation in political processes and institutional structure of democracy. Separate allocations are required to be made for this purpose. The need to link women's development programmes with Panchayat and local functionaries for effective participation of women in development.

Popular Participation

Popular participation has been conceptualised in relation to some form of political democracy and, equally broadly, in terms of involvement in processes of societal change and growth that term "development" suggests.[32] More commonly in development literature it is examined from the point of view of government intervention in development, and in this respect, terms such as "mobilisation" and "coercion" have been used to characterise the nature of the "participation". Conversely, where "participation" emerges as a result of some kind of bottom-up process, it is characterised as being "authentic" and focussing on distribution.

Recently, a National Conference was held at New Delhi to discuss the issue of women's participation in Panchayat Raj bodies. It is however, felt that mere reservation will not solve the problem unless women members are given commensurate powers to function effectively. The need to link women's development programmes with Panchayat and local functionaries for effective participation of women in development was also highlighted. The formal reservation of women in Panchayati Raj structures through reservation of seats, election, etc. is not a sufficient condition for their effective participation unless and until it is supplemented by measures which help in resolving the socio-economic pressures inhibiting them. The same can be realised by mobilising women through awareness campaigns and inter-personal communication by implementing the scheme which help them in attaining economic independence and by enhancing educational facilities at their doorsteps.

V. Conclusions and Suggestions

To summarise up, the condition of women crucially depends on the extent of economic independence and it has observed that Indian women are lagging behind in this sphere. The long term trend in economic participation of women indicates an overall decline in percentage of workers to total female population. Here, there is one aspect which need to be considered from a policy point of view, that there is a need to replace the traditional value system, which is based on an inequality of sexes where the females play a subordinate role, with a more egalitarian system. Even if there is no absolute equality between the sexes, there is need to bring about a betterment in the quality of life for women.

Recently, over twenty-seven schemes have been initiated by the Government for the welfare of women. The strategy is to tackle the issue on three main fronts—education, employment and health. It is observed that in most of the programmes women as a group have been neglected. Hence, it is suggested that Panchayat Raj institutions can act as a link between the service agencies at the higher levels and women's group.

It will be wrong to think that Panchayati Raj should be viewed as a God that has failed.[33] It has many achievements to its credit, the more important of which may be identified here. Politically its inception become democratic seed-drilling in the Indian soil, making an average citizen more conscious of his rights than before. Administratively, it bridged the gulf between the bureaucratic elite and the people. Socially, it generated a new leadership which was young having a modern and pre-social outlook. Finally viewed from the developmental angle, it helped rural people to cultivate a developmental psyche.[34]

As far as women's participation in the panchayati raj is concerned, it is not upto the mark. It is observed that mere reservation will not solve the problem unless women members are given commensurate powers to function effectively. However, in this regard the following steps have been suggested:

(*i*) all women members of panchayats and other executive bodies must be trained and empowered to exercise their authority;

(*ii*) particular attention must be paid to the development inter-personal communication skills amongst the trainess/community leaders;

(*iii*) effort are required to elicit participation of women through establishing links between the elected representatives and the development functionaries;

(*iv*) programmes meant for women's development should be linked with panchayat/local functionaries for more effective participation of women;

(*v*) despite being members of these democratic bodies or even their head, women's political participation may be severely constrained by various socio-economic pressures. It would, therefore, be necessary to supplement formal representation in institutional structures with other measures such as mobilisation of women and involvement of panchayats on specific socio-economic issues; and

(*vi*) there is need to organise women workers either in a cooperative or any other form whereby production and marketing are integrated. Government institutions or voluntary welfare organisations must come forward to organise women who are self-employed and reduce their exploitation and active participation in Panchayats.

REFERENCES

1. Government of India (1988): *National Perspective Plan for Women—1988-2000 A.D.*, Report of the Core Group set-up by the Department of Women and Child Development, Ministry of Human Resource Development, Govt. of India, p. 3.
2. S.P. Jain (1985): 'Rural Women Development in India through Last Decades', Background paper presented in an International 'Seminar on *Women & Development*, 13-16 February 1985, p. 1.
3. The Hindustan Times, October 24, 1989, New Delhi, p. 3.
4. G.K. Lieten (1988): 'Panchayat Leaders in a West Bengal District', *Economic and Political Weekly*, Vol. XXIII, No. 40, October 1, p. 2069.
5. *Ibid.*, p. 2069.
6. J.C. Johari (1981): *Indian Politics*, Vishal Publications, p. 424.
7. The Times of India, Lucknow, dated May 10, 1989.
8. PIB Feature (1989): 'Women's Participation in Panchayati Raj', *Yojana*, Vol. 33, No. 12, July 1-15, p. 14.
9. Ashok Kumar (1989): *Indian Women Towards 21st Century*, Criterian Publications, New Delhi, p. 40.

10. Govt. of India (1974): Report of the Committee on Status of Women in India, *Towards Equality*, Min. of Education & Social Welfare, p. 101.

11. R.H. Dholakia (1985): 'On Estimating Women's Contribution to National Product', *Manpower Journal*, Vol. XXI, No. 3, Oct.-Dec. 1985, p.1.

12. Ashok Kumar (1989): *op. cit.*, p. 48.

13. Office of the Registrar General, Census of India, 1981, Series-I, Paper 3 of 1981, New Delhi.

14. *Ibid.*, See Table 1.

15. *Ibid.*, See Table 2.

16. Nirmala Banerjee (1985): 'Women's work and Discrimination in Devaki Jain and Nirmala Banerjee (ed.) *Tyranny of the Household*, New Delhi.

17. Rohini Nayyar (1987): 'Female Participation Rates in Rural India', *Economic and Political Weekly*, December 19, 1987, p. 2214.

18. National Perspective Plan for Women –1988-2000 A.D., *op. cit.*, p. XI.

19. S.P. Jain (1981): 'Promoting Women's Participation in Development Programmes Role of Government, Voluntary Organisations and Panchayati Raj Institutions', Presented in a National Seminar on *Role of Women in Rural Development*, Organised by NIPCCD and BGMS on November 5-7, 1981, NIRD, Hyderabad, pp. 6-7.

20. Ashok Kumar (1989): 'The Jawahar Rozgar Yojana: An Appraisal', 'JRY-Old Wine in New Bottle', *Business Standard*, June 21, 1989, p. 5.

21. K.V. Rao (1989): 'JRY-Old Wine in New Bottle', *Business Standard*, June 21, 1989, p. 5.

22. J.S. Sodhi (1989): 'Jawahar Rozgar Yojana—Panacea for Rural Unemployment', *Economic Times*, June 10, 1989.

23. S. Chakravorty (1989): Current Programmes for Rural Women—The Theme.

24. Peter Oakley and David Marsden (1984): *Approaches to Participation in Rural Development*, ILO Geneva, p. 18.

25. Jain (1981): *op. cit.*, p. 15.

26. Govt. of India (1978): *Report of the Committee on Panchayati Raj Institutions*, Min. of Agriculture and Irrigation, Deptt. of Rural Development, New Delhi.

27. S.P. Jain (1983): 'Leadership Among Rural Women', *Social Change*, Sept. 1983, Vol. 13, No 3, pp. 9-10.

28. V.M. Sirsikar (1970): *The Rural Elite in a Developing Society*, Orient Longman's, New Delhi, p. 189.

29. S.P. Jain and V.K. Reddy (1981): *Rural Organisations: An Evaluation*, NIRD, Hyderabad.

30. Tahrunnessa Abdullah (1981): 'Women's participation in rural development: a Bangladesh pilot project', in ILO edited book *Women in Rural Development—Critical Issues*, ILO, Geneva, p. 36.

31. A. Pearse and M. Stiefel (1979): *Inquiry into Participation—A Research Approach* (Geneva, UNRISD), Pearse and Stiefel discuss this understanding of participation in terms of a "process of incorporation".

32. Asoka Mehta Committee Report.

33. E.V. Prakash Rao (1987): 'Operational Dynamics of Panchayati Raj', *Kurukshetra*, Vol. XXV, No. 9, June '87, p. 15.

PART B

CHILD DEVELOPMENT

10

Child As Human Resource: Towards A Strategy for Child Development in India

ASHOK KUMAR*
AND
HARISH**

The concepts of economic growth itself have taken a broader view of economic development in its institutional setting of socio-economic and political context. In this perspective, the choices of allocation of resources in planning investments in 'capital goods' as well as investments in 'human capital' are being revised so as to go into the problems such as rates of return from the competing claim of the two sectors.

Quite apart from considering human being merely as "capital assets" and their importance for promotion of productivity at different levels of the economic system, qualitative factors including social values, motivational patterns, potentials of developing entrepreneurial capabilities, their rights and and duties as citizens, creating social awareness and raising

*Faculty Member, at the National Institute of Public Cooperation & Child Development, Regional Centre, Lucknow.

**Research Scholar, CSRD/SSS, Jawaharlal Nehru University, New Delhi.

The views expressed in this paper are those of the author and not of the Institute to which he belongs.

levels of politicization are being considered as important areas of analysis to view Human Resource Development as an integrative process.

The importance of human resource development, therefore, is being increasingly realised in making a more meaningful of approaches towards integration of economic and social planning so as to view it is an independent variable and not treat it merely as dependent variable in the more classical, traditional, econometric models of development with GNP and Growth rates as their prime objectives. Human resource development also views development as a cooperative partnership between the government and the people through social institutions and organisations promoting voluntary action, giving a sense of self-direction to the local people and increasing self-reliance as important constituents of the development process itself.

Human Resource Development has to be an integral part of development planning so as to enable the poverty groups in rural areas to achieve a minimum level of living, a sense of belonging and opportunities for decision-making in issues that vitally affect them. At the "World Banking" Sector Policy Paper on Rural Development states:

Rural Development is a strategy designed to improve the economic and social life of a special group of people—the rural poor, Rural Development recognises that improved food supplies and nutrition together with basic services such as health and education, cannot only directly improve the physical well-being and quality of rural poor but can also indirectly enhance the productivity and their ability to contribute to the national economy".

Viewed in this prospective, Human Resource Development is the most important approach to raise the levels of aspiration and productivity and to break the vicious cycle of poverty at at the most vulnerable points. By releasing the "creative spirit" without which no wealth can be created, it can rightly be considered as the "critical input" for realising the pent up forces of progress.

By providing education, imparting new skills and supporting health, it opens up new avenues for vertical mobility in a rigid society rules by ascribed status. By making achieved status within the possible range of the poverty groups, it promotes new areas of entrepreneurship which require to be nurtured and developed as a part of public policy to promote equality of opportunity.

Another important dimension of human Resource Development is to make democracy more meaningful for the poverty-groups. Quite apart from the need for participation and fulfilment of basic human rights, democratisation of political, economic and social systems involves a change in structural relationships in a developing society. This is more likely to reduce tensions rather than to aggravate them as is commonly apprehended, for an educated and healthy citizen is more amenable to rationality than an ignorant and unhealthy one.

Social and political efficacy can thus be a powerful policy instrument to enable the rural poor to become active partners in development. The roles of rural economic, social and political institutions would thus undergo a rapid transformation from being maintainers of *status-quo* to promoters of development. In this context, the roles of cooperative, specially Farmers' Service Societies, Industrial Cooperatives, Service and Marketing Cooperatives, Voluntary Associations such as Youth Clubs and Mahila Mandals and voluntary agencies as accelerators of development become more significant.

There is a need to have a critical look at the linkages of human resource development with all other aspects of rural development in which a system approach appears to be the most useful one. The basic objective is to bring about a rapid improvement in the economic and social well-being of the people living in rural areas. The family has to be considered as the basic unit of planning and action in respect of rise in levels of living, employment generation and achievement of social and political status. Groups of families belonging to specific occupations such as small and marginal farmers, agricultural labourers and rural artisans, and being below the poverty line, have to receive the top priority. An integrated approach to target-group organisation and leadership development, human resource development, manpower planning and employment generation, transfer of technology and communication would require to be followed. Building up and re-organisation of the institutional frames work including administrative organisation participative systems including Panchayati Raj Institutions, voluntary agencies and rural organisations, delivery system including economic and social infrastructures such as input and credit supply, irrigation and road net-works, marketing and ware-housing facilities, education, health and drinking water supply, all these would have to be within the micro-level planning framework which would have to be supported by a multilevel planning and implementational system.

Development of children is a task area of planning and management which has changed a lot at different points of the planning era. However, the programmes directed at child development in India could be arranged in two major groups, *viz.*, (*i*) Programmes directed at developing/realizing full physical. mental, social and economic potential of the normal children. These are being undertaken by various sectoral departments/agencies dealing separately or collectively with education, medical care, sports and entertainment, culture and even industries and agriculture, etc.; and (*ii*) Programmes directed at helping different types of physically, mentally and socially handicapped of physically, mentally and socially handicapped children to overcome their handicapped existence, equip them with knowledge and skills to bring them functionally at per with the normal children.

However, these programmes are making an earnest effort to safeguard the rights of the children, protect them from various kinds of handicaps and help them in growing up in a manner which would make them responsible Indian citizens in their future adult life. Given the place of women in the Indian society, and also the fact that women and child development is yet to be recognised as a major task area for the governmental attention and consequent allocation of varied resources, this may be treated an assumption which is far removed from the empirical reality.

From the point of view of the child, three factors vitally affecting development, are the large proportion of urban mothers who working, the predominance of the nuclear family, and the phenomenon of child labour.[1] Each of these needs a little comment. In rural areas too, women in the lower economic strata are obliged to work, and it is a widely observed phenomenon than the nuclear family is more common as one proceeds down the economic scale. But in rural occupations, the family as a unit has a greater/chance to live and work and more together, with the mother often keeping the children close to her while working in the fields or forests. The nature of urban female occupations rarely allows for this women are mostly employed as domestic servants, hawkers and vendors, sweepers, unskilled labour (if at all they are employed outside their homes)--servicing, in other words, the more affluent sections of the urban population. This obliges them often to travel long distances and to be away from home at odd hours, and this leads to unavoidable neglect of the children.

Child labour in the exploitive sense, is again a phenomenon that is more associated with the urban areas.[2] With the exception of certain cottage industries like matches and *bidis* which are heavily dependent on children, child labour in rural areas usually refers to helping with the family tasks, Children are usually assigned such tasks as grazing cattle, looking after animals, fetching fuel and water, running errands, caring for young children and household chores. While this may often involve heavy work, it nevertheless, carries the conpensation of some dignity, freedom and responsibility which comes with being an active contributing member of the family economy.

In urban areas, fewer tasks of this sort need to be done and more and more children have to help the family by working, again in the unorganised sector, and again for an exploitative wage.[3] The urban child is caught up in a vicious triangle.[4] Hazardous health conditions in the squalor and misery of slums, poverty, lack of health care as a result of the ignorance and illiteracy of parents, and the insecurity and hardship of life form one side of this triangle;[5] the lack of adequate adult care, protection and guidance which can be attributed to the nuclear family and the absence of both parents and older siblings from the home is the second side,[6] the third side is the social and cultural milieu of the slums.[7]

In terms of policy, several departures have been made from the past practice for child development in India under the Five Year Plans. Important ones among them are: (*a*) For a change, the country level situation analysis an updated picture of how things are in terms of the nature, extent, causes and inter-relationships of major problem areas for each distinctive stage of the child's life; the effectiveness or otherwise of present attempts; the emergent areas of concern and the feasible directions for future action from which an action programme can be charted out—has been preceded by separate State-level analysis from different Indian States. This concedes the point that the notion of an Indian child is a myth and a more realistic dexcription of varied concrete realities for the children in different geographical, socio-economic-political-cultural locales must be given full weightage in deciding future action; (*b*) Relevant issues concerning the women will receive an in-depth attention as these have been deemed central to the development of children; (*c*) The perspective would not be narrow and blinkered but would review policies and programmes concerning economic development, infrastructure, social and other services development by the people, voluntary organisation and different limbs of the governments at various levels. In particular, it would attempt a better coordination and integration of different development programmes rather than establishing one additional set of schemes on an enormous load under which the people and the delivery systems are groaning.

The out-come of this approach, started by the ousted Rajiv Gandhi regime, is yet to be seen. It is yet not clear what the stances and priorities of the National Front Government would be on the question. However, based on the experience of the last 42 years, some general observations can now be safely made about the character of Indian child development programmes.

(*a*) Need of the Children and the Policies and Programmes Undertaken—A Mismatch

For the majority of Indian poor; rural as well as urban, the immediate concern is eking out a living. It not only consumes most of their time but-importantly enough, decides every thing else about their lives. Food, shelter, health, education, entertainment and politics take a back seat. Policies and programmes for the poor children, on the other hand, have been and continue to be framed by such professionale who have generally quite the opposite view of their needs. Some of these professionals have their own motives for offering peculiar solutions of the problems of the poor and the children. As a consequence, there is a mismatch between the need hierarchy as seen by the poor and the policies and programmes as articulated, formulated, operationalised, funded and implemented by the planners and politico-administrative personnel.

(*b*) Causes and Consequences—Mixed-up

Situation analyses and identification of critical areas for intervention through a set of programmes/schemes require, among other things, a very precise enunciation of the relationship between causes and consequences. Quite often, on the other hand, the planned programmes address themselves only to the symptoms rather than the root causes of the disease. Even in cases where the situation analysis does aim to identify the underlying causes, the *emphasis* appears to be getting placed on the *immediate* rather than the deep-rooted underlying causes.

(*c*) Problems and the Solutions

An ever expanding army of experts and programme planners has been displaying an amazing array of naivete in providing complex analysis of problems and yet culminating in over-simplified solutions quite far removed from the obtaining empirical realities. Programmes such as the ICDS are useful examples of these tendencies resulting in encouragement of any effective action at all. Therefore, whereas regorous analysis and improved understanding of the involved complexities are indeed very welcome, there is a strong case for a more realistic programmatic selectivity in programme design. Coaxed, cajoled and even coerced by international funding and other aid giving agencies, quite a few "intergrated" programmes for the children have been launched in India. However, in operational terms what programmes like the ICDS tend to do is to juxtapose tasks and resources from different agencies: integration is just not there and coordination is often left to an unworkable mechanism. There is also a second tendency of mixing up phasing of efforts in some programmes. A crucial programme like the EPI did not necessarily differentiate between the left-over targets for immunization from the past and the present and future immunization targets planned. The integration of tasks must result in a phased sequence of contributions over time by different sets of actors in a chain of steps designed to lay foundation for activities one after the other and ensuring inbuilt self-sustenance.

(*d*) Availability of Resources

Characteristically, some of the internationally assisted programmes for "child development" are so designed that a very large percentage of their allocation is consumed by the establishment created thereunder: only a meagre part is left for the software part of the programmes. The pattern of cooperation and assistance worked out between the international aid and giving agency(ies) and the Govt. of India on the one hand and between the Govt. of India and the state government(s) on the other sometimes ends up in bizarre situations. For the first part of these agreements, a large part of the outlays of programmes is consumed on the upkeep of the 'native' and 'international' staff stationed by the aid-giving agencies at national, regional, and local levels and their travel and *per diem*. The procedures of these international agencies sometimes make it obligatory to import equipment being used under these programmes from outside countries even though supplies or comperable quality and needed quantities are locally available. The Govt. of India—State government relationship also causes havoc in programmes like the ICDS for which the GOI provides funds for the establishment part and the State Govt. the allocation for nutrition component. In one major state where the Central directive of covering all the blocks with the ICDS and all eligible children upto 0-6 years age group, all adolescent girls and pregnant and lactating mothers to be provided nutrition at enhanced rate was to be implemented, the needed allocation for nutrition component of the VII Five Year Plan alone was put at Rs. 1465.02 crores. Its VIIIth Five Year Plan size was however, of Rs. 23,000 crores only.

Strategy for Child Development

The World Bank launched the so called strategy of "direct assault on poverty" in the mid-seventies, the hidden meaning of the touted goals has been evident to the discerning eye. This strategy ensures hedgemony of a world capitalist order. International aid-giving agencies and major industrialized countries control the very thrust of social-economic-political development in the developing nations through not only programmes of assistance of industrial, and agricultural development but, more importantly, of poverty alleviation, environmental control, etc. as well. These programmes make it possible for the international forces to keep the native national leadership—political, military, bureaucracy—in good humour and make poverty eradication also a flourishing business for both the sets. This is a God-sent opportunity where the poor continue to remain poor since the causation mechanism remains intact, and the rich continue to become richer by even direct assault on poverty programmes. It is precisely because of such an ideology that cosmetic nutrition programmes like ICDS get precedence over the subsidized feeding programmes in countries like India.

However, despite the popularity and effectiveness of the mobile health team it was clear that the replication of this specific service is not so easy. Before a new strategy was adopted the achievements of this team approach were assessed and the following points become very clear:

(*a*) the introduction of a simple cheap protein supplement made out of local ingredients for 25 np. each was very effective in reducing diseases of malnutrition;

(*b*) child care has become an indirect and probably a more effective and genuine method of family planning. The periodic recording of weight and height assured the mothers of their children's survival; and

(*c*) there has been a drop in the infact mortality rate in the project area.

The integrated approach to the basic needs of pre-school rural children which we have described above has, as its main objective, improvement in the quality of life through activities centred on the mother and child in the inter-related areas of health, nutrition and education. The change of attitude among the rural families who have participated in these programmes is encouraging and it seems likely that the new initiatives can become self-sustaining and have long-term effects because they have stimulated more intensive community involvement. Though it is not possible to draw any firm conclusions either about the methodology or the effectiveness of the programmes we have described above, it would seem that locally managed health, education and nutrition programmes for child welfare has a wider significance because it incorporates aspects—grass-roots mobilisation, the use of locally available personnel and the sharing of financial responsibility—that are capable of replication.

REFERENCES

1. Mina Swaminathan (1979): 'Children of the Urban Poor: Problems and Opportunities' in edited book of Alfred de Souza, *Children in India*, Manohar, New Delhi, p. 19.

2. *Ibid.*, p. 19.

3. *Working Children in Bombay: A Study* (NIPCCD) Mimeo, 1978, New Delhi.

4. S. Anandalakshmi, Editorial in *Ekalarya* (1973), Annual of Mobile Creches, New Delhi.

5. *Report on the Working and Living Conditions of Workers in the Building Construction*, Unorganized Sector Survey Series No. 1, 1977-78 (Simla: Labour Bureau, Min. of Labour) Mimeo.

6. *Working Mothers and Early Childhood Education* (New Delhi: NIPCCD, 1978).

7. M.K.A. Siddiqui (1969), 'Life in the Slums of Calcutta' *Economic and Political Weekly*, December 4, Oscar Lewis, *The Children of Snachez*; (London: Secker and Warburg, 1961).

11

Characteristics of the Developmental Programmes Related to Child Development

ASHOK KUMAR*

1. Background

After Independence, the government of free India initiated planned efforts for development of rural Indian and for the socio-economic growth of the rural poor/weaker sections. Since then, although there have been programmatic changes and shifts, in emphasis, the effort has been on, and considerable amounts of the country's scarce resources were being set and geared to year after year for achieving the objective. But in view of the giganticity of the task, and the thin spread of the benefits that have resulted from the efforts so far put in, we have still a long way to travel in order to see that the little communities living in our vast rural areas transformed into productive and forward-looking vibrant communities.

Rural development being multidisciplinery in nature and multi-sectoral in operation, is designated to fulfill multiple objectives, namely more production, more employment and more equitable distribution of income, wide participation in the development process, increased access to modern inputs and services and grater self-reliance and environmental awareness.

*Faculty member, NIPCCD, Regional Centre, Lucknow (U.P.)

Of later, several contradictions have arisen as various components of rural development plans and programmes have often been ill-concerned, fragmented and sometimes, almost unrelated. As a result, the question of rural development in recent years have loomed large and is being discussed, more with concern and attention than casual romantic euphoria, at the various national and international forums of academics, intellectuals, administrators, politicians and planners, etc.

Since last four decades, the rural development in India has witnessed Kaleidoscopic changes from time to time. In this context various programmes were introduced under different names, starting from Community Development (CD) to Integrated Rural Development (IRD) although their contents remains almost the same and also the fate of the people marked no substantial change. However, different approaches to rural development adopted during plan periods can broadly be grouped as:

COMMUNITY DEVELOPMENT APPROACH
- launched in 1952
- culiminated in Panchayat Raj structure, in 1955

GROWTH CENTRE APPROACH
- radiate employment income boosting projects
- reinforcing relationship between core & pesiphesy

SECTORAL APPROACH
- intensive sectoral development like Agriculture/ Industry etc.

TARGET SECTOR APPROACH
- IADP, MNP, SMFDP and package programme (Green Revolution launched)

PILOT PROJECT APPROACH
- pilot project evolved to assist small & marginal farmers as such SFDA & MFDA programmes launched

IRD APPROACH
- latest approach
- integrated development
- interrelation between different activities

From this perspective, the Indian rural development programmes have been reformist in nature. Here, instead of directly going to the root cause of rural poverty and hunger, so as to alleviate them, under the influence of Gandhism a reformist line was adopted which deterred and diverted the radical outlook.

However, as rural development is characterised by a combination of both a applied and theoritical aspects and the scope is primarily restricted to rural sector and encompassed all facets of rural life, it is subject-matter necessitates an appropriate understanding in spheres which are closely related to the development of the lives of the people. Further, it does not depend only on the promotion of social and economic activities but also on such other inputs which have close bearing on the lives of people such as health, nutrition, education and skill development.[2]

During the past four decades of plan development, social welfare as a plan component has acquired great significance, as evidenced by its widening interface with Government and increasing participation by voluntary agencies.[3] From the Fifth Plan onwards, emphasis has been on the promotion of preventive and developmental services. As a result several programmes in the areas of child welfare, *viz.*, nutrition, health, education and recreation for children have launched by the Government. Plan-wise rural development programme its objective, year of introduction, etc., related to women and children, are summarised in the Annexure I.

So far as child welfare is concerned, as a concept and practice it has deep historical roots in our country. In the earlier days as stated by Chowdhry (1984) 'Child Care services were confined to the voluntary sector. These services were mainly organised for victims of destitution, detinquency, abuse, etc. In mid-twenties, voluntary organisations such as Indian Council for Child Welfare, the Indian Red Cross Society, the All India Women's Conference, the Kasturba Gandhi Nation Memorial Trust, the Balkanji Bari, the Children's Aid Society, etc. organised programmes in the areas of care, health nutrition and education for children, etc.[4]

The status of Child indicates that children's programmes need the highest priority in the national development programmes. Earlier, child care had been the responsibility of the primary institutions of the society such as family and in most of the cases, the joint family. The Child's physical, psychological, social and cognitive development was assured by the resources aud the surrounding of the joint family. The transition from joint to nuclear family and changes in socio-economic status have brought many changes in society. Because of the new constraints, traditional care suffered progressive erosions. Child neglect, abuse and exploitation followed. As large number of families, both in rural and urban areas are below poverty line, these sections of the population are even to-day not in a position to provide the care and security needed for normal growth of their children. Intervention by the government, therefore, become imperative for their proper health care, nutrition, education and well-being.[5] It is in this view, the subject, at the same time, also requires a clear understanding of the planning process and the different rural development programmes which are being envisaged for the welfare of children from time to time.

After realising the significance of child development an attempt has been made in the present exercise to give a critical review of the programmes meant for this vulnerable group. The focus is primarily on rural development programmes only. The paper is spilit into five parts including the present one. The second part gives a brief sketch of child development during plan period. The third takes the vivid account of child development programmes whereas fourth examines the programmes critically. The final part offers a closing statement by highlighting same issues.

II. Child Development During Fire Year Plans

In the First Five Year Plan, the major responsibility of developing children's welfare services was placed on voluntary organisations; states too assumed greater responsibility and launched programmes for health, nutrition and primary education of children. Pre-primary education, however, continued to be the responsibility of voluntary organisations. The Second Five Year Plan reiterated that voluntary efforts in child welfare have to be supplemented by central, state and local authorities. The Central Social Welfare Board (CSWB) was given the responsibility of promoting and developing welfare services for women and children in the voluntary sector through grants-in-aids programmes. Welfare Extension Project programmes was expanded and coordinated with similar programmes of the Ministry of Community Development for women and children in community development blocks.[6]

In order to combat rural mal nutrition, Applied Nutrition, Programme was started during Third Five Year Plan—with the assistance of UNICEF, FAO and WHO. This was followed by supplementary Nutrition Programme in 1970-71 by the ministry of Social Welfare. Balwadi Nutrition Programmes funded by the government was also introduced in the same year.[7] However, there was no scheme for universal coverage of the rural pre-school children till the Fourth Five Year Plan.

In spite of launching a number of Child Welfare Programmes, the incidents of mortality, morbidity and malnutrition among children continued to be alarmingly high. A National Policy for children was formulated followed by the setting-up of a Nation Children's Board. The Ministry of Social Welfare Developed the Integrated Child Development Services Scheme (ICDS) in 1975 and 33 projects of ICDS were launched on an experimental basis in 1975-76.[8]

The Ministry of Rural Development has also introduced a scheme of Development of Women and Children in Rural Areas (DWCRA) as a part of the Integrated Rural Development programmes during Sixth Five Year Plan. During seventh Five Year Plan the wheat-based Nutrition Programmes was launched in 1985 by the department of women and child development.

However, after reviewing the programme launched during

different plan periods, we can examine the trends of the programmes in the past and in the current decade.

Thinking Trends of the Planners/Policy Makers

Before	Now
Social Welfare Oriented	Development Oriented
Child Development as some responsibilities and needs	Accept the children as human resource development in different socio economic set.up
Children s Programme Isolated from the main streas	Integration in the major programme for over all development
Oriented to the delivery of services	Participatory in nature

However, much ground needs to be covered yet to achieve the goal by way of creating an atmosphere of better understanding of the developmental needs for children in the context of national developmental strategy and a strong infrastructures and other supports to achieve the goal.

III. Rural Development Programmes in the Context of Child Development

In the early fifties, development of programmes for Women, children and youth in the rural areas was the responsibility of the Ministry of Community, Development (Annexure-I). However, because of limited resources in the community development did not get due importance in community development in the subsequent Five Year Plans. Children did not get as much attention as they needed nor did they get as much share of the increased income as they should have far their growth and development.

As a result, to cover this gap, different ministries of the government launched various programmes which aimed as raising the quality of life particularly of women and children. Broadly speaking the different rural development programmes related to children can be grouped as: (*a*) health; (*b*) Nutrition;

(*c*) education; and (*d*) integration of different services. Details of programmes are given in the subsequent paragraphs.

(*a*) Health Related Programmes

The situation of children in India is far from satisfaction with no access to proper food, shelter or sanitary facilities. Though most of the child health components are covered by CD programme, MNP and ICDS and very few are left like immunization, MCH and programme for some preventive measures. Some of these programmes are summarised here.

Immunization Programme. Public health programme in India has been operating at two planes. At one plane, an integrated curative and public health services are provided through the PHCs under the Health Department. At another plane big national programmes have been developed to tackle diseases like Malaria, Small pox, Tuberculosis, Leprosy, Filariasis and Trachoma. An *Expanded Programme of Immunization* (*EPI*) has also adopted for providing protection against Tetanus, Diptheria, whooping cough, Poliomyalitis and Tuberculosis. The programmes emerge at the initiative of the Central Government, and are executed at the states. The expenditure on these programmes is also borne wholly or largely by the Central Government. These constitute, so to say, the Central Contribution to the health services for the nation.

MCH Programme. In India, primary health centres are the backbone of rural health services. Within the limited resources primary health care is probably the best available alternative for providing MHC services in rural areas.

One of the factors which has a direct bearing on the rate of mortality is the type of medical attention received at birth. In rural areas, over 75 per cent births are attended by untrained medical practitioners or others and only about 8 per cent by trained medical practitioners.[9] However, with introduction of the latest scheme of providing at least one trained *dai* (Traditional Birth Attendent Programme) in each village is hoped that there will improvement in this situation.

CHV/VHG/CHW/Programme. The Community Health Workers or Village Health Guide Scheme is a step towards taking health services to the actual needy groups. Under this scheme an attempt is being made to make health services available to villagers at their doorstep.

(*b*) **Nutrition Related Programmes**

Several nutrition programmes are in operation in order to combat the problems of malnutrition. Most of them are short-term measures to supplement the diets of pre-school children, pregnant and lactating mothers. Some important among these are summarised here.

Applied Nutrition Programme (ANP). The Expanded Nutrition Programme (1959) was renamed as Applied Nutrition Programme and aimed at extending the services to the rural areas. Feeding, however, was limited to the volnerable groups, *i.e.*, Children in the age group of 0-6 years and pregnant and nursing mothers. Drought-prone and backward area were given priority over the others. It was implemented through C. D. Blocks. Organisation of poultry units horticulture, kitchen gardens, community gardens were the methods of production of food with the intention of bringing about greater awareness with regard to the production and consumption of protective foods. The feeding component was limited only to the use of food produced by vulnerable groups and was basically as a form of practical demonstration for the beneficiaries.

Intensive Development Programme (IDP). An IDP (1977-78) consisted of a package of inter-related basic services which could be delivered to specifically identified rural areas in order to improve the health and nutritional status of young children and their mothers. According, 23 on-going ANP blocks in 21 states were selected for intensive development with the UNICEF assistance for a period of two years. The programme under this experiment covered, in addition to ANP activities, safe drinking water, environmental sanitation, income generating activities for women, etc.[10]

Special Nutrition Programme (SNP). This programme was

launched as a crash feeding programme in 1970-71 to provide supplementary feeding to children below 6 years and expectant and nursing mothers living in urban slums, tribal, backward and rural areas and aims at bridging the existing nutritional gap in the target groups by providing supplementary feeding to the extent of 300 calories and 10-12 grams of protein for 300 days a year. Later on (during 5th Plan 1974-78), it was transferred to the state sector to be operated as a part of the Minimum Needs Programme with a special officer incharge of the programme under the Director of Social Welfare at the State Level.[11]

Balwadi Nutrition Programme (BNP) (1970-71). Children in the age group of 3-6 years from low income families of the rural areas are the main target groups of the BNP. It provides educational facilities for pre-school children and nutritional supplement to pre-schoolers with intention of elevating their nutritional status.

Mid-day Meal Programme (MDM). It was initiated in 1962-63 as a centrally sponsored scheme and later on transferred to MNP. Attempt is being made under this programme to offer a free meal to school-going children between 6-11 years from the weaker sections of society. The programme provides one meal containing about 80 gms. of foodgrains and 7 gms. of oil with a nutritive content of approximately 300 calories and 8-12 gms. protein for a period of atleast 180 days in a year per beneficiary.

Vitamin A Prophylaxis Programme. This programme was launched by the Ministry of Health and Family Welfare in 1970. The programme aims at reducing incidence of blindness occuring due to deficiency of Vitamin A. Children in the age group of 1-5 years from the target group and 200,000 I.U. of Vitamin A suspension in oil is provided to all the beneficiaries once every six months.

Prophylaxis Against Nutritional Anaemia (PANA). In order to meet deficiency of hoemoglobin level in pre-school children and pregnant women at later stages of pregnancy, the Ministry of Health and Family Welfare launched this programme. Iron and folic acid supplements to the extent of 60 mg. of iron as ferrous sulphate or ferrous furmarate and 0.5 mg. folic acid are provided to expectant mothers and 20 mg. iron and 0.1 mg. folic acid are given to pre-school children for approximately 100 days consecutively.

(*c*) Education Related Programmes

A number of committees and study groups were set-up from time to time suggest ways and means for pre-school education formalities. All these groups emphasised the importance of pre-school education but the recommendations remained mostly on paper. The CSWB initiated as a part of its welfare activities in the area not covered hitherto, the scheme of *Welfare Extension Projects.* But most of the children education programmes are integrated with the health and nutritional programme. However, a great impetus to the provision of pre-school education was provided by the declaration of a National Policy on children in 1974 which recognised children as the supreme asset of the nation. This was followed by the launching of Integrated Child Development Services Scheme.

(*d*) Integrated Programmes

Since the Fourth Five Year Plan integration of different services specially in the rural sector was started. At the outset Minimum Need Programme was first among the different programmes.

Minimum Need Programme (MNP). This programme was launched in 1972 with a objective to develop basic infra-structural facilities and to increase health and nutritional status of children and nursing mothers. It consists of the following elements:

(*i*) Elementary Education: 100 per coverage of children in the age-group 6-14 years.

(*ii*) Adult Education: Coverage of all adults in the age group of 15-35 years.

(*iii*) Rural Health: Establishment of PHC/subcentre and one CHV/VHG in each village.

(*iv*) Rural Water Supply: Coverage of all problem villages.

(*v*) Rural Roads: Linking of all villages with a population of 1000 or more.

(*vi*) Rural Electrification: Coverage of 60 per cent villages in each state.

(*vii*) House-sites for Landless: Provision of housing assistance to all rural landless labourers.

(*viii*) Nutrition: *SNP* to malnourished children, pregnant and lactating mothers, supplementary feeding to pre-school children for 300 days. *MDM*: Mid-day meals for one-fourth of children in the age-group 6-11 years to be served in schools for 200 days.

Out of eight components mentioned above only two components, *viz.*, elementary education and nutrition are directly related with the child development.

Integrated Child Development Services (ICDS)

The earlier efforts made to provide services to the pre-school child were sectoral and lacked necessary coordination.[12] It was felt that a programme may be evolved which was low in cost, economically more comprehensive and effective. As a result, the ICDS scheme was launched in 1975-76 after a series of inter-ministrial discussions. The scheme provides integrated services to (*a*) children below the age of 6 years; (*b*) the expectant and nursing mothers; and (*c*) women in the age-group of 15-45. The following package of services is provided on an integrated basis in the ICDS scheme:

(*i*) Supplementary nutrition;

(*ii*) Immunization;

(*iii*) Health check-up;

(*iv*) Referral Services;

(*v*) Nutrition and health education; and

(*vi*) Non-formal education.

The focal point for delivery of these services is the aganwadi centres.

The essence of the programme is 'integration', and is the first major child development programme in the country which has recognised the differential needs of the children 0-6 years age group. The services complementary to one another are integrated into a package to enhance the overall effect. The organisation is also integrated through coordination at various levels in the management of services by different departments/agencies running the programme which is intersectoral. The blueprint is well-drawn in terms of target groups, services, management, training and funding, the role of different functionaries, monitoring and evaluation.

Development of Women and Children in Rural Areas (DWCRA)

It is a sub-scheme under programme and is introduced on the realisation that income of the family is not merely dependent upon the economic programmes but has positive relationship with social inputs/services, *i.e.*, nutritional status of family, education, status of women, etc. It has drawn the attention on the needs of Rural women and has helped them to take up income generating activities and thereby look after their children better. Besides organising economic programme, emphasis in training will be given on organisation and management of child welfare services. Under this scheme, if the child care services are not available in the area under any other on-going programmes, it will be necessary to provide some facilities so that the children are not neglected while the mothers are at work. Another component of the programme is the provision of certain basic facilities for the care of children at NREP (now JRY) work sites. A provision of Rs. 5,000/- therefore, has been made for each block for creating temporary child care facilities at the work sites.[13] The programme is being implemented by DRDAs through block functionaries. The districts are selected in consultation with the state government on the criteria of backwardness, incidence of child mortality, level of literacy, etc.

A Critical Review

The programme envisaged under community development had a strong component for women and child development, social education, etc. But emphasis was more on community development. Even during First, Second, Third and Fourth Five Year Plans programmes for children did not receive any fresh impetus and continued on the earlier lines and were confined to the voluntary sector. But after Fourth Plan, Rural Development Programmes for children received high priority. In the present section we will critically examine the above mentioned programme launched for child development in the subsequent paragraphs.

The PHCs are conceived as focal points from which primary health care services could be provided through dispensaries and sub-centres. The operational responsibilities include medical care, control of communicable diseases, MCH, environmental sanitation, school health, health education, immunization, etc. But it is observed that because of lack of proper coordination the above mentioned services of different child health programmes are being ignored by the medical staff. Some of the services like; immunization, school health, etc. mentioned above are to be provided at the Anganwadi Centres and schools. But the health functionaries are not performing this responsibilities regularly and hence, it requires proper evaluation.

So far as the nutritional programmes are concerned, various reports and studies reveal that programmes have not succeeded to the extent desired in terms of improvement of dietary patterns and increase in production of protective foods. Poultry and fishery units (ANP) have failed to make any appreciable impact. Community, school and kitchen gardens had not been developed as they were envisaged in the scheme. Use of mass media and other means of communication for nutrition education in marginal. On the basis of there, it has been suggested that nutritional programme should be operated as a part of an overall rural development programme rather than as an independent one.

Involvement of local bodies, *viz.*, panchayati raj institutions, mahila mandals and other organisations in any of the programme in the promotion is observed to be very unsatisfactory as it was observed by Programme Evaluation Organisation (PEO) of the Planning Commission.

It has been observed that some of the programmes, services and inputs meant specifically for the children of weaker sections are utilised for the benefit of better-off setions because of weak delivery system. Supplies and services in PHCs or nutrition component of MNP in rural areas go to really a selected families who are known to the officials. Because of inadequacy of services and delivery system these services are not reach to the needy children. Despite of our efforts for raising the level of children, the rural development programmes do not bring results in proportion to which money is spent and efforts are made.

Among the different rural child development programmes, ICDS is single comprehensive and selective on clientele and therefore, economic programme. The services complementary to one another are integrated into a package to enhance the overall effect. The earlier programmes for pre-school children took it for granted that if a balwadi was started, related health and nutrition services will be forthcoming from the agencies like the PHC and ANP, but the ICDS Scheme ensures through the budget provisions the necessary direct inputs of health by strengthening the staffing pattern of the PHC, mechanism of proper coordination between health personnel and child development personnel, and organisation of training and orientation for these functionaries.

Despite the fact that the programme has many plus points, it has some weaknesses also. One is not so sure whether the children in the age group of 0-3 years do get the same attention as anganwadi children (3-6 years) in absence of any institution for them. In many project areas, the expected coordination and cooperation from the health staff or the block staff is not forthcoming for various reasons. Institutions have to be created and mechanisms have to be found by which the richer sections should pay for the services by contributing in cash and kind whereas the poorest sections could contribute in the form of voluntary service.

As far as DWCRA programme is concerned, some provision may be made out of its fund for the purchase of portable cradles, toys, pictorial books, etc. for the pre-school children. These services can be organised with the help of the community organiser and the gram sevikas.

The community organiser while being trained will also be familiarised with various other on going programmes supportive to the development of rural women and children so that she can help in coordinating these activities.

REFERENCES

1. Ram Bali Singh (1985): 'Concept of Integration in Rural Development', in edited book *Rural Development in India—Problems, Strategies and Approaches*, by K.N. Singh and D.N. Singh, National Geographical Society of India, Varanasi, p. 113.
2. S.P. Jain (1985): 'Rural Women Development in India through last decades', paper presented in an International Seminar on *Women and Development*, Jaipur, p. 129.
3. Govt. of India, Seventh Five Year Plan 1985-90, Vol. II, Planning Commission, Chapter 13, New Delhi, p. 306.
4. D. Paul Chowdhry (1984): 'Programmes for Youth and Children in Rural Areas' in a Silver Jublee edited volume of NIRD entitled *Rural Transformation—Readings*, NIRD, Hyderabad, p. 405.
5. *Ibid.*, p. 406.
6. *Ibid.*, p. 406.
7. *Ibid.*, p. 406.
8. *Ibid.*, p. 406.
9. *Ibid.*, p. 408.
10. Govt. of India & UNICEF: Assessing the Impact of Intensive Development Programme on Women.
11. Chowdhry (1984): *op. cit*, p. 412.
12. D. Paul Chowdhry (1985): *Profile of Social Welfare and Development in India*, M.N. Publishers & Distributors, New Delhi.
13. *Ibid.*, p. 76.

ANNEXURE I

List of Programmes for the Development of Women and Children Since Independence

Plan Period	Programmes	Year of Introduction	Implementing Agency/ Department	Coverage	Main Objectives
(1)	(2)	(3)	(4)	(5)	(6)
First Five Year Plan (1951-56)	1. Community Dev. Programme	1952	Distt./C.D. Block/ SEO	Complete C.D. Block	Multi-Dimensional/Mobilization of Human and material resources initially not included any prog. for women and child but latter on women component provided by SEO,

	2. Balwadis/Pre-Schools	1952	Voluntary Organisations, KGMNT, ICCW, AIWC	Dakshin Murti in Bhavnagar, Vedchi in Surat, Wardha in Maharashtra and some other parts of Western India	Pre-School/Nutrition and Immunization to children.
	3. Women and Children programme	1952	Deptt. of C.D.	2 to 10 villages	Ed./Nutrition and Health service to target group.
	4. National Extn. Service	1953	C.D. Block		Almost same as in 1.
	5. Welfare Extn. Projects (OP)	1954	CSWB/PIC	About 400 projects of 5 centres each	Home Sc. Approach.
Second Five Year Plan (1956-61)	6. Welfare Extn. Projects (CD)	1957	CSWB/PIC	About 400 projects of 5 centres each	Women's welfare, latter on handed over to Mahila Mandals in 1961-62.
	7. Khadi & Village Industries Prog.	1957	KVIC	—	Self-employment for women.
	8. Welfare Extn. Projects (Urban)	1960	CSWB/PIC	40 Projects	as in 6.

(Contd.)

(*Contd.*)

(1)	(2)	(3)	(4)	(5)	(6)
	9. Welfare Extn. Centres	1961	CSWB-Managing Committee of Voluntary Organisations	About 1600 Centres through 400 Voluntary Organizations	
Third Five Year Plan (1961-66)	10. Applied Nutrition Prog. (ANP)	1962	Min. of C.D./Block	1754 Blocks covering 63,318 villages	To provide Nutrition to women and children.
	11. Border Area Project	1963	CSWB/PIC	About 56 Projects with 280 Centres	
	12. Integrated Child Welfare Services Demonstration Projects	1963	DSW/Block	18 Projects	Child Welfare-Health Education, etc.
	13. Integrated Pre-school Project	1964	CSWB/PIC	23 Projects	Early/Pre-School Education to children 6 Years.
	14. Balwadis in Erstwhile Demonstration Projects	1965	CSWB/Balwadi Committee	11 Projects 249 Balwadis	

Annual Plan 1966	15.	Farmer's Training and Ed. Programme	1966			
Annual Plan 1967	16.	Family and Child Welfare Projects	1967	CSWB/Functional Committee	281 Projects of six centres	
	17.	Rural Work Programme	1967			
Annual Plan 1968	18.	Tribal Development Block	1968			
Annual Plan 1969	19.	Composite Rural Manpower Programme	1969			
	20.	Programme for Women and Pre-School children	1969	CSWB/PIC		
Fourth Five Year Plan	21.	Balwadi Nutrition Programme	1971	CSWB/Managing Committee of Voluntary Organizations	5033 Balwadis	To provide Nutrition to the target group.

(Contd.)

(Contd.)

(1)	(2)	(3)	(4)	(5)	(6)
(1969-74)					
	22. Cash Scheme for Rural Empl.	1971	Rural Development/ SFDA/Block		
	23. Small Farmers Development Agency (SWDA)	1971	Rural Development/ SWDA/Block	Blocks	Loan/assistance to small farmers.
	24. Minimum Need Programme (MNP)	1972	—do—	Blocks	To develop basic infrastructure like well, reads, electricity Health Centres Schools, etc.
	25. Special Nutrition Programme (SNP)	1972	DSW/Coordination Committee	69 lakh Beneficiaries	To provide Nutrition to the target group.
Fifth Five Year Plan (1974-79)	26. Scheme of Welfare of Children in need and protection	1974	DSW/Voluntary organisations	1550 Units	Forth welfare of children and mothers.

27. Creches for the children of Ailing/working mothers	1975	DSW/Voluntary Organisations	1385 Units	To provide creche facility for the target group.
28. Integrated Child Development Services (ECDS)	1975	State DSW/Health/ RD/TD/Block	1952 Projects (Till 1988)	1. To improve the nutritional/ health status of 0-6 years children. 2. Proper psychological physical and social development of child. 3. Reduce mortality, morbidity mal-nutrition and drop out. 4. Effective coordination of policy and implementation. 5. Proper nutrition and health education to mother.
29. Food for work prog.	1977	RD/SFDA/Block	Blocks	To provide food for work in rural areas.
30. Intensive Development Projects	1978	RD/Block	23	
31. Social Inputs in Area Dev.	1978	DSW/RD/Distt./Block	45	To provide Basic facilities to the rural people.

(Contd.)

(*Contd.*)

(1)	(2)	(3)	(4)	(5)	(6)
	32. Whole Village Development Programme	1979	RD/SFDA/Block	Blocks	
	33. Training of Rural Youth for Self employment (TRYSEM)	1979	RD/DRDA/Block	Blocks	Training for self employment.
	34. Integrated Rural Dev. Prog. (IRDP)	1979	RD/DRDA/Block	In all the Blocks/ villages	To provide assistance to below poverty line people to cross the poverty line.
Sixth Five Year Plan (1980-85)	35. National Rural Employment Programme	1980	RD/DRDA/Block	In all the Blocks/ villages	To provide employment to rural poor.
	36. PM's 20 Point Programme	1980			
	37. Tamil Nadu Integrated Nutrition Project	1980	State/DSW	One Distt. Six Blocks	To provide Nutrition.

	38. RLEGP	1982	RD/DRDA/Block	All the blocks/ villages	To provide employment to landless labourers.
	39. Dev. of Women and Children in Rural Areas (DWCRA)	1983	RD/DRDA/Block	50 Districts	To provide women's employment and income generating activities.
Seventh Five Year Plan (1985-90)	40. Wheat Based Nutrition Programme	1986	Deptt. of W. & C.D.	3 million beneficiaries in addition to already IIM ICDS	Supplementary Nutrition with a view to cover large number of beneficiaries in Tribal, Urban slums and Backward rural areas.

Source: Different Plan Documents. *Abbreviations*: RD—Rural Development, DSW—Deptt. of Social Welfare, D & CD—Women and Child Development, DRDA—Ditt. Rural Dev. Agency SFDA—Small Farmers Dev., Agency, TD-Tribal Development, SEO-Social Ed. Organization, CSDB—Central Social Welfare Board.

12

Promoting Child Development Through Rural Development Programmes: An Assessment

S. MISHRA*

Child as a human resource is a key factor in development. There is a worldwide consensus among psychologists, biologists and sociologists regarding the crucial significance of early years of life for the optimum development of the child. The foundations of man's physical, mental and social development are laid in this stage and damage on impoverishment suffered at this period is likely to be irreparable.[1] Timely services to meet the biological, emotional and intellectual needs of young children can make a positive impact on the development of the country by preventing or minimising the wastage arising from infant mortality, physical handicaps, malnutrition, stagnation in schools and inadequate development of mental capacities.[2]

Child development as generally means allround development of the child, physical, mental and social can only be enhanced, when the defined age group is provided with the basic services of both preventive and curative in nature in accordance with the needs and age of the child. The basic aspects which are to be looked after in order to stimulate early childhood development include:

1. Immunization
2. Nutrition

*Assistant Director, NIPCCD, Regional Centre, Lucknow-226020.

. Health
4. Early childhood education
5. Parental education.

Apart from specifically designed child care programmes, all most all rural development programmes (as mentioned in Annexure-1 of Reference Materials), have one or more such components of early childhood development.

The major problems that do not bring expected results of these programmes may be the rapid growth of population, lack of proper education and status of women in the present day situation in India.

Population. The size and growth of population has a strong bearing on social situation and process of human development. Every seventh person in the world is an Indian. With only 2.4 per cent of the global area, the country holds nearly 15 per cent of the world's population, over 20 per cent of the share of the developing countries. India ranks second only to China with a population of 685 million by the 1981 census, and 720 million as of 1983. Children constitute about 43% of the country's population, a major proportion which has remained almost constant through the past 70 years. This age distribution of the population is the combined effect of high fertility and steady decline in mortality. A crucial factor contributing to high fertility in India is the young age at which girls are married. In the absence of a foolproof system for marriage registration, data analysis reveals a small rise in age at marriage of girls from 13 years in 1901 to 15.3 years in 1951, 17 years in 1971 and 18.6 years in 1981.[3]

Education. Level of education also plays an important role in the process of human development, it is not only a basic need and human right but also a means of meeting other needs and for sustaining development itself. The progress achieved in literacy has been substantial but inadequate in relation to the size and growth of population. The percentage of literates to total population has improved from 16.67 in 1951 to 36.23

in 1981. If the estimated number of children below 5 years is excluded, the size of the illiterate population comes to around 340 million. While the literacy rate has slowly improved, the actual number of illiterates has been increasing due to the rising population and the backlog of adult illiteracy. With the pace of progress India has made, the literacy rate varies widely between males and females; between urban areas and rural interior; between scheduled castes and tribes on the one hand the rest of the population on the other; and between state and state.[4]

Status of Women. Women are subjects of development in their own right. They are also the principal providers of care and support for infants and children. The role of women in the economy and their status in society thus become crucial for children and for development. The trend noticed in relation to females in the demographic imbalance, unequal access to health and nutrition, dual economic role, educational neglect, legal protection and social solidarity are not autonomous but intimately interlinked. These trends are almost always adverse to women. This phenomenon can not be explained as distortions arising from poverty, but rather understood against a common denomination of inbuilt social prejudice and discrimination against women. Even if poverty were reduced, the situation of women is unlikely to improve unless social attitudes towards them change and their essentially dependent status given way to equality with men. The literacy rate for females has consistently been behind that for males, and by a big margin. And the female literacy rate in rural India, where three-fourths of the people live, has been around a third of the female literacy rate for the towns. Again, the proportion of illiterate females among scheduled castes and scheduled tribes is appreciably higher than for the rest of the national community.

The correlation between female illiteracy and infant mortality is equally clear. It is found that infant mortality was highest in the case of illiterate mothers both in urban and rural areas but much higher in the later. As education levels increased, the mortality rate declined. The lack of education of women limits their awareness of the benefits of learning for their children. Unless the women are educated, the efforts to open up learning opportunities to boys and girls from poor families is unlikely to succeed decisively. In fact, the most potent tool to create a social demand for early childhood development is the exposure to education of adults, particularly women.

Child cannot develop in vaccum. It needs support of the family and the community as a whole since the parents are the primary care takers of the child. The development of the child depends totally on the development of parents. A step to enhance child development through various rural development programmes is the inclusion of child development and parental education aspects as discussed earlier in the programme frame. The next step is to build up a sound community participation base for the successful implementation of the programmes. The following measures are to be taken care of to make Rural Development Programmes more child oriented:

— Parental awareness regarding the programme: objectives, services, beneficiaries, etc.

— Timely services.

— Adult education by incentive schemes, involving the literate beneficiaries.

— Steps to equality of women.

— Population education.

— Parental education to stimulate the development of the child in home situation.

— Use of media, innovative technology in educating parents.

— Involving beneficiaries in need identification, prioritisation of services, review and periodic assessment of the programme.

— Grassroot level organisational development and it's involvement in the programme.

— Inter-personal relationship between beneficiaries and programme functionaries.

The very purpose, promoting child development through rural development programmes explains the idea that child development should be considered in the context of family and the community, where the child lives. There is a need to include more child development aspects in rural development programmes and the parents, basically mothers should be equipped with required skill to stimulate the development of the child so that both work simultaneously to create a healthy, intelligent and socially viable child to make our country prosperous.

REFERENCES

1. Muralidharan, Rajalakshmi: Pre-school Education Profile of the Child in India: Policies and Programmes, Ministry of Social Welfare, Government of India, New Delhi.
2. Dayal, M.S.: Integrated Child Development Services, Profile of the Child in India: Policies and Programmes, Ministry of Social Welfare, Government of India, New Delhi.
3. UNICEF: An Analysis of the Situation of Children in India, 1984.
4. *Ibid.*

13

Integrated Delivery System for Child Development in India

ANJANI KUMAR SINGH*
POORNIMA SHEKHAR SINGH**

Children are an end and means of progress. It is high time to attend to the needs and rights of Children not as "a mere byproduct of progress but as an end and means of progress itself".[1] UNICEF's State of World Children 1989 report says that millions of Children the world over are growing up in circumstances under which they will never be able to fulfill the mental and physical potential with which they are born. This is a human tragedy which contains within itself the seeds of its own renewal. It is imperative to break the self-perpetuating cycle which is central to development process. Without this all other investment in food production, Community Services and Human Resource Development will be less effective because a significant proportion of people will neither be able to contribute fully to them nor benefit fully from them. According to the UNICEF's report the two tests of civilization is how well, it protects its Vulnerable and how well it safeguards its future; Children are both vulnerable and its future.

*Anjani Kumar Singh, is District Magistrate, Vaishali Cum Managing Director, North Bihar Industrial Area Development Authority, Muzaffarpur (Bihar).

**Poornima Shekhar Singh is former UGC Research Fellow, School of International Studies, Jawahar Lal Nehru University, New Delhi.

Percentage of living Child below 5 years not only varies among the countries of the World but also varies significantly within a State. Appendix-I depicts child life defence. It reveals that a Asia, it is as low as 70% in Afganistan and as high as 99% in Singapore. There is a positive co-relation between *per capita* national Income. Illiteracy rate and death rate among the Children below 5 years of age. Appendix-II compares a few selected countries on above mentioned indicators. Appendix-III compares, death rate among children below 5 years, reduction rate in illiteracy and growth rate of *per capita* National Income. The figures reveal that poverty and literacy are two most crucial factors which affect development of the Children.

Children are back-bone of a Nation. On their health and prosperity depends the health of a Nation. India has the second largest child population in the World. Out of the total population 68.31 crores according to the 1981 Census, about 27 crores (Two-fifths of the population) are children up to the 14 years of age. Children under 6 years of age constitute about 17% of the population and are about 11.6 crores in number.

Though planning for child development needs special care and falls in the category of target based planning. It is to be viewed in totality—as a part of national social well-being. India is a developing country and quite sizeable section of its population suffers from the problem of poverty, inadequate sanitation, sub standard housing, mal-nutrition and lack of education. Thus the development of the Children in this country will basically depend on over-all development of the Society and people of this country. The problem of Children Welfare thus can not be viewed in isolation.

Children in rural areas and tribal areas are more vulnerable category. During Fourth Five-Year Plan various programmes like nutritional programme, health programme, formal and non-formal educational programmes were launched-addressed to this section of population, but they were time and area specific programmes and sectoral in nature. They could not make desirable impact as there was no integration, and delivery system was defective. Much of the benefit could not reach to the target group and got siphoned in the way. It is in 1975 when the need for providing early childhood services in an integrated manner, specially to weaker and vulnerable section of the Community, was felt seriously. This integrated approach was meant to "help prevent or minimise wastage arising from infant mortality and morbidity and would be a positive contribution to the social and economic development of the country through all-round development of the individual".[2] The Children were declared *Supremely important asset* of the nation, whose nature became national responsibility. It was necessary to ensure children's full physical, mental and social development.

Integrated Children Development Scheme launched on birth day of Mahatma Gandhi in the year 1975, envisaged providing all essential services and in-puts to mother and Children at their door-step, especially in rural and tribal areas. Mother and Children together were taken as a unit; the assumption being, Children development is strongly co-related with the development of mother. ICDS was started in 20 blocks and 4 slums on experimental basis in 1975 and today it has expanded to more than 1500 ICDS Projects.

The main objectives of Integrated Child Development Services Programme are:

1. To improve health and nutritional status of children who are below 6 years and to create an environment for proper physical, social and psychological development of the Child.

2. To check and reduce the incidence of mortality, morbidity and mal-nutrition.

3. To make learning process for a Child an attractive and interesting affair and exposing them to the world of knowledge in play-full manner. Further to emphasise the need of education and to check drop-outs in Schooling.

4. To co-ordinate the activities of various departments engaged in rural development and general welfare of people. Further to achieve effective co-ordination of policy and implementation to promote child development.

5. To cultivate scientific out-look and an enhancing capability of mother to look after their own and their children's health and nutritional needs.

ICDS provides a package of services for Children and mothers. This package mainly includes supplementary Nutrition health check-up, primary health care/referral services, immunization nutrition and health education and non-formal pre-school education. Some of the activities figure very prominently in new 20 Point Programmes of Government of India. These are the core services under ICDS Programme. There are many related scheme like safe drinking water scheme, sanitation programme and adult literacy and non-formal education programme. Though above mentioned programme get implemented by different agencies but there is an urgent need for dovetailing of these schemes at ICDS Project level. Unless all these programmes move in unison the impact will not be quite visible. Without safe drinking water supply and proper sanitation, no child or mother can be disease free. Similarly Mal-nutrition can frustrate the benefits of health check-up and referral services. Good health, like good and adequate food is unevenly distributed over space.[3]

A child in rural areas on an average is less well fed than an average child in urban areas. Children who are inadequately fed for susceptible to many debelitating diseases. Hunger and mal-nutrition produce dangerous weakness in the body and lower the resistance to all kinds of diseases organisms. Thus proper nutrition becomes the key factor in any Child development programme.

Present delivery of services to the different beneficiaries group is as follows:

Beneficiaries	Service
1. Expectant and nursing mothers	(*i*) Health check-up. (*ii*) Immunization of expectant mothers against tetanus. (*iii*) Referral Services. (*iv*) Supplementary Nutrition. (*v*) Nutrition & Health Education.
2. Other women 15 to 45 years	(*i*) Nutrition and health education.
3. Children below 1 year of age	(*i*) Supplementary Nutrition. (*ii*) Immunization. (*iii*) Health-Check-up. (*iv*) Referral Services.
4. Children between 1 and 3 years of age	(*i*) Supplementary Nutrition. (*ii*) Immunization. (*iii*) Health check-up. (*iv*) Referral Services.
5. Children between 3 and 6 years of age	(*i*) Supplementary Nutrition. (*ii*) Immunization. (*iii*) Health Check-up. (*iv*) Referral Services. (*v*) Non-formal pre-school education.

Protecting Children from various fatal diseases, many vaccination programmes have been launched. The most important drive used in this programme are vaccination programmes which saves Children from Diptheria, Polio, Typhoid, Tetanus and measles. Appendix-IV shows population of Children below one year of age and extention of vaccination among a few selected countries.

The following simplified model depicts organisation and implementation of ICDS programme in India:[4]

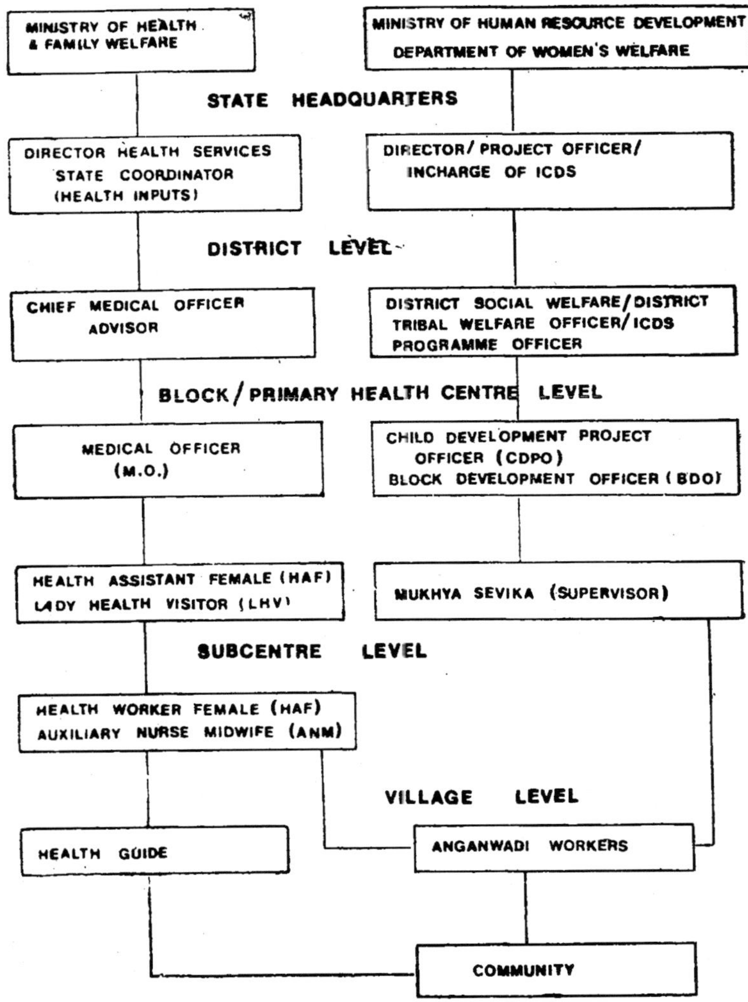

From the above mentioned model it will appear that Aganwadi is the model point for delivery of package of services to mothers and children in rural areas. Similarly a Child Development Project Officer, who is in over all charge of each ICDS Project, is the key-personnel. At the district level Co-ordination among various departments is done by the District Collector. Another important characteristic in this scheme is that the services are rendered at door-step.

A delivery system compromises the set of agencies (whether Government, private or Cooperative) and the procedures followed by them for providing services/advice to the clients which in the context of Child Development Programmes, would include persons below 15 years of age. Delivery system for each item/service has got its own peculiarity and varies from State to State and some times from one region to another, even within State.

To make the delivery system more efficient and productive, it is imperative to have clarity in role play, better co-ordination among various departments, developing linkages with other similar and allied activities. The programme will succeed only when the delivery system is able to take benefits directly to the beneficiaries at their door-step. For example group demonstration, techniques of lectures, practical demonstration of nutritious, recipes, utilising the locally available nutritions food should be conducted using mobile vans. The emphasis has to be on the proper utilisation of locally available foods in improving the nutritional status of the community. The importance of improving the cooking techniques, personal as well as environmental hygine has also to be brought home to the people.

The use of audo-visual aids has to be made extensively to deliver the massage of nutrition education.

How linkages between two programmes can be achieved, can be shown by taking the following example. The linkages between Anganbaries and primary schools can develop like: this. The Anganbaries should generally be located in close proximity to the Primary Schools. Girls above 10 years of age should be involved in Child Care in Anganbaries for atleast twice a month. The pre-school children in Anganbaries should transit to the Primary Schools in a natural fashion.

Further the Child Development programme should benefit by better utilising the existing strength of field staff of Welfare and Health Departments We can take an example of local birth attendants. He/She can easily do the following jobs under ICDS.

1. To identify pregnant mother.
2. To visit anti-natal mother and provide anti-natal care.
3. To prepare mothers for delivery.
4. To conduct delivery using modern knowledge/ techniques.
5. To provide post-natal care.
6. To assist ANMs.

Thus efficient co-ordination among departments, better utilisation of existing resources and developing proper linkages among programmes related to Child and Mother development, will lead to better implementation of Child Development programme. The Child development programme should be viewed as programme of the Community, specially of parents for their own children and mother.

The Child development programme should not be viewed merely as one more Government programme. It should be a Community programme with Government as one of the aiding Organisations. Much of its success will depend on quantity and quality of Community participation.

ACKNOWLEDGEMENT

The authors wish to acknowledge with gratitute generous help provided by senior officials of Welfare Department, Government of Bihar.. We also thank Mr. Yadunath Roy, Senior Dy. Collector, Dist. Vaisahali (Bihar) for help in collecting data. Mr. Zeyaur Rahman, Senior P.A. to M.D., North Bihar Industrial Area Development Authority, Muzaffarpur (Bihar) also deserves credit for typing this article neatly. Special thanks is due to our son Sukant who remained the motivating factor for writing this article.

REFERENCES

1. NIPCCD News letter, National Institutor of Public Co-operation and Child Development, New Delhi. Vol. 9 No. 2, Nov.-Dec. 1988, p. 8.

2. Department of Women and Child Development, Ministry of Human Resource Development, Government of India. A guide book for Anganwari workers, New Delhi, 1986, p. 3.

3. Harm J. Dubly: Human Geography: Culture, Society and Space, Wiley International, New York, 1976. p. 63.

4. Ministry of Social Welfare, Govt. of India, New Delhi: Integrated Child Development Services and Functional Literacy for Adult Women, 1983, p. 94.

APPENDIX I

Child Life Defence

Asia	Percentage of Living Child Below 5 Years
Singapur	98.8
Malasia	96.7
Koria (P. Republic)	96.6
Koria (Republic)	96.6
Sri Lanka	95.5
China	95.5
Thailand	94.9
Mangolia	93.9
Philipins	92.5
Papua New Ginea	91.5
Vietnam	90.9
Burma	90.2
Indonesia	88.0
India	84.8
Lao (People Republic)	83.7
Pakistan	83.1
Bangla Desh	80.9
Bhutan	80.0
Nepal	80.0
Campuchea	79.2
Afganistan	69.6

Source: UNICEF report on State of World Children, 1989.

APPENDIX II

Per Capita National Production, Death Rate Among Children Below 5 Years and Illiteracy Rate

1986-87	1987 Death Rate Children Below 5 Years	1986 Per Capita National Income	1986 Illiteracy Rate
India	152	290	57
China	45	300	31
Zambia	130	300	24
Sri Lanka	45	400	13
Nigeria	177	640	57
Camaroon	156	910	38
Brazil	87	1,810	21
S. Africa	101	2,010	—
Yugoslavia	28	2,300	8
USSR (1980)	30	4,550	0
Spain	11	4,860	5
Oman	149	4,980	70
Trinidad	24	5,360	4
Libia (1985)	123	7,170	34
Singapur	12	7,410	14
Italy	12	8,550	3
U.A. Emarat	33	14,680	47
America	13	17,480	1

Source: UNICEF report on State of World Children, 1989.

APPENDIX III

Death Rate Among Child Below 5 Years, Reduction Rate in Illiteracy and Growth Rate of Per Capita National Production

	Death Rate Among Child Below 5 Years			Reduction in Illiteracy			Per Capita National Production
			Average Yearly Reduction Rate			Average Yearly Reduction Rate	Average Yearly Production Rate
	1965	1986	1965-66	1970	1985	1970-85	1965-86
Argentina	71	39	2.8	7	5	2.2	0.2
Togo	261	159	2.3	83	59	2.2	0.2
Bangladesh	244	194	1.1	76	67	0.8	0.4
Zimbabway	171	118	1.8	45	26	3.6	1.2
Burkina Phase	338	241	1.6	92	87	0.4	1.3

Costa Rica	106	24	6.8	13	6	5.0	1.6
India	258	156	2.4	66	57	1.0	1.8
Nigeria	299	180	2.4	75	58	1.7	1.9
Pakistan	255	173	1.8	80	70	0.9	2.4
Sri Lanka	102	46	3.7	23	13	3.7	2.9
Algeria	249	115	3.6	75	50	2.7	3.5
Thailand	130	53	4.2	21	9	5.5	4.0
Brazil	144	89	2.3	34	22	2.9	4.3
Yaman	347	200	2.6	95	85	0.7	4.7
Singapur	38	12	5.3	26	14	4.0	7.6

Source: UNICEF report on State of World Children, 1989.

APPENDIX IV

Country	Population of Children Below 1 Year of Age (In Thousand)	B.C.G.	Diph.	Polio	Measle	T.T.
India	20,983	46	58	50	17	47
China	19,571	85	75	77	97	—
Nigeria	4,908	41	20	21	31	12
Indonesia	4,744	82	69	70	61	33
Bangladesh	4,144	14	9	8	6	7
Pakistan	3,934	72	62	62	53	27
Brazil	3,861	68	57	90	55	—
Maxico	2,506	71	62	97	54	—
Ethopia	2,086	28	16	15	13	5
Vietnam	1,770	59	51	54	42	—

Pbilipins	1,705	92	73	73	68	49
Iran	1,694	56	74	74	76	12
Egypt	1,526	72	82	88	76	12
Turkey	1,409	34	71	70	50	7
Zaire	1,360	54	36	36	39	26
Thailand	1,270	97	80	80	60	61
Kenya	1,184	86	75	75	60	37
Tanzania	1,161	95	81	80	78	60
Burma	1,063	45	23	13	14	24
Sudan	954	46	29	29	22	12
Korean Republic	944	47	76	80	89	—
Algeria	903	95	66	66	59	—
Columbia	844	80	58	82	49	40
Uganda	793	74	39	40	48	13
Afganistan	786	27	25	25	31	6
Standard Average		62	58	59	46	21

Source: UNICEF report on State of World Children, 1989.

14

Towards A Strategy and Approach for Child Monitoring System in India

A.K. JHA*

India has more children than all the 46 countries of Africa put together. There are around 270 million children and an estimated 120 million are under 6 years of age. An analysis of the situation of children in India reveals that less than half of them have access to an essential minimum of nutrition, health care and early learning opportunities. This is caused by the material poverty of the families, accentuated by the effects of ignorance, ill health, isolation and prolonged by the structural inequalities in the society. More than a tenth of the 23 million born each year die during the first 12 months. Two-fifths of infant deaths occur in the first month, and nearly half the deaths in the first month are in the first week. While the overall death rate has been falling, the proportion of deaths occurring in the first 5 years has been on the increase. It is estimated that almost half of all deaths are now in the 0-5 age group. There is a need to accord high priority to the needs of children in the formulation of the country's development programmes in order to enhance their survival and development. The

*Lecturer, SNSRKS College, Saharsa, Bihar.

The views expressed in this paper are those of the author and not of the Institute to which he belongs.

National Policy for Children (1974) aims "to provide adequate services for children, both before and after birth and through the period of growth, to ensure their full physical, mental and social development.[1]

In the Seventh Five Year Development Plan (1985-90), specific national objectives have been set for the end of the decade and for 2000 A.D. in a number of fields all of which are relevant to child survival and development. The crucial importance of a child monitoring system at the country level as an integral part of the national endeavours to promote child survival and development can hardly be over-emphasized.[2]

At the country level child monitoring system involves the timely collection, compilation, analysis and dissemination of key indicators of child survival and development to monitor overall progress towards its promotion. If the system has to serve the intended objectives then it is important to collect data at approprite time intervals on selected indicators disaggregated by small geographic areas and specific socio-economic population groups so that necessary action-oriented policies can be directed or rather redirected in favour of the most disadvantaged areas or groups that are identified through indicators.

A child monitoring system should be treated as independent of programme/project monitoring systems, since it reveals the trends in indicators of child survival and development which are influenced and determined by a complex of known and unknown socio-economic factors. It aims to provide information on the changing conditions of children in different regions of a country. The data provided by a child monitoring system cannot be adequate to assess the impact of specific programmes for improving child survival and development. Although such programmes may be among the factors which have a bearing on the indicators of child survival and development. The objective of a child monitoring system is not to establish casual relationships between specific programmes and changes in the indicators. The latter effort involves an indepth evaluation.[3]

A child monitoring system must facilitate the generation of information on two major aspects (UNICEF, 1986):

(*i*) Are children surviving and developing?

(*ii*) Which factors are contributing to and are responsible for their survival and development?

When the data on these two aspects are available it is possible to know not only the progress towards child survival and development but also which contributing factors require special further attention.

Conceptually, the first part of the first question concerning the survival of children is relatively simple and straight forward. But the questions relating to the development and factors responsible for child survival and development are not easy to tackle since "as yet there is no clearly established overall theory about what causes survival and development, what causes those causes and how they can best be controlled". Despite this uncertainty, it is still possible to identify a few factors, based on existing knowledge, which are highly probable causes of early mortality and inadequate development of children.

A tentative list of indicators of child survival and development should include (UNICEF, 1986):

(*i*) Infant mortality rate,

(*ii*) Child mortality rate,

(*iii*) Nutritional status,

(*iv*) Percentage of infants who are underweight at birth,

(*v*) Incidence of infectious diseases,

(*vi*) Percentage of children immunized,

(*vii*) Maternal morbidity.

The factors or conditions conducive to child survival and development would include safe delivery of healthy infants, nutrition and nurturing, safe physical environment and educational opportunities. These conditions are in turn determined by a number of factors (determinant indicators) operating at the household and community level.[4]

Child Monitoring: Some Strategy and Approach

To review the data systems that already exist with a view to assess :

—their ability to generate data disaggregated by small geographic areas, age, sex and other characteristics;

—their ability to generate data at the desired frequency;

—their ability to provide data which are reliable (relative reliability is more important than absolute reliability to measure trends and differences among regions and groups).

Review of existing data systems and agencies, date generated, methodology and process of data collection, and an assessment of their strengths and weaknesses indicates the following (UNICEF, 1986):

(*a*) The National Census is carried out once 10 years with a time lag of 3-7 years. Vital Registration Systems and Sample Registration Systems provide data at state level. In the case of SRS, the methodology and sampling procedures are designed to obtain data by states and not for smaller regions like districts or blocks. Both the systems suffer on account of poor quality of data and time lag of 2 to 3 years between data collection and analysis.

(*b*) The health information systems, at national and state level, suffer from many deficiencies including the poor quality and lack of reliability of data, as also large time lags.

(*c*) The National Sample Survey Organisation, an organ of the Ministry of Planning, Government of India, is always heavily loaded with many sample surveys of sorts sponsored by the Ministry of Planning as well as other Ministries/Departments of the Central and state governments. It carries out sample household surveys once in 5 years with a time lag of more than 5 years. There are also gaps in the quality and reliability of data contained in the reports.

(*d*) Many state governments are making efforts to establish monitoring systems for monitoring progress of plan projects. The performance till now has not been satisfactory because of many operational difficulties. A review of the systems in various states by the Planning Commission has identified a number of deficiencies.

In any case, the systems cover sectors like irrigation, power, agriculture and rural development and industry. A few states like Karnataka and Gujarat seem to be making a headway in monitoring the progress of the 20-Point Programme including the number of beneficiaries covered in the ICDS projects. None of the State monitoring systems includes any aspect of child monitoring. In the light of this, it will be difficult to involve the state monitoring units in efforts to set up the child monitoring system in the foreseeable future.

(*e*) There are many demographic and population research institutions in the country, funded by Central/State governments and international and bilateral agencies. They undertake comprehensive baseline and special surveys in small areas on a continuous and periodic basis to collect demographic and related data. Some of them (especially those located in Gandhigram in Tamil Nadu, Bangalore and Bombay) enjoy high reputation for professional standards, quality of work, and timely completion of projects.

(*f*) The National Institute of Nutrition, Hyderabad, is a reputed institution having wide experience in research and studies in the fields of nutritional status and surveillance and evaluation of national nutrition programmes. The National Nutrition Monitoring Bureau, established by ICMR, is a part of NIN and is engaged in continuously monitoring the nutrition and diet situation in 10 states on an annual basis. Discussions with NIN have indicated that they will be willing to undertake regular surveys to monitor the nutritional status indicators as a part of the proposed child monitoring system.

A review of the existing data systems has revealed that there is a gap between the data requirements of a child monitoring system and the scope for utilisation of many of these existing systems. This situation would suggest that the implementation of a child monitoring system through the existing data systems covering all indicators discussed earlier is a formidable task and is certainly impossible in the present circumstance. It is therefore desirable to initiate the effort in a small and humble way, and a phased approach is the best strategy for introducing the system. To begin with, in the first phase, it should be possible to select a few core indicators and the best data mechanism and agencies, which can be enlarged later in Phase II to include other important indicators by involving, hopefully, other data systems and ther agencies.

In the Indian situation where 80 per cent of births occur at home, it is impossible to collect data on weight at birth. Height by age, although perhaps measurable, cannot be a meaningful indicator across the regions and population groups in the country, since the genetic and geographic factors have an impact on the height of children irrespective of their nutritional intake. The choice therefore falls on weight by age which can be measured by the anthropometric standards developed by the Indian Council of Medical Research.[5]

Nutritional status as measured by weight for age is the most important and appropriate indicator of child development since it reflects the impact of many factors responsible for child development including food intate and infection conditions which in turn are influenced by incomes, female education and other determinant indicators.[6]

Keeping in view the limitations and handicaps of the National Census, Vital Registration Systems and the health data systems at national and state level, the choice of the sample household surveys as the data collection mechanism in Phase I offers the best solution in the prevailing circumstances. Sample household surveys are relatively superior in many ways:

—They are less expensive, and it is therefore feasible to conduct surveys at short intervals.

—They can be easily organised and implemented.

—They are flexible in the sense that a wide range of data on CSD can be collected with minimum incremental effort.

A major problem with sample household surveys is in respect of the sample size and the margins of sampling errors. However, this is not a major disadvantage because the non-sampling errors in the other data collection mechanisms may tend to be even more serious.

The next important issue is about the choice of the agencies and institutions which can be involved in the task of monitoring the indicators. The possibility of involving the National Sample Survey Organisation can be straightaway ruled out for reasons outlined earlier. The choice must fall on the population research centres and the National Institute of Nutrition to undertake surveys on infant and child mortality rates and nutritional status, respectively.

REFERENCES

1. UNICEF (1986): 'Towards Establishing a Child Monitoring System in India', in (ed.) Bose, A.B. (1986), *Monitoring Survival and Development of the Young Child,* NIPCCD Pub., New Delhi, pp. 189-190.
2. *Ibid.*, p. 190.
3. *Ibid.*, p. 191.
4. *Ibid.*, p. 192-193.
5. *Ibid.*, p. 194.
6. S.N. Ray and R.D. Agarwal (1986): 'Monitoring Child Survival and Development through National Sample Organisation', in (ed), Bose, A.B. (1986), *Monitoring Survival and Development of the Young Child,* NIPCCD Pub. New Delhi.

15

An Appraisal on Child Health : A Case Study of Kumaun

S. S, KHANKA*

Let us start with the trite proposition that: "A healthy mind rests in a sound health". Health is, therefore, the starting point of all development. Child health is of crucial importance for future development of any economy. The situation of child health and also its improvement is directly related to the structure and performance of an economy. The poor health situation of children in India is evinced by this fact that of the more than 270 million children of India, the number who has not access to a minimum of nutrition, health care and learning opportunities may be more than half.[1] The squalor of poor child health considerably varies across the regions depending upon their varying levels of development. Kumaun Division of Uttar Pradesh consisting of Almora, Pithoragarh and Nainital districts, represents one such special case of economic backwardness and poor child health.

Situation analysis in a context of change in different regions is, undoubtedly, a continuing process. The main objective we have set for ourselves in this paper is, therefore, to reflect the panoramic view of child health in Kumaun Division of Uttar Pradesh. The facts and figures on which the analysis is based

*Dr. S.S. Khanka, Lecturer, Department of Commerce, Kumaun University, Nainital.

are derived mostly from the official sources of government and partly from published findings of professional research.

REFLECTION ON CHILD HEALTH

Demographic Features

Like elsewhere in India, the age-structure of Kumaun Population is characteristically bottom-heavy tapering to top. In every 10 persons, 4 are children below 15 years (see table 1). A relatively high birth rate combined with a low and declining rate of infant mortality account for this phenomenon. One evil effect of this broad-base population can be seen in a high dependency ratio of the order of almost 1:1. A bulk of resources are needed to gear towards the rearing of this mass population which has not been feasible in a resource scarce economy like ours. As a result, this mass seedling of human resources is deprived of even minimum of life necessities. The heavy dependency ratio produces two inevitable consequences on the structure of child population in the rural areas. First, most of the children start to help their parents in their family chores. Second, some migrate to the plains to eke out their livelihood as also to support their families in the villages. What these children do in the plains is as restaurant and house servants. The plight of children is impending.

Education

Education is a key input to all development. Viewed from this angle, the Kumauni children particularly in a rural interior are also found at a disadvantageous position. In every 10 children below 15 years, there are only 5 children literate (see Table 1). Again, the literacy for females has consistently been behind that for males, and by a big margin. Girls education is given lesser importance in so far as the priorities of the parents are concerned. While the male children are sent to school even if located in remote places, and they are not supposed to do domestic work. The girls, on the other hand, are compelled to drop out from schools at initial stages in order to help mothers in their domestic work including baby-care. When we deny educational opportunities to girls, we deprive our country of good mothers who could guide the courses of future generations.

TABLE 1

Indicators Reflecting Child Health in Kumaun

Sl. No.	Indicators	Almora	Pithoragarh	Nainital
1.	Percentage of children below 15 years to total population, 1981	40.87	39.68	41.91
2.	Literacy rates of children (in %), 1981 Boys			
	Girls			
3.	Percentage of villages with junior basic schools at 5 km. or more, 1987	14.75	12.18	2.23
4.	Women literacy rates (in %), 1981	20.3	20.3	27.1
5.	Women work participation rates (in %), 1981	36.6	44.8	11.6
6.	Percentage of villages at 5 km. or more from a Primary Health Centre, 1987	53.4	65.8	40.5
7.	Percentage of villages at 5 km. or more from Family and Maternity Child Welfare 1987	44.5	39.5	18.0
8.	Villages per 1,000 inhabited villages with clean drinking water facilities, 1986	679.03	722.17	982.83

Not only that, schools for girls are few and far between in the interior/rural Kumaun. Nearly 81 per cent villages in Almora district, 63 per cent villages in Nainital district and more than 91 per cent villages in Pithoragarh district have schools for girls at a distance of more than 5 kilometers. These long distances in rugged terrain and difficult slopes are formidable barriers in the pursuits of girls education. Literacy status females of has an important bearing on their age at effective marriage in rural Kumaun. Nearly 55 per cent of illiterate females consummated their marriage at the age below 17 years against about 45 per cent with some education.[2]

There is no systematic governance of the schools and not very unoften, teachers do not attend the schools regularly. Remoteness and fragmented habitations involve exorbitant administrative costs while the schools lack in even the basic facilities like black-boards and floor mattings. These adversely tell on child education, resulting in poor health of children.

Health

Life is not mere living but living in health. Health can be defined as "a state of complete physical, mental and social well-being". In India even in very ancient times, it was believed that physical, mental and spiritual health are intrinsically interwoven. This is the basis of the science of yoga also. Health is not the absence of illness but a glowing vitality, a feeling of wholeness with a capacity for continuous intellectual and spiritual growth.

Health is an obvious function of nutrition. Malnutrition in the family emerges as one of the underlying causes of ill health. That a variety of infections and infestations play havoc with health should not be a surprise in a situation where economic and environmental factors are adverse to the large numbers of the people. Their insufficient awareness about health and about less than appropriate behavious in health-related matters are also traceable to this social situation. The relationship between age and height indicated that the children had lower height than the values assigned to normal Indian children. In boys, the percentage by which the height was less than the

Indian standard ranged from 10.7% for year old boys to 17.8% for 13 year old boys. In girls, this value ranged from 13.9% for 6 year old girls to 19.3% for 12 year old girls.[3] In general, the girls' heights were less than the boys heights in comparison to the Indian standards. Several genetical and environmental factors, such as nutrition and diseases are attributed to limit the height of children and women in this mountain region. Thus, a sizeable number of all children in the region is reported to have a low weight for age. It is also reported that nearly a quarter of infants are born each year weighing less than 2500 grams.

Meagre network of health amenities available in mountains is yet another factor adversely telling on child health (see table 1). For example, service of allopathic hospitals can be obtained in rural area of the Almora district after crossing mountainous tract of above 5 kilometers in more than per cent villages. A similar distance has to be covered for reaching a maternity centre. Even in Nainital district, which includes the plains area of the Tarai and Bhabar, nearly per cent villages are situated at at a distance more than 5 kilometers from the hospital or dispensary. In district Pithoragarh, the scenario is more worse where nearly per cent villages are more than 5 kilometers away from a public dispensary. The primary health centres and child welfare centres in the hills are so remotely located that the villages can hardly make of their use. What is more alarming that whatever health network is available in the official records remains often without health workers and doctors.

Nutrition

Nutrition is basic to health. The root cause for poor health, therefore, lies in malnutrition in terms of calory intake and protein. Our region is specially plagued by this malnutrition predicament. As against the standard requirement of 2430 kcal/person/day, the actual per head per day food in take during 1986-87 in uplands, midslope and Dunfloor of Kumaun is reported at 1925-61, 2,392.07 and 2,413.66 kcal respectively.[4] Similarly, a recent study at the National Institute of Nutrition shows that against a calory coefficient of 0.5 for children between 1-3 years, the actual intake was only 0.33 for children in the group 4-6 years the actual intake was only 0.47, as against the coefficient of 0.62.[5] The most common cause of malnutrition is a demand factor, not a supply factor—it is a straight forward lack of purchasing power. This argues that employment of the poor has to be expanded and their productivity increased, if they are at all to participate in the development process.

On the whole, the commonly noted effects of malnutrition on the hill population are: (*i*) reduced activity (saving on energy consumption); (*ii*) reduced growth of children, *i.e.*, reduced height for age (stunting) and reduced weight for height (wasting); (*iii*) increased susceptibility to, and more serious effects from, some infections like measles, or disorders due to non-absorption of micro-nutrients like iron causing anaemia, poor use of vitamin A because of low energy intake leading to eye impairment and in time blindness; (*iv*) death in case of severe and prolouged malnutrition.

The gross malnutrition in Kotadun, representing the entire Kumaun's Case is illustrated in Table 2.

The evil effects of malnutrition on mortality and morbidity of the sample population are presented in Table 3.

Environment

Environmental degradation, the major concern of the time, has also its deleterious effects on human health including child health. The massive deforestation at an rate of per cent has narrowed down the food variety, particularly of the seasonal wild fruits. The scarcity of fodder meant reduction in the livestock size per household in turn meant reduction in the availability of milk. This also has resulted in the reduction of manure input and decline in agronomic productivity per unit area. Thus, as time progressed, with increasing population both the quality and quantity of food produced for the land declined. The input of foodgrain can only partly fulfil these deficiencies. Very often the foodgrain import necessitates the selling of milk and fruits raised by the villagers. Another serious problem arising from the forest depletion is that the

TABLE 2

Nutritional Deficiency in Kotadun, 1986-87

Estimates of Diet	Standard Requirement	Dunfloor (Patkot) —Deficiency +Surplus	Midslope (Amgarhi) —Deficiency +Surplus	Uplands (Sigarhi) —Deficiency +Surplus
(1)	(2)	(3)	(4)	(5)
Energy kcal	2430.0	— 16.34	— 37.33	—504.39
Protein gr	66.0	— 8.06	— 1.88	— 2.05
Fat gm	50.0	— 8.73	— 10.78	— 25.49
Carbohydrates gm	430.0	— 50.54	— 47.60	— 65.51
Calcium mg	800.0	—110.46	77.88	—266.56

(Contd.)

(Contd.)

(1)	(2)	(3)	(4)	(5)
Phosphorus mg	1400.0	+156.16	−207.75	+254.18
Iron mg	40.0	− 11.37	− 10.57	− 12.26
Carotene ug	960.0	− 59.49	−334.46	−696.17
Thiamine mg	1.8	+ 0.18	+ 0.07	+ 0.16
Riboflavin mg	1.5	− 0.65	− 0.64	− 0.72
Niacin mg	16.0	+ 5.74	+ 0.50	+ 0.15
Ascorbic Acid mg	50.0	− 19.10	− 26.29	− 17.37

Source: B.R. Pant *et. al., op. cit.*

TABLE 3

Mortality and Morbidity, 1986-87

Sample Village	Energy Per Head Per Day (kcal)	Percentage of Morbidity to the Total Population	Percentage of Mortality to the Total Patients
Dunfloor (Patkot)	2413.66	8.52	10.42
Midslope (Amgarhi)	2392.62	11.35	13.51
Uplands (Sigarhi)	1925.64	25.64	20.00

Source: Same as of Table 2.

people especially women have to devote more energy and time to fodder and fuelwood collection. In addition to the stress on human energy, this leads to deterioration in the child health care and in children's habits relating to health, hygiene and general cleanliness. Further, forest depletion has led to extinction of springs, which means scarcity of water for maintaining the overall cleanliness.

Thus the foregoing analysis suggests that the various elements of child health development, namely, education, nutrition, health, environmental sanitation and fertility reduction are closely inter-related. Therefore, improvements in one area can facilitate improvements in others and reinforce all aspects of development. The task of child health development can much better be facilitated if the nutrition worker, the health worker, the sanitarian, the water technician, the school teacher and the environment worker work together for this cause.

REFERENCES

1. UNICEF: *An Analysis of the Situation of Children in India,* United Nations Children's Fund, Regional Office for South Central Asia, New Delhi, 198[illegible], 'Foreword' by David P. Haxton, Regional Director of UNICEF for South Central Asia.

2. J.N. Srivastava: *Determinants of Age at Marriage*, Series-C, Analytical Report, Demographic (now Population) Research Centre, Lucknow University, Lucknow, 1982, pp. 60-64.

3. Deepa Singh: Human Health with Special Reference to Women and Children in Relation to Environment, In: S.P. Singh, *River Gaula Catchment* (Central Himalaya) *Ecodevelopment Project*, Final Technical Report, Department of Botany, Kumaun University, Nainital, p. 95.

4. B.R. Pant, R.C. Joshi and D.S. Jalal: Nutritional status and Deficiency Diseases of Kotadun, Kumaun Himalaya, *The Indian Geographical Journal* (in press).

5. B.N. Rao: *Development of Salt Fortification Programmes to Prevent Iron Deficiency in India*, National Institute of Nutrition, 1984.

16

Voluntary Efforts in Child Development

ASHOK KUMAR*

India has made rapid strides in a number of fields including science and technology. But, it has also been experiencing travails of transition which a developing country is bound to face. However, for over several decades, transformation of the rural communities has been the concern of the government, the voluntary organisations, and the people. An active role in the field of child. Development, largely in the inaccessibly parts of the country, was played by the religious missionaries since the middle of the 19 century, who aimed at an all-round development of their followers.

However, successive plan documents, reports of the commissions and committees,[1] apart from delineating the role of voluntary organisations in the field of child development in context of their terms of reference, have analysed the positive dimensions of the functioning of these organisations. The concern of the state in seeking the cooperation of these people's institutions is expressed in the plan documents. The Mid-Term Plan (1978-83) states, "the voluntary agencies who are engaged in social and developmental work are close to the

*Faculty Member at the IAMR, New Delhi.

The views expressed in this paper are those of the author and not of the Institute to which he belongs.

people and have the capacity to motivate the rural population for community participation in developmental programmes. With a view to utilising this potential, it is contemplated that as a policy, voluntary organisations doing social and developmental work in child development areas should be induced to into integrated development approach so as to provide a foil to the completely departmental approach to the problem.[2] However, in the present exercise, in broad terms, an attempt has been made to examine the role of some National Level Voluntary Organisations in the field of child welfare activities.

Voluntary Organisations—Its Concept

According to Lord Beveridge, voluntary organisation[3] as 'one which, whether its workers are paid or unpaid, is initiated and governed by its own members without external control'. Such organisations, however, are only ideal forms. In practice, some mode of control exists either by the state or by the funding agency or by both. In some cases enlightened public opinion also acts as a check on its functioning.

Some scholars have drawn distinction between non-official organisations and voluntary organisations. To them, all non-official organisations are not necessarily voluntary. The test for voluntariness is that the organisations has to try and stimulate voluntary action in the served community. It has to also progressively incorporate enlightened individuals belonging to the community to serve in the higher echelons of its decision-making machinery. Another distinguishing point made out between these bodies is that the voluntary organisations are spontaneous in their origin whereas the non-official agencies may be sponsored by the state.

A voluntary agency may be interpreted as an organisation set-up by a group of persons on their initiative or partly on outside motivation to help the people of a locality to undertake activities in a self-reliant manner, (partly or wholly) to satisfy their felt needs. It is a non-profit body, has flexibility and is manned by dedicated persons who have human touch. Thus, for our purpose voluntary agencies are formed by the people to meet their own needs and solve their problems with resources primarily from the community (grants-in-aid in the nature of supplementation only). A voluntary agency is responsible to the community which supports it and to the Government to the extent it receives grant.

A voluntary agency has the following main features[4]:

(*i*) It should be voluntary and created by the people themselves at the grass-root level;

(*ii*) It should have a legal status through registration under an appropriate Act;

(*iii*) It should have a Managing Committee elected/nominated by members;

(*iv*) It should have considerable autonomy and flexibility in planning and management of its programmes and services;

(*v*) It should have a sense of commitment to human development/welfare;

(*vi*) It should understand people's needs and help to solve their socio-economic problems;

(*vii*) It should plan and implement its own programmes through its own voluntary and paid workers;

(*viii*) It should raise its funds from the community; and

(*ix*) It should maintain its accounts and be accountable to people and the Governments so far as it receives grants.

Voluntary Organisation—Retrospect

As voluntary organisations had necessary flexibility, adaptability and voluntarism in them, they came forward to organise child welfare programmes much before the government initiated these programmes through its five-year plans. These voluntary organisations have been serving children in the area of health, education, nutrition, welfare and recreation.[5] They have provided both institutional and non-institutional services.

Balkanji Bari was the first children's organisation formed in the year 1920 with its headquarters in Bombay. It started nursery schools, children's club, play grounds, children's literacy programmes, child's arts and crafts. In 1924, the Guild of service launched its child welfare service in Madras and South India. In 1927, the Children's Aid society, Bombay, established residential institutions for vagrant children. In the year 1942, Kishore Dal in Bihar was founded, Nanhi Duniya was set-up in 1946 and Bachhon Ki Biradari was formed in Delhi in 1946.[6] These organisations organised Shishu Bhavan, Children art exhibition, play centres and distributed milk to children.

During First Five Year Plan, Child health, nutrition education and family planning were the main programmes undertaken by voluntary organisations. With establishment of Central Social Welfare Board, Voluntary effort in child welfare programmes get fillip. The Second Five Year Plan emphasised that voluntary effort in the field of social welfare have to be supplemented by the Central, State and local authorities.

The Central Social Welfare Board while phasing out the community development projects consequent on the introduction of the panchayati raj system handed over balwadis in around 1500 villages to the voluntary organisations and the local mahila mandals in 1961-62 onwards. As part of the grants-in-aids of the Central Social Welfare Board, around 5,000 balwadis and equal number of creches are being run by voluntary agencies with assistance of the Board. Some important National Level voluntary organisations in the field of child welfare are summarised here:

(*i*) Indian Council for Child Welfare (ICCW):	Established in 1952 under societies Registration Act 1860. Its prime aim was to mobilise voluntary activity in every state in favour of all aspects of children's need.
(*ii*) Balkanji Bari:	National Level organisation established in 1920. Supplementing home and school activities to children.

(*iii*) The Children's Aid Society: The society was founded in 1927 at Bombay. Rehabilitation of destitute children was the main objective.

(*iv*) Harijan Sevak Sangh: Set-up in 1932 in New Delhi with aim to educate Hindus on the need of removal of untouchability. Since 1971 it runs Balwadis and creches.

(*v*) SOS Children's Village: It provides non-institutionalised form of child care. It has provision for cottage type residential care with mixed groups and provides near family atmosphere.

Some other important voluntary organisations working in the field of child welfare are the Bhartiya Adimjati Sevak Sangh, Indian Red Cross Society, the All India Women's Conference, Bhartiya Grameen Mahila Sangh, Kasturba Gandhi National Memorial Trust, the Royal Common Wealth Society for the Blind (Bombay), Children's Book Trust (New Delhi), Child Welfare Workers Association (Bombay), Children's Film Society (Bombay), Society for the Care, Treatment and Training of Children in Need of Special Care (Bombay), and Society for the Rehabilitation of Crippled Children (Bombay).

Since last decades several innovative projects have been undertaken in voluntary sector in different points of the country to meet the needs of children. Some of these projects are as follows.

(*i*) Indo-Dutch Project for Child Welfare: Experiment in an Integrated Approach: At the Chevilla block of Range Reddy district aims at overall development of children, a joint venture of the Nitherlands Foundations, Govt. of India and State Government started in 1969.

(*ii*) Integrated Mother and Child Health Nutrition Project:	Started in 1974 to deliver integrated health and nutrition services to on going children and mothers programmes.
(*iii*) Comprehensive Rural Health Project, Jamkhed:	Project initiated in 1970 is located in Jamkhed village, in Ahmed Nagar district. To meet the basic health needs of the population by providing parental care, immunization of children and mothers.
(*iv*) Integrated Health Services Project, Miraj:	It was designed to provide medical and health care in an integrated pattern for a vast rural population. A joint project of the Govt. of Maharashtra, Sangeli Zilla Parishad and Miraj Medical Centre.
(*v*) Vikasvadi Project Kosbad:	A simple pattern for pre-school care in rural areas. It aims at providing these services through a trained village women in basic principle of early child care including nutrition, immunization and play techniques using ordinary local equipment. These services are provided to village children between the ages of three and six.
(*vi*) Project Poshak:	A micro pilot project on integrated health nutrition for pre-school children in rural and tribal areas of Madhya Pradesh. Based on principle of take home food for children upto three years and pregnant

	and lactating mothers with supportive services of child care, education and health. The project was administered by CARE India. Financial assistance was provided by USAID and the UNICEF.
(*vii*) Other Innovative Projects:	Cooperative Rural Dispensaries Services, Kerala, which functions as a self contained medical unit rendering day to day medical care both curative and preventive is yet another innovative project in the voluntary sector which provides medical services to people. Other projects include Padha Hospital community Health Project in Betul district of Madhya Pradesh, Community Health Development Project, Kanyakumari, Child in need Institute in Daulatpur village, South of Calcutta, Nutrition Rehabilitation Centre and village child care centres, Madurai, etc.

However, apart from providing services to the needy, voluntary organisations have also done commendable work in the field of training. In this context, the name of Kasturba Gandhi National Memorial Trust needs to be mentioned. The trust trained Gram Sevikas, Mukhya Sevikas and Mid-wives. Thus, voluntary organisations have been responsible for the organisation of many child welfare programmes. The Government has enhanced its support to them by providing necessary funds. Their role have not only been to promote participation of the community in the provision of services but also increase awareness of the community in regard to child care education.

The Changing Role of Voluntary Organisation

There are huge number of spiritual inspired organisations which have done commendable job particularly in the areas of health and education with a degree of dedication and devotion which other cannot hope to attain. Most of the organisations are concentrated due to a variety of historical reasons, in the Southern and Western parts of the country.

The Sarvodaya Movement, under the inspiring leadership of the late Vinoba Bhave, was able to attract a good number of leaders like Jayaprakash Narayan. The objective of Sarvodaya is to instil faith in man and his future. To reduce tension and coersion in society, sharing together of good things that are produced by common endeavours are indispensable.[8] Sarvodaya aims at replacing the present 'competitive' economy by a social economy based on cooperation.[9]

Voluntary organisations are capable of performing a wide-variety of tasks. The aims, motivations, ideology, dedication, quality of work, personnel, etc. differ from one agency to another. All the agencies are involved in development work in one way or the other, but they exhibit marked differences in the context, direction and quality of this involvement. Some voluntary agencies may not take up development programmes, but serve the people indirectly by placing checks on corruption and inefficiency that are usually associated with development administration.

However, the voluntarism of the post-independence India yielded place to a new kind of professional voluntarism distinct from professional politics. As a result, a new class of professionals has entered the field of voluntarism-economists, sociologists, engineers, agronomists, veterinarians, communicators, architects, managers and the rest. This professionalism of voluntarism marks a new departure. These people are committed to development, socio-economic transformation and social justice. Voluntarism has drawn talented professionals and angry youngmen seeking social revolution through social action. These are the militant professionals of voluntarism, social dynomos of considerable potential.[10] Social mobility and change brought about by social movements lead to social transformation thereby changing the traditional balance of power.[11] The increasing role of voluntary agencies in the local level planning can be attributed.[12]

—the need to help a specific target group, *e.g.*, women, children and the landless;

—imparting certain skills through training to augment the income of the target groups, *e.g.*, handicrafts, new varieties of seeds or crops;

—to popularise social activities aimed at improving the quality of life for the disadvantage groups, *e.g.*, adult literacy, nutrition, education, basic health and sanitation and family planning; and

—to popularise appropriate technologies by improving indigenous machines, tools, artifacts and demonstrating their superiority.

Depending on the approaches they adopt and the priority they give, voluntary agencies have been classified into seven categories by J.B. Singh.[13] This means that generally voluntary agencies operate in seven distinct areas. These are:

(*i*) Charity:	giving food, clothing, medicine, slums, in cash and kind, land, buildings, etc.
(*ii*) Welfare:	providing facilities for education, health, drinking water, roads, communication, etc.
(*iii*) Relief:	responding to call of duties during natural calamities like floods, drought, earthquakes and man-made calamities like refugee influx, ravages of war, etc.

(*iv*) Rehabilitation:	Continuing and follow-up of the work in areas struck by calamities and starting activities durable in nature.
(*v*) Services:	building up infrastructure in depressed backward areas. Tractor hiring services, providing or facilitating credit, supply of seeds, fertilisers, technical know-how, etc.
(*vi*) Development of Socio-economic Environment around human being:	Socio-economic transformation on area basis-covering all people in a given area or concentrating only on a particular group of people normally neglected and in need of help.
(*vii*) Development of Human Beings:	Conscious raising, awakening, raising conscience, organising, recording of priorities to suit social justice, redeeming the past and opening doors to opportunities to the oppressed and the exploited.

Approaches 1 to 6 are related to delivery system and 7 is basically related the 'receiving mechanism'. However, the voluntary agencies generally follow four clear cut strategies. These are:

Strategy-I:	Simple charity, supplementing welfarism on the state.
Strategy-II:	Encouraging people's participation and in implementing programmes lunched by the Government for larger benefit of the community or village.
Strategy-III:	Involving people in programme planning, raising resources, implementing activities and sharing fruits of development.

Strategy-IV: Conscience instilling and organising people enabling them to demand and undertake planning and implementation of development programmes beneficial them.

It is evident that voluntary agencies adopting strategy-I generally suffer from inferiority complex and a feeling of helplessness. It is based on 'giver and receiver' relationship. Most people believe that it is paternalistic in nature and cause human degradation—not upliftment of human spirit. The active role of voluntary agencies in limited to the last two strategies. Most voluntary agencies are following these two strategies with varying degree of success. The choice of strategy depends on the ideology, motivation, capability of the organisation, experience of the workers and the actual situation in a given area.[14]

Concluding Remarks

The voluntary agencies have to bring about a healthy environment for the steady progress. The provision of inputs in the right time and in required quantities may be important, but no less important, is the change in the attitude of the people towards development. There is need for external animators to create awareness of a better life outside the rural scene and to sustain interest and participation in the face of social tension that are bound to emerge whenever programmes for the welfare are intensified.

The role of voluntary agencies needs to be emphasised. The role is not of middleman but of midwife. All the voluntary agencies may not be able to provide assets or direct services to the target group they are serving. But, the voluntary agencies may help the people take advantage of the opportunities available to them. There is need for promoting development consciousness among the people. The voluntary agencies alone can undertake this important but time-consuming task.

There is one important reason because of which the

voluntary agencies have entered the development field is that rural development administration is far from satisfactory. The delivery system is imperfect. Most developing countries have not yet evolved an appropriate institutional set-up to help the rural poor. The need of the hour is to adapt administration to rural needs. We should, therefore, study, the imperfections, associated with rural development administration.

REFERENCES

1. In this context, the report of the team for the Study of Community Projects and National Extension Service, Committee on Plan Projects (Coop.) Vol. Nos. I, II, III, Planning Commission, New Delhi, 1975, *Report of the Study team on Social Welfare and Welfare of Backward Classes*, Government of India, 1959, *Block Level Plans and Programmes for Rural Development by Participation of Voluntary Organisations, Voluntary Action*, XX-8, 1978 and the successive five year plan documents may be of interest.
2. *Draft Five-Year Plan* (1978-83), Government of India, 1978, and the Draft of the *Sixth Five-Year Plan* (1980-85), Government of India, 1980.
3. A discussion on the concepts of voluntary organisation and voluntary action is provided in D.P. Chowdhry's *Voluntary* Social Welfare in India, Sterling Pub. (P) Ltd., New Delhi, 1971; B.K. Roy Burman, *Role of Voluntary Organisation in the Welfare of the Tribals* (*Mimeo*), Min. of Home Affairs, Government of India, 1968, V.M. Kulkarni, Voluntary Action in a Developing Society, IIPA, New Delhi, 1969.
4. D. Paul Chowdhry (1985): *Profile of Social Welfare and Development in India*, M.N. Pub. and Distributors, New Delhi, p. 225.
5. *Ibid.*, p. 226.
6. *Ibid.*, p. 226.
7. *Ibid.*, p. 226.
8. Archana Sinha (1978), *The Social and Political Philosophy of Sarvodaya*, Janaki Parkashan, Patna-4, p. 194.
9. Jayaprakash Narayan (1978), *Towards Total Revolution*, Vol. 1, p. 144.
10. B.G. Verghese (1979): 'Voluntary Action: A New Mission for the New Missionaries' in R.P. Mishra and K.V. Sundaram (Ed. 1979), *Rural Area Development: Perspective and Approaches*, Sterling Publishers Pvt. Ltd., New Delhi, p. 235.

11. M.S.A. Rao (Ed. 1978), *Social Movements in India*, Vol. I, 'Peasant and Backward Classes Movements', Manohar Publications, New Delhi-2, p. X.

12. R.P. Mishra (Ed. 1978), *op. cit.*, p. 62.

13. *Yojana*, November 1984, p. 46.

14. *Ibid.*, p. 47.

17

Is ICDS A Better Alternative for Child Development—A Case Study of Saharsa Distt. (Bihar)

ASHOK KUMAR*

I. Introduction

Indias' developmental efforts, through successive Five Year Plans, have contributed a great deal towards commendable improvements in the health indices of the country. As a result of these efforts the death rate is now one third of what it was in 1921, and the life expectancy has gone up from 24 years in or around 1901 to about 52 years in 1981.[1] Children who constitute the most vulnerable section of the population have also benefitted and infant mortality, has also been brought down from as high as 2?0 per thousand live births in 1921 to 94 per thousand live births in 1988.

Successive Five Year Plans have laid special emphasis on providing at least minimum health facilities integrated with family welfare and nutrition for women and children, side by side with the acceleration of women's education. The Sixth Plan has not only continued but expanded the maternal and child health schemes including ante-natal, natal and post-natal

*Faculty Member, at the National Institute of Public Cooperation & Child Development, Regional Centre, Lucknow.

The views expressed in this paper is entirely those of the author and not of the Institute to which he belongs.

services. The nutritional status of child at birth is influenced by the nutritional status of his mother. 'It is well documented' as the Sixth Plan says, 'that a vast majority of pregnant and nursing mothers, especially belonging to the low socio-economic group, live on diets which are inadequate'. The high incidence of pre-maturity, low birth weight of babies and neo-natal mortality can be attributed to poor nutritional conditions among the mothers.[2]

Considering the above problems, in persuance of the national policy for children, the scheme of ICDS was launched in 33 projects on experimental basis on October, 1975. Encouraged by the evaluation of the programme by the Programme Evaluation Organisation (PEO) of the Planning Commission and the All India Institute of Medical Sciences. The concept and the performance of the programme over the years had attracted wide attention not only in India but abroad too. However, several studies have been conducted on the impact of services delivered through ICDS projects. The Planning Commission conducted a Baseline survey of the ICDS Projects for the reference period of 1976-77 to find out the state of preparedness of these projects to deliver the services effectively and whether necessary infrastructural support was available for that. The Repeat Round was undertaken of the projects for the reference period of 1977-78 to evaluate the extent of coverage of target population and the impact of the scheme on beneficiaries.[3]

The research studies conducted on ICDS observed that the scheme helped, by and large, in improving the health and nutritional status of children and mothers in the target groups. On the other side, it was observed that the concept of pre-school education was not correctly understood by the ICDS functionaries, the component of health and nutrition education has not received adequate attention; and the community contribution and participation in the ICDS programme was negligible. Lack of effective supervision of the programme at the Anganwadi level for functional coordination at different levels of the project, and lack of involvement of local leadership in the programmes were identified as some of the operational constraints in the effective implementation of the ICDS Scheme.[4]

Effective delivery of services under the ICDS scheme depends to a large extent on the organisational system designed for providing the, services and on the utilisation or management of inputs available for them. Again, the functioning of an organisation is not merely dependent on the internal structural arrangements but also on the external factors and environment—social, political and economic. However, ideally the organisational system might have been designed to deliver the services, its effectiveness will equally depend upon the attitude of the people in general and the target groups in particular, and the commitment of local leadership to the objectives of the project. Similarly, effective use of resources for achieving the project objectives will mostly depend upon the leadership. The administrative procedures prescribed by the government provide broad guidelines to implement a project, but the achievements of its objectives will depend to a greater extent on the project incharge and his/her managerial abilities and skills in harnessing the human and material resources for the project and utilising them.

The Scheme

An ICDS scheme was launched in 1975 for providing opportunities of physical and psycho-social development to children in the age-group 0-6 years through an integrated package of early childhood services.[5] These services include supplementary nutrition, immunization, health check-up, referral service and treatment for minor illness for these children and expectant and nursing mothers, pre-school education for children in the age group of 3-6 years, and nutrition and health education for all women in the age-group 15-45 years. The services are provided through the ICDS projects located mostly at the Block level. With its expansion in successive Five Year Plans, ICDS is today a major programme of child development at the national level with the following main objectives:

(*i*) to improve the nutritional and health status of children in the age-group 0-6 years;

(*ii*) to lay the foundation for proper psychological physical and social development of the child;

(*iii*) to reduce the incidence of mortality, malnutrition and school dropout;

(*iv*) to achieve effective coordination of policy and implementation amongst the various departments to promote child development; and

(*v*) to enhance the capability of the mother to look after the normal health and nutritional needs of the child through proper nutrition the health education.[6]

The objectives are sought to be achieved by delivery on integrated package of early childhood services comprising supplementary nutrition, immunization, health check-up and referral services for children (0-6) and for expectant and nursing mothers; by providing health and nutrition education to mothers; and by imparting non-formal pre-school education to the children in the age group 3-6 years.[7]

The objective of the scheme are implemented through the projects located at the block level.[8] Launched initially with 33 ICDS projects on 2nd October 1975 on experimental basis in 22 States and the Union Territory of Delhi, the scheme covered 164 projects by the end of March 1987.

Objectives

The objectives of the study were following:

— to examine the organisational patterns for the implementation of ICDS projects and study their relation to the effective delivery of services;

— to analyse the processes of management obtaining under different organisational patterns and compare their effectiveness in the delivery of services; and

— to suggest a more effective organisational system for better implementation of the projects.

Scope

The study was confined to rural IÇDS project to make it feasible. It was undertaken in Mahisi block of Saharsa district, Bihar, where the Department of Social Welfare and Health and Family Welfare respectively were the nodel departments for the implementation of the ICDS scheme, with the objective of comparing the effectiveness of delivery of services under two different organisational and administrative systems.

Criteria for Selection of Project

The project for the study were selected from among those sanctioned during the Sixth Five Year Plan (*i.e.*, during the year 1984-85) taking it as the cut-off point as the project should have completed five years of operation by the time of study, a period long enough for a project to stabilise. Accordingly, the ICDS Project at Mahisi (Rural) in the Saharsa district of Bihar was selected for study.

Methodology

Data were collected through personal interviews with the help of interview schedules prepared separately for officials, beneficiaries, community leaders or voluntary workers involved in or associated with the implementation of the project. The data thus, obtained were supplemented by:

— Observations on the implementation of the programme at the Anganwadi level and proceedings of the meetings of project staff and coordination committees.

— Information collected through secondary sources are; circulars, district census Handbook, District Statistical Handbook, administrative reports, monthly and quarterly reports, etc.

Sample for the Study

The major consideration underlying the selection of the villages was the location (distance from project/PHC/Block) and their representative character. The first group represented the villages which were near the Project/PHC/Block while another group represented those which were far from the project headquarters. A third group was formed with villages which were neither very near nor very far from the project office. Two other groups were also formed. However, the creterion for forming these five groups were as follows:

Group	*Distonce Criteria*	*No. of Villages Selected*
(*i*) Near from the Project	0-10 kms.	2
(*ii*) Far from the Project	40 kms. and above	2
(*iii*) Medium distance range	10-20 kms.	2
(*iv*) Near the Sub-Centre/ Dispensary	0-10 kms.	2
(*v*) Remote village (No facilities)	40 kms. & more	2
	Total	10

The villages were grouped according to the norms specified above. Having listed the names of the villages in each group, the final selection of villages was made in consultation with the CDPO on the basis of the population/number of households. The sample for the study included 13 per cent (two from each group) of the Anganwadi villages. It was also ensured that the selected Anganwadi villages were geographically well distributed in the project area and the sample included centres located in the interior. The respondents comprised Anganwadi Workers (AWWs), beneficiaries and community leaders from the selected centres/villages. From each centre/village two beneficiaries and two community leaders were selected following purposive sampling technique. Besides, the respondents included all the other ICDS functionaries, *viz.*, CDPO, Medical Officer and BDO.

The number of different types of respondents interviewed

in the field during the course of the survey in project under study may be seen below:

Types of Respondents		*No. Interviewed*
1. Project Level Functionaries		
(*a*) ICDS-CDPO		1
Anganwadi worker		10
(*b*) Medical Officer		2
(*c*) B.D.O.		1
2. Local Community		
(*a*) Representative of Panchayat, village leaders, teachers, etc.		20
(*b*) Beneficiaries		20
	Total	54
3. Number of Anganwadi Centres covered		10

In addition to this, efforts were also made to collect and discuss the concern officers posted and district level, *viz.*, Welfare Officers, DSO, etc.

Limitation of the Study

As the study was confined to only one rural ICDS project of Saharsa in Bihar, the observations cannot be generalised in the case of other rural projects. However, the findings may at the most indicate the trend in the case of other rural projects in the State and to that extent some of the suggestions given in respect of the project may be of relevance to them.

II. THE PROJECT MANAGEMENT

The administrative chart of Central, State, District, Block and village functionaries for the ICDS Scheme is given in Annexure-I.

At the district level, the District Development Commissioner (DDC) who is a senior officer of the IAS cadre, Deputy Director, Social Welfare (posted at the commissionary level) and District Welfare Officer at the district level is responsible for coordination of programmes under the scheme. The Health Department being the nodal department for the implementation of ICDS projects, the CDPO and the Supervisors who are on the regular cadre sometimes treated as on deputation while Bihar, unlike in many states, where Deputy Collectors (selected through State Public Service Commission) are being posted as CDPO. Another significant aspect of the system is that the DDC (a senior IAS officer equivalent to Collector in Status) exercises overall administrative control, and thus, facilitating coordination and cooperation among the officers concerned with ICDS at the district and project levels.

The organisational set-up of ICDS in Saharsa is given in Annexure-II. The ICDS project at Mahisi covered 95 Anganwadi Centres (AWCs) and five sectors but at the time of the study one sector Supervisor was transferred. There were therefore, four supervisors and 95 workers in position and each workers was assisted by a Helper. The project was headed by a Child Development and Project Officer (CDPO). The CDPO was responsible for supervising and guiding the work of project team including Supervisors and Anganwadi Workers. He was to maintain close functional laiscn with the BDO and PHC Incharge and other functionaries at the block level to avail the already existing infrastructure and resources for development for the effective implementation of the ICDS project. The CDPO was functioning as the drawing and disbursing officer for the project.

However, the staff position as on 6th February 1990 at the ICDS Project Mahisi is as follows:

Category	Sanctioned	In Position	Trained	Under Training
(i) CDPO	1	1	1	—
(ii) Addl./Asstt. CDPO	—	—	—	—
(iii) Supervisor	5	4	4	—
(iv) Anganwrdi Workers	95	95	91	4
(v) Medical Officer	5	4	—	—
(vi) LHVs	2	2	2	—
(vii) ANMs	25	20	20	—

Source: ICDS Project Mahisi.

As mentioned above out of Anganwadi Workers only 91 are trained and 4 workers had been for training to Ranipatra Training Centre, Purnia, but the training programme was postponed.

The informations regarding infrastructural facilities available at the CDPOs office and Anganwadi Centres are also collected and presented below:

(a) At the CDPO's Office

Item	*Availability*
Jeep	One
Trailor	—Nil—
Typewriter	—Nil—but required
Duplicator	Yes (One)
Slide Projector	Yes (One)
Slides/Film Strips	Yes
Office furniture	Yes—but inadequate

(b) At the Selected Centres

Weighing scales	Adequate
Coloured strips for UMAC	—do—
Registers	Inadequate

Health Cards	Inadequate
MPR Forms	Adequate
Guide book for AWW	—do—
First-aid kit	Inadequate
Materials for pre-school activities	—do—

It was observed during field visit and also suggested by the CDPO that there should be one operator for slide projector and first-aid kit and materials for pre-school activities were fairly inadequate in all the selected Anganwadi Centres.

III. THE STUDY AREA

(*a*) Block Profile

District Saharsa has been bifercated from the old Bhagalpur district in 1954. Three sub-divisions, *viz.*, Saharsa proper, Supaul and Virpur and 16 blocks constitute the district. It is located in the North-eastern part of India from 26° 34″ to 25° 27″ latitude and 86° 12″ to 87° 80″ longitude.

The ICDS project Mahisi (which is a block also) is situated 18 kms. north of Saharsa which is one of the most backward blocks of the district with a literacy rate of 18.46 per cent (as per the 1981 census). The population of the project area was 95,154 (48640 male and 46514 female) in 1981, out of which 20,370 belong to scheduled castes. Though the project was identified as a rural one, 79 out of 81 villages (per cent) were inhabited.

The detail block profile of the selected block Mahisi (Saharsa) is given in Table 1. The project area was mainly inhabited by Hindus with agriculture as their main occupation. There were also large section of Muslim inhabitants. Wells and handpumps were the main source of drinking water in the project village. In about 30 per cent of the villages, the drinking water was considered not safe as open wells were the main source of water supply. Diarrhoeal diseases and malaria were reportedly common in the area. The project had a total

TABLE 1

Block Profile—Mahisi (Saharsa)
(As Per 1981 Census)

Items		Number	Percentage
A. Total Number of Villages			
(a) Inhabited		79	—
(b) Uninhabited		2	—
B. Area (in sq. kms.)		222.9	—
C. Population—Total (1981)		95,154	—
	Male	48,640	51.11
	Female	46,514	48.89
D. Literacy (1981)	Total	17,572	18.46
	Male	14,028	14.74
	Female	3,544	3.72
E. Scheduled Caste	Total	20,370	21.40
	Male	10,434	51.22
	Female	9,936	48.77
F. Work Force			
(i) Total Main Workers		33,078	34.76
(a) Cultivators		13,361	40.39
(b) Agricultural workers		17,976	54.34
(c) Workers engaged in household Industry, construction and repair works		254	0.76
(d) Other workers		1,487	4.49
(ii) Marginal workers		3,533	3.71
(iii) Non-workers		58,543	61.52
G. (a) Registered Birth (1979)		675	—
(b) Registered Death (1979)		257	—

number of 95 Anganwadi Centres (covering 79 villages) grouped under five sectors with a supervisor incharge of each sector.

However, Panchayats were functioning in the project villages. There were no Mahila Mandals and youth clubs in the project area.

(*b*) **Village Profile**

A brief profile of the selected Anganwadi villages is presented in Table 2. The 10 Anganwadi villages under study had a population varying between 960 to 1250. A close perusal of the table reveals that villages dominated by scheduled castes population are having very less infrastructural facilities. Whereas villages of high castes are having all the facilities. Most of the (7 out of 10) were connected by transport. Handpumps and wells were the main sources of drinking water in most of the villages. The villages falling in 'diara' land of river Kosi, however, had problems of drinking water due scattered nature of houses. The villagers had to walk long distance to fetch water.

Out of 10 only 2 villages had high school, 4 had middle school and 6 had primary school. The health infrastructure in the project covered one PHC at Mahisi, the block headquarters and sub-centres at different places. However, only 4 sample villages were having this facilities in the village itself and remaining villages were located five to 12 kms. away from the sub-centre (Table 2).

Although State of Bihar has a strong system of Panchayati Raj but involvement of Panchayats in the project area was almost nil except helping functionaries in providing accommodation to AWCs. The villages under study had no Mahila Mandals nor any Yuvak Mandal.

In the Minimum Need Programme (MNP) and also in Rural Electrification Programmes (REC), there is a provision to provide electricity to the scheduled castes villages on priority basis. But out of 10 villages under study five villages were dominated by scheduled castes and none of them were

TABLE 2

Profile of the Selected Anganwadi Villages Under the ICDS Project, Mahisi (District Saharsa, Bihar)

Items	Teghara	Ramsala	Maina	Baluwaha	Belahi	Arrapatti	Telwa	Jalai	Lahuwa	Rajanpur
1. Population—Total	1065	1015	1000	1250	1075	1125	1025	1100	1175	960
S.C.	1065	—	960	—	300	425	1025	1100	900	—
O.B.C.	—	215	40	345	775	200	—	—	275	60
2. School— High	—	yes	—	—	—	—	—	—	—	yes
Middle	—	yes	—	yes	—	yes	—	—	—	yes
Primary	—	yes	yes	yes	yes	yes	—	—	—	yes
3. Whether connected by transport	yes	yes	no	yes	yes	yes	no	no	yes	yes
4. Road to AWC (K=Kutcha, P=Pucca)	—	P	K	K	P	P	K	K	K	P

5. Whether had sub-centre (Y=Yes, N=No)	N	Y	N	Y	N	Y	N	N	N	Y
6. If sub-centre is not located, distance from the nearest one (in Kms.)	5	—	8	—	5	—	8	10	12	—
7. Whether electricity is there or not?	no	yes	no	yes	yes	yes	no	no	no	yes
8. Drinking water facilities	yes	yes	no	no	no	yes	no	no	no	yes

Source: Field Survey

electrified. However, based this brief village profile it can be inferred that scheduled castes and other backward community are still lagging behind as far as availing of government developmental efforts are concerned.

The Anganwadi Workers

Among the 95 Anganwadi Workers of the project area, a little more than one-fifth (21) or 22.10 per cent belonged to the scheduled castes community. Population-wise five out of the 10 selected villages under sample were predominantly inhabited by the scheduled castes. However, this did not coincide with the fact that five of the 10 Anganwadi Workers who belonged to the scheduled castes were coming from the same villages where the scheduled castes population was high. Notwithstanding, in two villages where the SC population was predominant, the Anganwadi workers did not belong to the SC community.

A brief profile of Anganwadi workers is presented in Table 3, which exhibit that more than one-third or 36.86 per cent workers belonged OBC (other backward castes) category followed by SC (22.10 per cent) and Hindu low castes. Hindu high castes and Muslim community had the equal share, *i.e.*, 10.52 per cent, as far as caste-wise representation of Anganwadi workers is concerned.

Age structure of Anganwadi workers was biased towards young. Majority of the Anganwadi Workers (45 or 47 per cent) were in age group 21-25 years followed by 26-30 years (35 or 36.84 per cent). About 16 per cent workers were in the age group 31 and above and none of the workers were from the age group 15-20.

As far as educational structure of the Anganwadi workers is concerned, a little less than two-third or 62.12 per cent were educated upto middle only. About 36 per cent were below high school standard and only 2.10 per cent had crossed this bar. However, none of them were illiterate. A total of 91 underwent job training for the Anganwadi workers and four were untrained. Their experience as Anganwadi Workers

TABLE 3

Profile of Anganwadi Workers

Variables	No. of AWWs	Percentage
Age: 15-20 Years	0	0.00
21-25 Years	45	47.38
26-30 Years	35	36.84
31 and Above	15	15.78
Total	95	100.00
Caste: S.C.	21	22.10
S.T.	0	0.00
Sub-Total	21	22.10
Other Backward Caste	35	36 86
Hindu High Caste	10	10.52
Hindu Low Caste	19	20.00
Muslim	10	10.52
Others	10	10.52
Total	95	100.00
Education: Upto Middle	59	62.12
Below High School	34	35.78
High School and Above	2	2.10
Illiterate	—	—
Total	95	100.00

(*Contd.*)

(Contd.)

Work Experience:	Less than 1 Year	4	4.21
	1-3 Years	24	25.26
	3-5 Years	32	33.68
	5 Years Plus	35	36.85
	Total	95	100.00
Training:	Trained	95	95.78
	Untrained	4	4.21
	Total	95	100 00

Source: ICDS Project, Mahisi, Saharsa.

varied from less than one year to more than 5 years. Majority of them (35 or 36.85 per cent) were having more 5 years experience.

Eight out of 10 Anganwadi Workers were local (staying in the same villages where their respective Anganwadi Centres were located) and rest two were coming from the neighbouring villages situated at a distance of one to 5 kilometers. The details regarding this are as follows:

	Numbers
Local	8
Non-Local (coming from a distance of 1-2 kms.)	1
Non-local (coming from a distance of 3-5 kms.)	1
Total	10

Functioning of Anganwadi Centres

Time devoted by the Anganwadi workers on different activities and informations regarding functioning of the Centres were also collected. The services provided under the project included supplementary nutrition for children in the age group 0-6 years and pregnant and nursing mothers, health check-up, immunization and referral services for them, health and nutrition education for mothers and non-formal pre-school education for children in the age group 3-6 years. The Anganwadis, the focal points for the delivery of services under ICDS, were functioning from 10.00 a.m. to 2.00 p.m. With the following schedule of activities:

Time devoted by AWCs	*Activity*
10.00 a.m. to 11.00 a.m.	Bringing of children to the AWC by the helper.
11.00 a.m. to 1.30 p.m.	Pre-school activity.
1.00 p.m. to 1.30 p.m.	Washing of hands and face of children.
1.30 p.m. to 2.00 p.m.	Distribution of supplementary food.

However, it was observed during field visit that in almost all the selected Anganwadi Centres, the above mentioned programme schedule was followed except washing of hands and face of children. The programme schedule given above was broad and flexible in the sense that the Anganwadi Worker could adjust it keeping in view the local situation and take initiative in conducting the activities in a more interesting and effective manner. On the whole, it was observed that the Anganwadi Workers were not giving proper attention in washing of hand and face of children.

IV. THE BENEFICIARIES

The beneficiaries under the ICDS Scheme are categorised

under expectant mother, nursing mothers, children (6 months to 3 years) and children (3 years to 6 years). However, under those categories number selected for supplementary nutrition and number of children registered for pre-school education in the complete ICDS project area were also selected and given in the table below:

TABLE 4

Number of Beneficiaries Under the ICDS Project

Category of Beneficiaries	No. Selected for SNP	Percentage	Children Registered for PSE
Expectant mothers	570	1.225 (6.03)	—
Nursing mothers	570	1.225 (6.03)	—
Children (6 months-3 years)	4,507	(47.70)	—
Children (3-6 years)	3,800	(40.22)	3,800
Total	9,447	9.92	3,800

Source: ICDS Project Matusi, Saharsa (Bihar).
Note: Figures in bracket are the vertical percentage.

Above Table 4 shows that only 9,447 or 9.92 per cent of the total population were the ICDS beneficiaries for SNP in the block. As far as expectant and nursing mothers are concerned they were having equal share, *i.e.*, 1.225 per cent. Among the total beneficiaries, children below 3 years (6 months to 3 years) were having good share, *i.e.*, 47.70 per cent. The corresponding figure for children 3 years to 6 years was 40.22 per cent. A total of 3,800 children in the ICDS project area were registered for pre-school education.

It was observed during the field visit to the selected Anganwadi Centres that the attendance of children was very low. Only 10-20 children were present in majority of the Anganwadi Centres (6 out of 10) for both the programmes. The number was less than 10 in one Anganwadi Centre. However, a detail information regarding this is presented in Table 5.

TABLE 5

Attendance of Children at the Anganwadi Centres

No. of Children	No. of AWCs Showing Attendance of Children	
	As Per Register	During Visit
31-40	3	0
21-30	5	3
10-20	2	6
Less than 10	0	1
Total	10	10

The number of children was more in three of the Anganwadi Centres, where the pre-school activity in an innovation way, was going on. In none of the Centres more than 30 children were seen though the number of children enrolled at various centres varied from 15 to 60 and 20 to 50 for children in the age groups 6 months to 3 years and 3 to 6 years respectively.

Having noticed the poor attendance of children at the Anganwadi Centres, the reasons thereof were also identified, from both parents as well as Anganwadi Workers, which are as follows:

— At the time of field visit, supplementary nutrition was suspended due to interruption in food supplies (State Food Corporation).

— At some places children were not interested in having

'Khichudi' only. And through out the year they were given 'Khichudi' and supplementary nutrition.

— The community were not properly educated about the ICDS programme. Because in PSE activities they were expecting something else and so not found it worthwhile to send their children to Anganwadi Centres.

— In the villages predominant by higher castes, parents preferred to send their children to school than Anganwadi Centres (even 3 years of children).

— In the Scheduled castes families, older chilren had to stay back at home to look after their younger siblings while both the parents went out for work.

— It was also complained by the villagers that Centre used to remain close for longer period (10-15 days) in a month so they found it not worthwhile to send their children.

— This problem was discussed by the ICDS functionaries. As per their statement children will only come to the Centre when supplementary nutrition will be provided to them. Interruption in food supply leads to the poor attendance of children at the Anganwadi Centres.

Supplementary Nutrition

Under the programme, supplementary nutrition food was used to serve (not regularly) to the children and the pregnant and lactating mothers. Mostly they were given "Khichudi" of rice and *dal*, which were locally available. However, the Anganwadi Workers were expected to see that the children wash their hands before the food under SNP was served to them. Though this was the practice at most of the Anganwadi Centres, the children observed were by and large untidy. The Anganwadi workers found fault with the parents for not keeping their children neat and clean. It was, however, observed that no effort was made by the Anganwadi Workers to keep the children clean. The children were sent back home as they were at the end of the Anganwadi Programmes. If the Anganwadi Workers send them neat and tidy, it would give the parents a feeling that children are developing good habits while attending the Anganwadi Centres.

Most of the parents reported that they were sending their children regularly to the Anganwadi Centres, but it was observed that many of them were not doing so particularly when supplementary food could not be served due to delay in supplies. This was more so with the parents of the SCs community for whom the main attraction at the Anganwadi Centres was the food that was distributed. At one of the Centres it was observed that not even a single beneficiary was present.

The timing of food distribution was found not suitable, it being afternoon by that time, the parents were expecting a full meal for their children and therefore, they had a feeling that the quantity of the food given was not sufficient.

As far as pregnant and nursing mothers are concerned, very few of them were going to the Anganwadi Centres for taking their share of supplementary nutrition food. Some of them felt it below their dignity to go to the Anganwadi Centre just to have a little share of food while others did not find time to go there as they were busy in their fields or household work. It was also observed that not many women were aware that supplementary nutritions food was provided to pregnant and nursing mothers through the Anganwadi Centre. They were not educated properly about the Services available at the Anganwadi Centre.

By and large, the Anganwadi workers were not getting any help from the beneficiary mothers in running the Centre. They were only coming sometimes to leave their children at the Centre and take them back at the end of the Anganwadi activities, as they used to keep themselves busy in own household/agricultural work. They were of the view that the Anganwadi worker does not require their help as she was provided with a Helper to assist her. They, however, expressed their willingness to help the Anganwadi worker, if at all she required any help from them. These observations suggest that the mothers were not clear on how they could participate in the

Anganwadi activities. It could be that the Anganwadi Workers were not clear that how they could involve mothers in conducting the programmes of they did not like to involve them.

Food supplies under SNP to the Centres were generally irregular (as per the responses of both the workers and local people) and their quality unsatisfactory. It was also reported that warm-infested food material was supplied on one or two occassions. As reported by the ICDS functionaries, the community people were not at all in a position to contribute anything being very poor and affected by natural calamities like drought, floods (Koshi river), etc., in the case of Anganwadi Centres not approachable by road, the village people were not helping the Anganwadi Worker by picking up the supplies from the roadside and delivering them to the Centre.

However, supplies of food material for SNP and medicines to the Anganwadi Centres were not regular as reported by the Anganwadi Workers. Four out of 10 Anganwadi Centres studies had inadequate facilities for storage of supplies. The article in these Centres were kept at a neighbouring house to avoid theft. All the Anganwadi Centres were provided at the beginning with very few utencils/equipments for running the programmes, one-third of the Anganwadi Workers felt that certain items like bucket, rope, plates and spoons should also be provided at the Centre.

Pre-School Education

The next important activity of the programme is the preschool education (PSE) with having the following main objectives[9]:

— developing adequate muscular coordination and basic motor skills in the children;

— develping creativity and aesthetic appreciation and elementary hygienic sense;

— providing opportunity for interacting with other children of the same age-group:

— developing in the child the ability express his thoughts and feelings influent, correct and clear speech; and
— developing the habits of attending the AWC regularly.

The programme content of pre-school activity is, therefore, centred on play activities as "play is the main activity by which child learns and develops". These play activities should be based on indigenous material and culture.

However, in the project under the pre-school activity was being conducted generally from 11 a.m. to 1.00 p.m. The activity, starting with a payer, included recitation of nursery rhymes, teaching of numbers and narration of stories. It was observed that Anganwadi workers were not having sufficient kit materials to perform this activity. Many of the Anganwadi Workers were of the view that the play material became unusable and required replacement.

In most of the centres, the children were asked to recite the same old prayers, poems, and tell the same old stories narrated to them when the project started functioning. However, the workers were making efforts to involve children in outdoor games. They were trying to develop the concept of number, shape, colour, size, etc. But it was observed that in almost all the centres those activities were repeatitive. Thus, the pre-school activity, although conducted regularly, were repetitive and monotonous and not attractive enough for the majority of the Anganwadi Centres. It was also unattractive for them as the same old charts and play material provided when the project started functioning were used for these activities.

Health and Nutrition Education

Health and nutrition education to the target groups were mainly given by the Female Health Worker (FHW)/ANM, Multipurpose Health Worker, Anganwadi Worker and LHV as mentioned by the beneficiaries. Under this component ANMs were suppose to motivate the people for adoption of family planning practices and were suppose to educate them on the need to get their children immunized and keeping their surroundings clean.

It was however, observed that very few were imparting health and nutrition education to the people. Very few of the Health Functionaries make the visit of their alloted area/villages as reported by the villagers.

Health Check-up, Immunization and Referral Services

As in the case of health and nutrition education, these three activities are also the main responsibility of the Primary Health Centre (PHC) and its dispensaries and sub-centres. In the project there was no regular health check-up at the Anganwadi Centre. The Medical Officer (MO) was conducting an overall health check of children to identify infectious diseases, etc., when, immunization services were provided through mass campaigns.

Although weighing scales were available at each Anganwadi Centres but the weights of children were not taken as per the schedule. Growth charts and Health Cards were distributed to AWCs long back when the project started. It was also observed during the field visit that the mothers were usually not present when the weights of their children were taken at the Anganwadi Centre except in the case of those who were in the age-group of 6 months to 2 years. However, the mothers should be required to be present when the weights of their children were taken irrespective of their age-group as they could help in Anganwadi Worker in taking the weights. Their presence world also help in creating health awareness among them.

As regards immunization, services were being provided for mothers and children through the sub-centres. The children of Anganwadi Centres were usually immunised twice in a year against different diseases. The targets and achievements of the complete area of the PHC is given in the Table 6.

It is evident from Table 6 that for none of the items achievements are more than fifty per cent. This problem was discussed with staff posted at PHC level. As per their statement the poor

TABLE 6

Targets and Achievements Under Different Items of PHC Mahisi, Saharsa (Bihar) 1989-90

Item	Target	Achievements	Percentage
(1)	(2)	(3)	(4)
DPT	3950	1820	40.07
D.T.	3900	1630	41.79
B.C.G.	4077	895	21.95
Polio	4077	1685	41.32
T.T.	5233	1925	36.78
Vitamin 'A'	—	75 Bottles	—
Iron Tabs. (Children)	—	88,000	—
Iron and Folic Acid Tablets for (Women)	—	78,000	—
Simple Drugs	—	Adequate	—

Source: PHC, Mahisi.

achievement is because of the lack of manpower at both the level; field as well as PHC/dispensaries. However, supply of vaccines and medicines for each items are adequate.

So far as the referral services are concerned, services were not provided in a regular and systematic manner. The FHWs/MPWs on their visits to villagers, advised the parents of children suffering from typhoid, dehydration, etc., requiring special attention to go to the nearest dispensing centre or PHC or district hospital as the case may be. But there was no regular follow-up of such an advice as there was no formal referral service system at the project through a referral card or slip. There were no referral services or regular follow-up even in the case of malnourished children.

Very few people were approaching the sub-centre for treatment of minor ailment through they were aware of the facility available there. The beneficiaries however, by and large unaware of the referral services due to the reason that these were not effectively provided. Similarly, they were not aware that the health check-up of children and mothers was a part of the services delivered through the Anganwadi Centre as it was not done regularly.

The opinion of parents varied in regard to the benefits received from the services rendered through the AWC. Most of them (60%) felt that their children benefitted from the SNP. Next in order were the immunization and pre-school services (65%). Only about one-third of them mentioned that their children benefitted from the service of health check-up. None of them was aware of the referral services provided through the AWC.

Services	*Benefitted*	*Not benefitted*	*Don't know*	*Total*
S.N.P.	12 (60%)	4 (20%)	4 (20%)	20 (100)
P.S.E.	13 (65%)	7 (35%)	—	20 (100)
Health Check-up	7 (35%)	—	13 (65%)	20 (100)
Referral Services	—	—	20 (100)	20 (100)

Most of the parents particularly those belonging to the scheduled castes community, could not, however, spell out how the services benefitted their children. Only a few of them specified the benefits received as follows:

— they learnt good manners;

— developed school going habit;

— learnt the correct usage of words, etc.

Visits of Functionaries to the Anganwadi Centres

For proper functioning of the centre, the Anganwadi Workers required the guidance and Supervisors. It is, therefore, the information regarding visits of different functionaries (their frequency) to the AWCs were also collected and presented in the Table 7.

TABLE 7

Visits of Functionaries to AWCs During 1989

Frequency	Functionaries Visited No. of AWCs				
	CDPO	MO	Supervisor	ANM	LHV
2-5 times	6	8	3	7	9
6-9 times	2	1	3	3	1
10-14 times	2	—	2	—	—
Total	10	10	10	10	10

The above Table reveals that the supervisor (ICDS) most frequently make visit of the Anganwadi Centres. Five out of 10 studied centres have reported that ICDS Supervisor had made visit of their Centres more than six times. High frequency of visit was followed by the CDPO. The Anganwadi Workers said that their Supervisors helped them in solving some of the problems. They persuaded the parents to send their children regularly to the Anganwadi Centre. They explained different columns in the registers/reports and guided the workers in filling the requied information, etc.

Coordination at Different levels

As the ICDS scheme adopts an inter-sectoral approach involving more than one department or agency of the Government, panchayats and voluntary agencies, there is all the more need for coordination of their efforts in delivering the package of services for children and mothers. Coordination will help maximum utilisation of the available resources. The scheme provides for formal mechanisms through the constitution of coordination committees at the State, district and project levels.

It was observed that at the district level there was no coordination committee formally constituted. However, the DDC/DHO and Deputy Director Social Welfare holds periodic review meetings with the health and non-health functionaries. At the block/project level, BDO/Pramukh (elected Chairman) at the Block is the Chairman and CDPO is the Convenor of the Committee. The project level committee is expected to meet on 28th of every month. It was however, observed that the meetings of the committee were not convened regularly. The project level meeting was generally attended by MO, CDPO, LHV, ANMs and Supervisors. But as the minutes of these meetings were not available in the office of CDPO, it was not possible to find out specifically what problems were discussed there. However, as reported by the CDPO, getting the accommodation for AWCs and getting articles from the SFC, etc., were some of the problem discussed in the last meeting.

On the whole, it was observed that at the block level BDO, CDPO and MO were having good coordination between each other but at the grass-root level coordination between the health functionaries and AWWs were not so.

Community Participation

The community participation in the effective implementation of the programme is a very important aspect which cannot be ignored. For the purpose of present study, representatives of Panchayat, village leaders and influential persons of the village were considered. The primary-school teacher who is usually a source of information and an agent for creating community awareness was also included under the category of leaders.

A total of 20 community leaders were interviewed. However, their observations may only indicate the general trend. Most of them said that they were visiting the Anganwadi Centre twice a month and some of them stated almost every alternate day. The functionaries who consulted them mainly included the CDPO, Supervisors, AWWs and ANMs. They sought the advice of the leaders on various matters like improving the attendance of children at the AWCs, creating community awareness about the programme.

However, by and large, it was observed that the community participation was poor in programme implementation. None of the Anganwadi Centre's building was donated by the community. Neither they were helping the functionaries in repairing the same. The conditions of all the visited centres were very poor. The AWWs used to keep the articles in nearby houses. During field visit "Mukhia" of the village panchayat was also consulted in this regard and few of them were agreed up on it and givins assurance that under the Jawahar Rozgar Yojana they are going to construct the building for Anganwadi Centre.

V. SUGGESTIONS & RECOMMENDATIONS

(*a*) About Proper Functioning

— The primary school teacher or one of the fellow villagers or elders or local persons should supervise/guide the helper in the distribution of supplementary nutrition food when the Anganwadi workers are on leave or even in normal course also;

— The local people should help the Anganwadi worker in procuring the articles for Anganwadi Centre;

— For running the Anganwadi Centres more affectively in regard to programmes and activities, role of functionaries, supplies and equipments, support and participation of the beneficiaries and the village panchayats should also be enhanced.

— The community should be made more aware of the activities and programmes of the Anganwadi Centres;

— The priority should be given to the local girls for recruitment of Anganwadi workers so that she can put more efforts in running the Centre;

— The Supervisors and the CDPO should make frequent visits to the Anganwadi Centres and provide necessary guidance to the Anganwadi Workers; and

— The Anganwadi Centres should be provided with adequate number of utencils and containers for storage of food material.

(*b*) About Supplementary Nutrition

— Food supplies under SNP by the State Food Corporation were very irregular and their quality were unsatisfactory. It was reported that worm-infested food material was also supplied on one or two occasions. Hence, it is suggested that the food supplies should be regular and of a better quality;

— It was observed that since last one year only "Khichudi" distribution of rice and dal was going on in all the Anganwadi Centres. There should be variety in the supplementary food given to mothers and children.

— When there is delay in food supply community should contribute the locally available food for the Anganwadi Centre;

— It was suggested by the parents that children may also be given sweets and biscuits sometimes in place "Khichudi"

(*c*) About Pre-school Education

— It was observed that pre-school activity, although conducted regularly, were repetitive and monotonous and not attractive enough for the children. It was also unattractive for them as the same old charts and play material provided when the project started functioning. Hence, it is suggested that some more teaching materials through the help of UNICEF should be supplied.

— Parents were in the opined that Anganwadi Worker should give more emphasis on teaching numbers and alphabets to children. Thus, in this regard parents need to be educated by the functionaries on the concept of pre-school education.

— Toys may be provided or should be prepared by the AWWs/ Community through waste materials for children at the Anganwadi Centre to attract and educate them simultaneously.

(*d*) About Health & Nutrition Education

— Under this, the ANMs/FHWs were motivating the people only for adoption of family planning practices to achieve their targets. They should also give emphasis on the need to get their children immunised and keeping their surroundings clean.

— Very few of the Anganwadi Workers were imparting health and nutrition education during their home visit. But they should use puppets and posters to educate the community on the evils of alcholism, drug addiction, etc., through group meetings of the beneficiaries.

(*e*) About Health Check-up, Immunization and Referral Services

— The mothers should be required to be present when the weights of their children were taken irrespective of their age-group as they could help the Anganwadi Worker in taking the weights. Their presence would also help in creating health awareness among them.

— The health functionaries working at the grass-root level (like, ANM/FHW, an MPW) should make regular visit at least twice in a month for health check-up and once in six months for immunization.

— Local people had a feeling that the Anganwadi Centre is only to look after the children, so at least the ANM should be provided the required medicines during home visits.

— Long back when the project was started a medicine kit box was supplied to the Anganwadi Workers through UNICEF after that neither any medicine nor tool kits were given to the workers. It is therefore, suggested that atleast first-aid medicine should be supplied at the centre.

— Referral services, were not provided in a regular and systematic manner. The beneficiaries by and large, were unaware of the referral services due to the fact that these were not effectively provided. However, grass-root level health funcnaries should given special attention and advisee the parents to go to the nearest dispensing centre or PHC or district hospital as the case may be.

REFERENCES

1. *Manual on ICDS*, 1983, NIPCCD, New Delhi, p. 4.
2. *Ibid.*, p. 4.
3. L.S.N. Murthi & Sunita Mathur (1988): *Project Management—A Study of ICDS Projects*, NIPCCD, New Delhi, p. 7.
4. *Ibid.*, p. 7.
5. *Ibid.*, p. 1.
6. India, Ministry of Social Welfare, *Integrated Child Developmeut Services Scheme*, (Revised), New Delhi, 1982, p. 2-3.
7. Murthy & Mathur (1988), *op. cit.*, p. 4.
8. The block is an administrative unit covering about 100 villages with an average population of one lakh.
9. Murthy & Mathur (1988), *op. cit.*, p. 27.

ANNEXURE I
ICDS PROJECTS

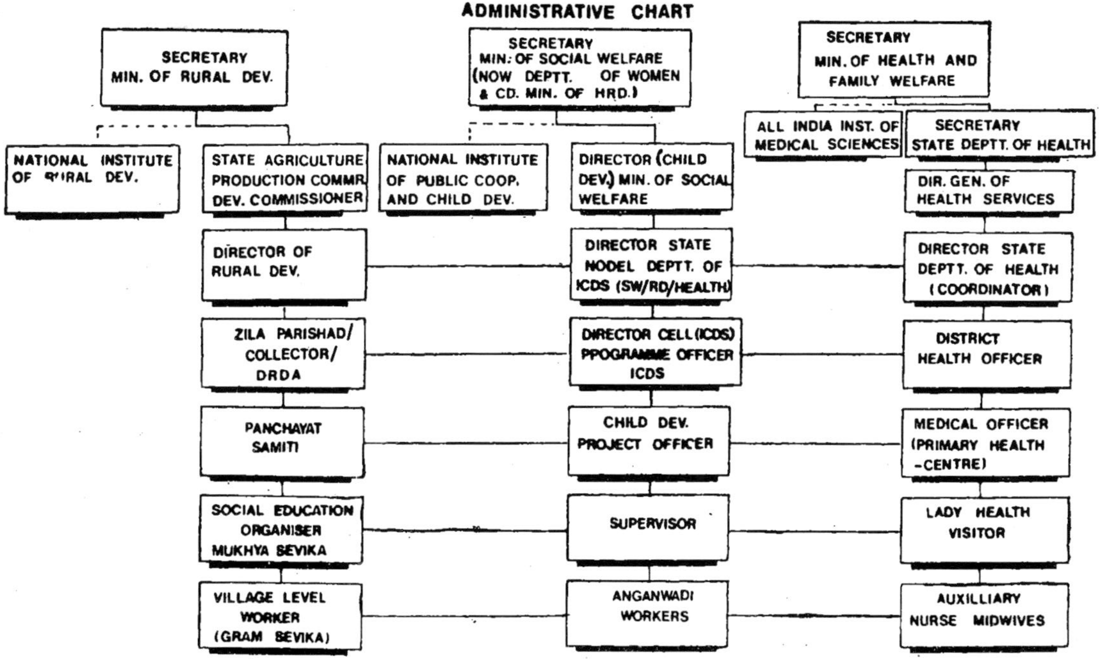

Source: National Institute of Public Cooperation and Child Development, Manual on Integrated Child Development Services, New Delhi, 1984, p. 169.

ANNEXURE II

ORGANISATIONAL SET-UP OF ICDS IN SAHARSA (BIHAR)

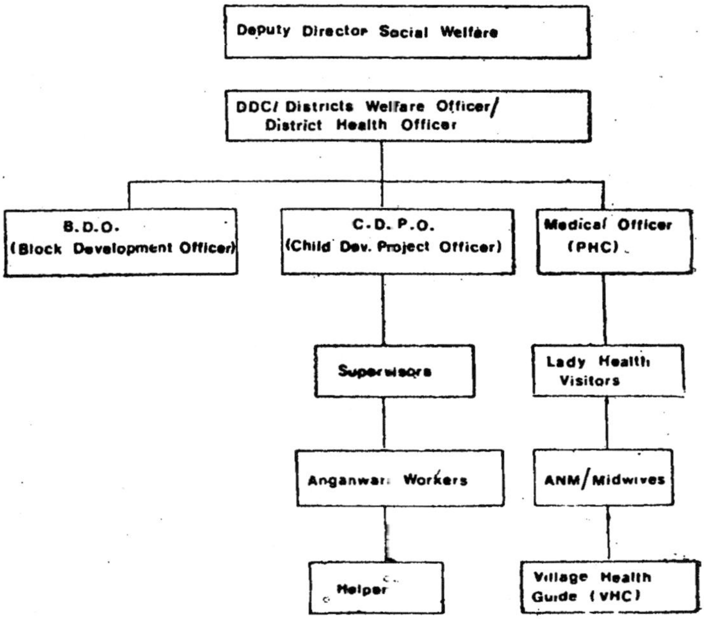